The Night Before Me

The Night Before Me

BY CONSTANTINE FETTEL
AND ERIC TYSON

NEW ENGLISH LIBRARY
TIMES MIRROR

To Ena

Until the day break, and the
shadows flee away, turn, my
beloved, and be thou like a
roe or a young hart upon the
mountains of Bether.

Song of Solomon 2.17

Chapter One

It began like many another Sunday, that summer day that was to change my life. An early awakening, in the tent that served as my weekend quarters, by the blinding light of the rapidly-rising Egyptian sun. A wash and shave in the ablutions block, followed by breakfast with some of the refugee friends I had come to visit. An impromptu game of football after the midday meal. A tea-time stroll to the Arab-owned café, half-an-hour's walk away, where the refugees of El Shatt idled away much of their endless days. And, all the time, the interminable talk.

By nine o'clock it was almost time for me to depart, back to the army base at El Kantara, thirty miles away, where I was stationed with the 1st Battalion Royal Yugoslav Guards. Like Cinderella, I had to be home by midnight, the time my weekend pass expired. The uncomfortable, dust-choked journey, by the same army transport that had brought me to El Shatt the previous day, was not an experience to which I looked forward with any sense of pleasure.

The cool that always came when the sun went down had already begun to creep through the desert camp. Outside the neat rows of tents, a hundred or more, army issue and dirty white, the refugees were sitting in family groups, talking over the day's non-events, grateful for the sudden drop in temperature after the burning heat of the day.

Inside the tent allocated to Vinka and her family, however, it was still uncomfortably hot. Even though I was wearing my lightweight overseas uniform, sweat meandered among the hairs underneath my open-neck khaki shirt. Dark stains, damp and unpleasant, were appearing yet again under my armpits and behind the knees of my thin cotton trousers. I loosened the webbing belt round my waist, picked up the cheese-cutter cap lying across my knees, and placed it beside me on the bed.

Vinka was the main reason I had gone to El Shatt that weekend. She and her family were Yugoslavs, the same as I. It was only to be expected that Yugoslav soldiers stationed nearby should seek to spend their weekends with friends and families of the same nationality living at the refugee camp. If the friends concerned happened to be of the opposite sex, or if the families included the added attraction of a pretty daughter of the right age – or even a not-too-repulsive female of any age – then, for soldiers stationed so far away from home, the joys of social intercourse with their fellow countrymen and countrywomen knew limitless bounds.

The light of the oil-lamp hanging in the middle of the square-shaped tent glinted deep within Vinka's pale blue eyes and flickered among the brown hair that tumbled round her shoulders. In the bright red cotton skirt and white blouse that she had made herself, she looked even younger than her twenty years. The smiling, oval face was even more beautiful than I remembered from my previous visit.

She smiled at me from the other bed, a shy smile that wondered if we might be alone together just once more before I had to return to camp at El Kantara. The hope, however, seemed a forlorn one. It was too late, and too dark outside, for us to stroll arm-in-arm to the banks of the Suez Canal, an hour's walk away. And the café, only half the distance, would be closed. There was just one possibility left that might result in Vinka and me being able to talk to each other the way we wanted to, private talk that was reserved only for our ears. Her parents, who were sitting next to her on the bed, might decide to visit friends on the other side of the camp, and the couple sharing the bed with me, a husband and wife from another tent, might go along, too. That possibility, however, was receding with each passing second. The four of them were engrossed in a deep and serious conversation.

It was 21 July 1946. The war in Europe had ended more than fourteen months before and in the Far East more than ten months before. The Allies were victorious, the fighting had ended and men were at peace. Yet, for millions of people, the world at peace was an equally chaotic, uncertain and frightening place in which to live – or exist – as it had been for all of the previous seven years. Thousands of men and women were still in uniform, scattered in strange countries throughout the world, longing for the distant day when they would be demobilised and returned to their families. Thousands more men and women, many of whom had never worn a uniform, yet who had suffered no less from the terrors and the ravages of war, were dispersed throughout equally strange countries, condemned to the primitive conditions of refugee camps, certain in the knowledge that they would never see their homes, or their homelands, again.

For Yugoslav refugees in camps all over the world, the Communist take-over of Yugoslavia following the defeat of the Nazis presented a considerable dilemma. Some, because of previous political adherences, were unable to return under the new regime, either for fear of reprisals or because they were declared *persona non grata*. Others simply could not countenance returning to a peacetime Yugoslavia dominated by the Communists. A few were undecided.

Although I had been born in Istanbul and had lived in Turkey all my life, my nationality was that of my Yugoslav father. In December 1941, despite apparently conflicting loyalties, my duty had been clear. Italy, my mother's country, had been fighting on the side of Germany since June 1940. Yugoslavia, my father's country, had been overrun and vanquished by Germany in April 1941. Turkey, my family's adopted country, had signed a treaty of friendship with Germany two months later. Yet my allegiance, and that of my family, had been with Yugoslavia and the Yugoslav royal family. There had been no hesitation about my decision to join the Royal Yugoslav Guards just as soon as I was able, just as soon as I had taken my final examinations and had left school. I had volunteered and, on 15 December 1941, had left Istanbul, a boy of seventeen, to join the 1st Battalion at Agami, near Alexandria, in Egypt.

Three years later, I had been faced with a decision that was less clear. King Peter of Yugoslavia's army had renounced him and committed itself to the Communist cause. The victorious Marshal Tito had been officially recognised by the Western Powers. Officers and men of my own regiment had been offered the choice of returning home, joining the fight against the Germans with a battalion of Tito's army, or remaining loyal to the king in the sadly depleted ranks of the Guards. My decision had become clearer when I remembered the wise counsel of my father when I was a boy; that, once I had started something, I should always finish it. I had known that he would have wanted me to remain with the regiment, to stay with the king until the purpose for which I had joined the army had been accomplished. I had known, too, that my conscience compelled me to remain a royalist. Since then, the tattered remnants of the 1st Battalion had served on attachment to the British Eighth Army. What was to become of us, almost a year after the end of the war, nobody knew. Nor did anyone know what was to become of the refugees of El Shatt, and the conversation of the four Yugoslavs in

Vinka's tent graphically reflected their mood of bitterness, frustration and despair. The man next to me on the bed blamed Tito. They would all have been back home by then but for him, he said. His wife thought the Allies were to blame for letting Tito take over, doing nothing about it, and then letting the Communists get rid of the monarchy. King Peter's government in exile was the legal one – still was, she claimed – and the Allies should have made sure he got his throne back.

'They couldn't very well – not with the popular support they knew Tito had,' said Vinka's father, not unreasonably.

'They owed it to the king,' she replied. 'They should have insisted that Peter went back.'

'They owed more to Tito for getting rid of the Nazis. And what were they supposed to do when Tito refused to have him? Use force to put him back?'

The woman was subdued for a moment by the logical and reasoned argument of Vinka's father.

'The British will regret it, anyway,' she said at last. 'They can't afford to lose another monarchy in Europe.'

'The Reds won't stop at Yugoslavia,' said her husband. 'It's just a start.'

Vinka's mother, a small, crumpled figure in her home-made skirt and blouse, held up her hands.

'All the time politics!' she complained. 'I'm sick of politics. Nobody talks about anything else any more. The politicians have been talking for years, but it hasn't got us out of here.'

She sat staring sadly into space. Her grey hair topped what seemed an even greyer face, a face lined and wrinkled with worry and the hard life she had led in the refugee camps, a face full of sorrow and suffering. Despite the difference in years, there was still a definite likeness with the young girl sitting next to her. The similarity produced in me a distinct feeling of unease. Was it possible that, with the passing years, Vinka would grow even more like her mother?

'Kosta!'

The voice, loud and commanding, appeared to come from behind me, from over my left shoulder. It was a voice that I did not recognise and one that was far more audible and penetrating than the normal conversational tones being used in the tent. Despite that, however, despite the curious direction that it had come from, and despite the fact that the only people present were all visible to me, my immediate – and illogical – impression was that the voice belonged to one of my companions in the tent. I turned my head instinctively in answer to my name.

As I did so, a considerable quantity of liquid struck me in the face. It splashed against me with some force, as if thrown from a container. It soaked the top of my head and the left side of my face, ran on to my forehead, dripped from my eyebrows, seeped down my neck, and trickled on to my left arm and chest.

The initial surprise, rather than shock, was followed by brief seconds of perplexity which, in turn, gave way to the relieved conviction that somebody was playing a game and had thrown water over me as a joke.

That optimistic conclusion was quickly proved incorrect, however, when in every part of my body touched by the liquid, my skin began to tingle. Within seconds, the tingling had increased in intensity until the sensation was no longer one of tingling, but of burning; burning that progressed from a dull glow to a fierce flush and from a fierce flush to an almost unbearable, fiery heat.

Suddenly, there was a loud scream, a frightened scream, that appeared to emanate from somewhere close to my left ear. Like a startled gazelle that has scented the first faint whiff of danger, the woman sitting next to me sprang to her feet, scattering the glasses on the table between the beds and almost overturning the table itself. She clutched the back of her neck and screamed again.

The shocked silence that had followed the first scream was quickly dispelled by the frenzied panic occasioned by the second. In the bewildering confusion of babbled voices, I was vaguely conscious of my own voice, somewhere, making a pathetic plea for enlightenment.

'What is it? What's happened?'

'What's wrong? Where did it come from?'

'Sit down. Let's have a look.'

'Jesus!'

I was unaware of why the woman had screamed or why she was still screaming and, what was more, I did not care. I was aware only of the fact that my face was burning, that my head was on fire, that the pain was increasing with each passing second, and that the help I so sorely needed was unlikely to be forthcoming from the other occupants of the tent. They were crowded round the woman, attempting to silence her, attempting to pacify her, apparently too busy attending to her needs to attend to mine, or oblivious of them.

In spite of my confusion and involuntary inability to concentrate my thoughts on anything but the searing pain, my brain was still capable of realising the necessity and the urgency of obtaining qualified medical help. It was clear, however, that in the absence of immediate assistance from Vinka or her parents – and they were still helping the man to calm and reassure his wife – I would not be capable of running, or even walking, to the camp first-aid post four hundred yards away.

As anxiety mounted in my troubled mind, mounted and ran wild until it had attained a gravity amounting to near-panic, my thoughts turned to the one certain source of succour that I knew was close at hand and would not fail me – Pavlo Dushamanovitch. Pavlo and his wife, Maria, were Yugoslavs from Turkey, the same as I was, and, as a result, we had become good friends. If anyone would help me, they would.

I hurried out of the tent and into the desert night. The sky was scattered with a million stars but, on the ground, it was dark, almost inky-black. The darkness, however, was a minor obstacle in locating Pavlo's tent. I was well acquainted with the layout of the camp and with the tent's exact situation. From where I was standing, outside Vinka's tent, it was two rows away and on the left; no more than one hundred and twenty yards. I could find it with my eyes shut.

As the words flashed into and out of my thoughts, I realised for the first time that, although my eyes were not shut, but wide open, my vision appeared hazy and blurred. Everything around me – the stars, the silhouettes of the tents, my hands outstretched in front of me – seemed somehow indistinct, almost as though a film was forming, or had formed, over my eyes. For the first time, too, I realised that my eyes were hurting, smarting, and that tears were welling into them and spilling on to my cheeks. The agonising pain that had engulfed my face and head had undoubtedly engaged my attention to such an extent that I had been unaware of the increasing discomfort in my eyes.

A dog, one of the many mongrels that roamed the camp scavenging what food they could, scurried away from under my feet and disappeared into the darkness. To my left, a cat, almost certainly a disdainful tabby rejecting the advances of an over-amorous tom, hissed and spat angrily, sending the prowler scuttling shamefacedly over the hard-baked sand.

I ran past the two rows of tents, turned along the row in which I knew Pavlo's tent was situated, and shuffled towards the figure of Maria, sitting outside on a camp stool, silhouetted against the brightly-lit interior. To my surprise, the figure surveyed me coldly, and there was no response to my pleadings for help.

'You're drunk!' she said at last.

With a shock, I realised that it was not Maria's voice. It was not Maria, nor even Maria's tent. Maria must have been about forty, but this woman was nearer sixty. In my panic, in my confusion, in the darkness, and with my failing vision, I had not only mistaken Maria, but the tent as well, and probably even the row. Despite my natural indignation at being so unjustly accused, I was not completely able to disregard the increasing conviction that there might well be sound reasons for her judgement. I was swaying on my feet, rocking from side to side, backwards and forwards. It was enough, certainly, to provide at least a basis for her suspicions. I knew that I was not drunk, however, and, knowing that, what puzzled and perturbed me was the fact that I could not comprehend the reason for my unsteady condition.

I stepped forward into the light from the tent. Immediately I did so, the woman screamed, stared like a frightened rabbit mesmerised by a snake, and screamed again. At that moment, I neither knew nor cared why she was screaming. All I knew, and all I cared about, was that she appeared to be as incapable of rendering any assistance in my moment of need as Vinka and her family had been.

'Take me to my friends,' I urged her. 'The Dushamanovitch tent.'

She took my elbow and guided me away. She held my arm tighter as I stumbled and almost fell. I could not understand why I should stumble on the hard sand, so solid and smooth, so flat and level. I could not understand where the stars had gone, all those millions of bright, sparkling diamonds that only a few minutes before had littered the black velvet ceiling that was the desert sky; now there was nothing but an unrelieved and funereal darkness. I could not understand why the night seemed blacker than when I had left Vinka's tent, why my eyes did not appear to be becoming accustomed to the darkness, and why the night seemed darker, so much darker, with my left eye than with my right.

'Here's Kosta!' It was Maria's voice and she sounded pleased. 'Come in, Kosta!'

I entered the tent and was met by a shocked silence, followed by the same hysterical reaction that, by then, I had come to expect. Pavlo appeared to be only a little less distressed than was

Maria. I explained that something had been thrown at me and that my face was burning. A man whose voice I did not recognise shouted for some flour as, he said, flour was good for burns. A woman, probably his wife, was weeping noisily, and Maria was crying, too.

They guided me to a bed and I lay down. Hands unfastened my belt and tugged my shirt out of the waist-band of my trousers and over my head.

Their reaction to the sight of my face, and the reaction of the woman I had mistaken for Maria, made me realise, for the first time, the gravity of my situation. Even in the shocked and dazed condition to which, by that time, I had been reduced, I knew that whatever had happened to me was more serious than I had hitherto suspected.

'Get the ambulance, Pavlo,' I urged. 'Get it quickly.'

I was aware of Pavlo instructing his son, Yiogi, who was fourteen, to run as quickly as he could to the camp first-aid post, four hundred yards away, and call out the Red Cross ambulance. I was aware of people crowding into the tent and milling round the entrance and of Pavlo pleading with them to let Yiogi through.

The flour arrived and hands patted it on to what, by then, I was certain must be raw flesh. The initial agonising effect was quickly followed by a distinct easing of the pain. To my immense relief, the flour did, indeed, appear to possess considerable cooling and soothing qualities that immediately removed the intense feeling of burning and replaced it with a bearable, hot glow. The relief, however, was not to last. No sooner had the pain diminished than the application of the flour began to have a different, and far less agreeable, effect. A feeling of tightness began to envelop my face. It was as though the skin was shrinking, shrivelling, being stretched, being drawn tight across the cheekbones, nose and forehead, and around the eyes. An identical tight feeling spread across my chest and arm, everywhere the liquid had burned, everywhere the flour had been applied. At the same time, the pain began to return, pain that was every bit as severe as previously, more severe than previously, more excruciating than any I had ever experienced; pain that resembled the effect of a red-hot iron being pressed against my face, pressed hard and turned so that it was well ground in, pain that was becoming more agonising with every passing second, that made me long to cry out, that made me wonder how I could stop myself screaming, that made me ask myself how long it would be before I could hold the screams inside me no longer.

Someone bent over me. I reached out into the darkness of a tent that I knew was brightly lit by Pavlo's oil lamp. I grasped a wrist, a male wrist, judging by its thickness and its hairs.

'It's all right, Kosta,' said Pavlo's voice. 'The ambulance is on its way.'

'Pavlo,' I said. 'I can't see.'

Chapter Two

Through a protective haze mercifully bestowed by Nature to minimise the worst effects of the pain and the resultant anxiety, I was vaguely aware of the sound of a petrol engine, brakes being applied, a heavy vehicle drawing to a rumbling halt, and the voices of two men speaking in English. I was aware that they had pushed their way into the tent and were asking questions about what had happened and what had been thrown at me.

Hands lifted me from the bed, held me firmly under the armpits, and guided me out of the tent, into the fresh air, and into the ambulance. I could see nothing, but I could feel the same hands easing me into a lying position and placing blankets over me, and I could hear the door slamming, the engine spurting into life and the vehicle leaping forward. A few moments later, the silence that followed the switching off of the engine, the sound of the ambulance doors opening and the feel of the same hands helping me down the steps told me that we had arrived at the first-aid post.

Inside, my clothes were removed and I was placed naked on a bed. More blankets were pulled over me and a hard pillow was slipped behind my head. I could hear another English voice, a woman's voice, inquiring about my condition and the two men explaining the little they knew about what had happened. From their conversation, it became apparent that the application of flour – commonly held to be a correct emergency treatment for burns – was, in fact, probably the worst action my friends could have taken. Far from alleviating the situation, it had caused the fluid to burn even deeper into the tissues.

'Is the pain very bad?' It was the woman's voice.

'Very bad.'

'We'll give you a morphine injection. It won't hurt – and it will take away the pain.' Her voice was calm and reassuring.

The needle went in and stayed there for a moment before being withdrawn. The sharpness as it punctured the skin was negligible compared with the pain in the rest of my body.

Cotton wool, cold and clammy, doubtless soaked in boric acid, was gently propelled by unseen fingers over my face, round my nose, in my eyes, over my scalp, in and behind my ears. More cotton wool was smoothed over my chest, down my left arm, back again round the eyes, squelching, dripping, washing, cleaning.

'As soon as we've finished here we'll send you in the ambulance to the 13th General Hospital at Suez,' said the woman. 'The pain will be gone in a few minutes – just as soon as the morphine takes effect.'

Her comforting words, and those of the two men, vaguely rekindled for me the memory of some distant first-aid lecture, one of many such lectures inflicted upon new recruits during the first months of my army service five years before, and I realised that they were carrying out the recognised prescribed treatment for patients suffering from severe shock – administer morphine, lie patient flat on back, wrap in blankets and seek to give reassurance.

It was not reassurance I needed, however. It was sleep. The pain had gone. I was tired. Drowsy. Peaceful. I was happy in the knowledge that I would soon be in a comfortable hospital bed, and that the doctors would smooth soothing ointment on to my face and put healing drops into my eyes. The burns would soon heal and new skin would form. The drops would soon soothe my eyes and I would be able to see again. I would soon be fit and well and back on guard duty with my battalion at El Kantara. And I would soon collect another weekend pass and visit Vinka at El Shatt again.

Even though my body had received a liberal dose of morphine, I was unable to sleep. The lack of made-up roads between El Shatt and the Canal – the only land communication was by way of tracks through the desert – made sleep impossible. I longed for the ambulance to reach the smooth, concrete roads at the other side of the water.

Two incidents on the journey served only to aggravate the considerable confusion of mind, occasioned equally by the shock and by the morphine, that had taken hold of me. The ambulance came to a halt close to the Suez Canal because of – according to an attendant sitting beside me – a hold-up at the bridge. When the engine re-started and the ambulance moved off once more, I innocently inquired how long we had been stopped. His reply – half-an-hour – both shocked and perplexed me. It seemed impossible. To me, in my confused state, it appeared to be only a few minutes, three at the most. I could not understand the discrepancy between his answer and my conviction. Weird suspicions began to creep into my mind and I concluded that, for some inexplicable reason, the man was lying. The second incident occurred no sooner than, it appeared to me, we had crossed the Canal and, to my relief, had begun to travel for the first time on smooth roads. Again the ambulance stopped and, when I inquired the reason, I was told that we had arrived at the hospital. I knew that the 13th General was at Suez and that Suez town was some distance from the Canal. As a result, I could not understand how we could possibly be at the hospital so soon after crossing the bridge.

It quickly became clear that, despite my doubts, we were, indeed, at the 13th General. I was lifted into the air, carried down steps and placed on a flat surface. The horizontal movement and the squeaking of wheels told me that I was being pushed on a trolley. I could hear doors opening and murmured voices. Then I became aware of a light, a dim yellowish light that I realised was probably from an electric bulb, creeping in underneath the gauze that completely covered my face. People were moving about and I sensed that someone was bending over me. There was the click of forceps near my ear and a corner of the gauze was lifted and then peeled gently from my face. Bright lights glared down at me and I guessed that I was in the operating theatre.

'Christ!' said a man's voice. 'What a bloody mess!'

Hands behind my head lifted me up and a cold rubber covering was slipped underneath. Warm water was sponged over my hair and liquid soap poured on and rubbed in. There was the rasping of a razor shaving off my hair, leaving me completely bald. More warm water was sponged over my face, chest, arm and eyes. A light, brighter than the ones above, was shone into my eyes. Fingers wearing rubber gloves parted my eyelids, held them open and let them go again. There was the sound of scissors close to my face. The blades seemed to clash together with all the ferocity of shears attacking a privet hedge. Skin was snipped from my face and from round my eyes, nose and ears. More skin was gripped by surgical instruments and torn away. Damaged and dead tissue was cut from my head, neck, chest and left arm.

'Right. That will do for now,' said the same man's voice. 'Bandage him up.'

Bandages were wrapped round my head, face, neck, chest and arm, totally enveloping me, even my ears and chin, leaving nothing uncovered except my mouth. The bright lights disappeared. It was darker even than when the gauze had been covering my face.

'Take him to the ward now,' said the man. 'He can have an injection to make him sleep.'

The needle went in and soon I did not care about anything any more. It was true that I could not see at the moment – not the operating theatre, not the faces, not even the scissors cutting the dead skin from my face. But I could tell there were lights shining overhead and I knew when the flashlight was shining in my eyes. It was true that I could not actually see the flashlight itself, but that was doubtless a temporary condition brought on by the fluid running into my eyes, and one that would soon be remedied by the treatment I would receive.

There was one matter, however, that made me a little uneasy – that remark by the doctor. *Christ! What a bloody mess!* What did he mean?

Chapter Three

It was not my first experience of hospital since that day in June 1924 on which I was born, to be followed an hour later by a sister. Much had happened in the twenty-two years that had passed since then.

My parents named their twins Constantine and Helen, but, in the family, called us Nino and Nina. By the time we were five, Nina and I, together with Lucia, our elder sister by two years, regularly swam in the sea that gently lapped the walls below the front garden of our house at Yeşil Köy – it means Green Village – an hour's drive from the centre of Istanbul. At meal times, we left the water reluctantly at my mother's call.

We were a close family. My father owned an import-export business in the city, leaving home each working day at 8 o'clock and not returning until the cool of the evening. Over dinner, for which we all sat down together, my mother used to discuss the events of the day with him. If I had been disobedient or had misbehaved, she would tell my father during the meal. I dreaded her disclosures of my childhood escapades. I loved and respected my father and the sight of the reproach in his face was more hurtful to me than any corporal punishment.

Soon afterwards, we moved into the city, into a second-floor apartment with six rooms in a block near Taxim Square. After the quiet of Yeşil Köy, I was fascinated by the sights and sounds of Istanbul – the calls to prayer from the many minarets, the street vendors with their emaciated horses, and the clatter of metal wheels on metal rails as the trams rumbled their way along the twisting streets. The vendors' horses were laden with baskets bulging with green peppers, tomatoes, celery, grapes, melons, cherries, peaches and plums. Men with wooden yokes across their shoulders offered yoghurt for sale from huge tins suspended from ropes on either side. My favourites, however, were candy floss and toffee apples – and *simit*, a doughnut shaped pastry sprinkled with spices, hung from sticks which each held as many as fifty pastries, lined up in a row like tasty-looking hoops at a fairground hoop-la stall.

When I was seven, I started school at the College of Saint Michel, run by *Les Frères des Ecoles Chrétiennes* – The

Brothers of the Christian Schools. During the long summer holidays, my parents used to rent a villa on the island of Büyük Ada – which means Big Island – an hour away by steamer. My mother and aunts ran the villa, my father sailed each day across the water to Istanbul to carry on his business, and we children went boating, fishing and swimming. They were beautiful, warm days filled with laughter and gaiety. September, when we had to sail back to Istanbul and school, always came too soon.

One day in November 1932, when I was eight years of age, I awoke with an agonising pain in my left ear. The doctor diagnosed mastoiditis, and arranged an immediate operation at the hospital of Saint George, which was run by German nuns. In those days there were no antibiotics, and my first impression of hospital was one of fear and pain. I remained in hospital for two months. My mother stayed with me in my room for the whole of that time. Apart from the comfort she afforded, my only happiness in hospital was derived from flying gas-filled balloons, brought to me by my mother on long pieces of string, from the verandah.

I completed my schooling when I was seventeen, having passed an examination equal to the General Certificate of Education in Britain, and was launched on the world. One by one, Yugoslav boys with whom I had been at school joined the army, and I watched them go with growing envy and patriotic feelings. Finally, I broke the news to my parents that I wanted to be a soldier. At first they were hurt and shocked, especially as they had expected me to take over the business from my tired and ageing father. Eventually, however, following considerable persuasion, they relented and reluctantly agreed. The day my parents accompanied me to the Yugoslav consulate in Istanbul was a happy one for me. My father gave his written permission for me to join the army and I signed with an eager flourish.

If only I had known what was to happen to me five years later, I would not have signed with such youthful enthusiasm. For that signature to enter the army was to change my entire life.

My mother did not come to the railway station to see me off. She kissed me goodbye at home and then turned away, hoping that I would not see her tears. My father, two sisters, aunts and cousins waved as I hung out of the carriage window. Haydarpasa Station was a sad place that day. It was 15 December 1941, and it was the last time I was to see my beloved father.

The carriage was cold and the wooden seats were hard. The discomfort was to last for four days – the time it took to reach my destination, a transit camp at Haifa, in Palestine. By that time, my youthful enthusiasm had begun to be tested. I missed home and the good food. I even missed being reproved by my mother.

My creased and travel-soiled civilian clothes, and those of the other raw recruits – mainly Poles – were replaced by soldiers' uniforms, in my case a baggy battle-dress and cheese-cutter cap bearing the Royal Yugoslav emblem.

Four weeks later, I was one of a small band of recruits who travelled by train to Agami, the headquarters of the 1st Battalion Royal Yugoslav Guards, in Egypt. By then, I was less homesick, and off-duty visits to Alexandria, the nearest big town, made me feel even more at home. It was two miles from Agami and, like Istanbul, cosmopolitan. The sounds and smells were similar to those of Istanbul, too.

After three months' basic training at Agami, we were posted to the Western Desert. On the way, the troop train screeched to a sudden halt, an alert was sounded, and orders were given to abandon it immediately. Out of the sky, Italian dive-bombers swooped down. Their target was the train. Bombs plunged towards it, some scoring direct hits and sending shattered pieces of carriages hurtling through the air, others exploding in the sand on either side. We huddled in the sand, our heads almost buried in it. The explosions tore at the ground and damaged the train badly. I knew then what war was like.

Our battalion set up camp at a place called Hellfire Pass, behind the lines of the British Eighth Army under General Montgomery. The tank force of the German General Rommel attacked and we were forced to retreat. Our battalion of infantry set out on another arduous journey, to Saida in Syria. There, attached to the King's Own Rifles and the Gurkhas, we were given more intensive training than we had received at Agami. In between training and weapon instruction, I played a lot of sport. Football was my passion and before long I captained my team in matches against other battalions. I was promoted to corporal and given the job of training the men in football, unarmed combat and physical training. One day, King Peter of Yugoslavia visited the camp. Spit and polish – literally – shone our boots even in such dusty surroundings. Following an official inspection, I captained the battalion football team in a match played before the king. As team captain, it was my honour to escort King Peter and introduce him to my team-mates. It was a proud moment, and a proud day, for me – especially when my team won.

After eighteen months at Saida, I was posted with the remnants of the battalion on attachment with the British Eighth Army at El Arish, in the Egyptian desert. The camp was mainly for refugees, Yugoslavs and Greeks, and our battalion was assigned to look after them. I was promoted to staff sergeant and put in charge of the stores. My job was to organise supplies of food and drink for the five hundred refugees. The cool evenings were beautiful and the village, surrounded by palm trees, was like the sort of exotic, faraway place I had previously seen only in photographs. It was easy to forget that a war was still in progress.

Six months later, the refugees were moved from El Arish to El Shatt and, soon afterwards, my unit was posted to do guard duties at the British army depot at El Kantara.

It was from there that I made, more than a year later, that fateful final journey to see Vinka at El Shatt.

Chapter Four

I awoke in hospital not knowing what time it was. The bandages swathing my head made it impossible to tell whether it was daylight or still the night. From the total silence around me, I guessed – correctly, as it turned out – that I was not in a ward but in a room by myself.

Eventually, a nurse entered. She washed my hands, injected penicillin into my rump and handed me a glass of warm milk. I was hungry and told her so. She explained, however, that I was permitted only liquids for the whole of that day. Provided I was feeling better, I would be able to have light solids the following day. She tried to slip a straw into my mouth to make it easier for me to drink the milk but, somehow, had difficulty in doing so. I knew that the bandages completely covered my face and that the hole they had left for my mouth was only a small one, but the difficulty experienced by the nurse seemed to be not in negotiating the bandages but in inserting the straw between my lips. When she succeeded, the straw emerged from the right-hand corner of my mouth at an angle of forty-five degrees, making it not only difficult to drink the milk but uncomfortable, too.

'I'm the ward sister,' said a newcomer. 'The first thing we must do is to put some drops in your eyes. You must have them every two hours.'

It seemed to me that by the time they had unwound the yards of bandage from round my head, put in the drops and bandaged me up again, the two hours would be up and it would be time to start all over once more. I told her what I was thinking and there was a laugh in the darkness.

'We won't have to take the bandages off each time,' she said. 'There are two little flaps over your eyes. See?'

I felt a movement over my right eye. Daylight flooded in. I could see. I could see the sister bending over me, smiling, her hair tucked behind her cap. I could see that she was wearing the uniform of a British army nurse, of the Queen Alexandra's Royal Army Nursing Corps, and I could even see that sewn across her tunic was a row of brightly-coloured medal ribbons. There was, however, something not quite right. The ribbons, her uniform, sister's face, the room – everything – was red. Bright red. She bent lower, a dropper in her hand. The drops flooded into my eye and the pad was closed. The flap over my left eye was lifted. I could see nothing. Not sister's face, nor her ribbons, nor her uniform. Not even in red.

The sister was the last woman, the last human being of any sex or age, I was to see for twenty-one years.

Mid-way through the morning, I pulled back the bedclothes, lifted the mosquito net, ducked underneath it, felt for the wall, collided with the locker and eventually found my way to the door. The floor was cool and refreshing on my bare feet after the heat of the day and of the bed, made worse by the mosquito net. No sooner had I entered the corridor outside the room than sister intercepted me. My explanation for my action was peremptorily dismissed and she insisted that I return to bed, did not get up again without permission, and rang for a bedpan in future.

The thought of using bedpans and bottles was one that horrified me far more than did the thought of what I must look like with my head shaved and my face burned. Like, I should imagine, many young men of my age, I was appalled at the prospect of going through my bodily functions lying down in bed, knowing that members of the opposite sex were liable to walk in unexpectedly and see me in such undignified circumstances. How could I possibly face them afterwards, especially knowing that they would have to take away and empty the unpleasant contents? The future was too distressing even to contemplate. Fortunately, as events turned out, the acute – and understandable – embarrassment of those first few weeks in hospital was not to last.

As the years passed, as the number of hospital confinements increased, and as the number of occasions on which I used bedpans and bottles reached treble figures, I found it was quite possible, even natural, while moving my bowels or emptying my bladder, to hold perfectly normal and intelligent conversations with women without the slightest trace of embarrassment. At that time, however, I was not only embarrassed, I was angry, too – angry because they were treating me like an invalid who had lost the use of his legs and who had to be confined to bed, when all the time I was young and strong with powerful leg muscles from playing football, and perfectly capable of walking to the lavatory. All I had was a burned face and some burns on my chest and arm, not paralysis of the legs. What I did not know, of course, was the severity of the burns, and what I did not appreciate were the after-effects, such as shock, that could result.

I was still grumbling inwardly at being confined to bed when, some time later, a doctor came to see me. He lifted the flap over my left eye. Light flooded in, but only light. There was still nothing visible. I sensed a dark shadow near my eye. There was a click and a flashlight switched on.

'Hmmm!' said the doctor.

He lowered the flap and opened the one over my right eye. I could see nothing. Not the doctor bending over me, not the flashlight he held close to my eye, not the sister hovering in the background, not the room, not even vague shadows. Only the sensation of light flooding in when the flap was lifted.

'Hmmm!'

They spoke in lowered voices, sister and the doctor. I listened carefully, hoping to hear what they were saying, but it was professional talk in medical terms I had not heard before and my knowledge of English was not sufficiently good to understand.

'I'll see you again, old chap,' he said in a louder voice.

He patted me on the shoulder, the door opened and he and sister left. I lay back on the pillow and considered the implications of the doctor's visit. An hour before, possibly two, when sister had opened the flap over my right eye to put in the drops, I had been able to see. I had seen sister herself, smiling down at me, seen her cap and uniform, even the medal ribbons sewn on the tunic. But, when the doctor had opened the same flap, I had seen nothing. I pondered what could have happened in the intervening period but I came to no conclusion. I wondered why I had not begun to panic, like they did in the films at the cinema when they found they could not see, before breaking down and weeping. The reason, I told myself firmly, was that I knew I was going to see. Perhaps, for the moment, I could not see faces, but it was not totally dark. I could tell when the flaps were opened and daylight flooded in.

The door opened and sister brought in a visitor.

'Good afternoon, Kosta,' said a voice.

'Major Rapotec!'

Major Rapotec was my commanding officer, in charge of the Yugoslav unit assigned to guard duties at the British army depot at El Kantara.

'You recognised my voice.'

'Straight away.'

'Are you feeling better?'

'A little.'

'It's a terrible thing, Kosta,' he said. 'Terrible. A tragedy.'

Major Rapotec was not normally a man prone to exaggeration or over-dramatisation and I could not understand the meaning of his words. The damage to my face and eyes was serious enough, certainly. That much I knew. But *tragedy*?

'It was good of you to come all this way, Major Rapotec.'

'Not at all, Kosta – not at all. The least I could do – the very least.'

He sat on a chair at my bedside and told me of events at El Kantara since I had left on my weekend pass, of plans for what was left of the battalion and of news from Yugoslavia. A nurse entered and Major Rapotec stood up to leave, presumably at an unspoken signal from her.

'Don't worry about anything, Kosta,' he said. 'We'll see to everything for you.'

'Thank you, sir.'

'I'll tell your friends to come and see you.'

'Thank you, sir, but I don't think that will be necessary,' I told him. 'I hope to see them all soon back at camp.'

Major Rapotec cleared his throat.

'Goodbye, Kosta,' he said.

As Major Rapotec left, three doctors walked in – the one who had examined me earlier in the day and two others, one of them, according to sister, the chief eye specialist. The flaps were lifted once more, lights were shone into my eyes and the flaps were closed. There was a murmured discussion between the three of them, again in medical language that I did not understand. Then they were gone.

At 6.30 the following morning, a nurse opened my room curtains, washed and dried my hands and sat at the side of the bed, a tray resting on the bed between us. The blackness behind my eye pads remained the same. I could see nothing of the light that must have invaded the room.

When I spoke to the nurse, the words came out in a sort of mumble, seemingly from the right-hand corner of my mouth and, when she tried to feed me the porridge she had brought, I found that I could not open my mouth at all. My lips seemed stuck together, sealed tight, and when I tried to part them, the pain forced tears into my eyes. Despite persuasive noises from the nurse, my mouth stayed closed. She pressed the spoon gently against my lips at the right-hand side and found a gap where the lips were not completely sealed. The spoon slid partway inside but, when it reached the point of its greatest width, would go no further.

'It hurts!' I told her.

'I'll fetch sister,' she said.

Sister seemed unimpressed by my mumbled explanation of the difficulty.

'We know all about your mouth,' she said. 'It's nothing to worry about.'

She had brought a teaspoon with her and that proved small enough to go inside. When the porridge was finished, I tried to question her. She was, however, decidedly unforthcoming.

'You mustn't worry yourself,' she said. 'It's nothing – no problem. A little snick with a knife and it will open again.'

It seemed clear that my lips were stuck together because of the burning, like two pieces of rubber, or many other surfaces, would stick together after being heated, or burned, and then pressed against each other. Sister had not explained. She had given only the sort of non-committal, diplomatic answer she was trained to give. It was no problem. A little snick with a knife. That was all.

On the Wednesday, my third full day in hospital, the daily routine continued – eye drops every two hours, penicillin injections every four hours, bedpans approximately every six hours and bottles, it seemed, more frequently than any of them.

Outside, I knew, the sun would have climbed into a clear, blue sky and would be scorching down on Suez town, on the canal and on the hospital. The temperature would already be soaring into the eighties. Inside the hospital, the burning heat was uncomfortable. Inside the mosquito net, inside my bandages, it was unbearable.

The routine and my consciousness of the heat were relieved by a visit from Lieutenant Mitar Djuritch, a friend from El Kantara, an officer in the same unit of the Royal Yugoslav Guards and a friend of my father's from back home in Istanbul, where he, too, a Yugoslav citizen working in Turkey, lived. With him came Private Milan Milanovitch, another friend. They sat on chairs, one on either side of the bed.

'How are you, Kosta?' Milan said. 'How are you getting on?'

'I don't know,' I said. 'Nobody tells me anything.'

'Don't you ask?'

'I ask – but they seem too busy to tell me.'

'A terrible thing to have happened,' said Mitar. 'Terrible.'

'I don't know what happened,' I complained. 'Nobody has told me.'

'You don't know anything?'

'Only that we were sitting in the tent, talking, when something hit me. I've been on fire ever since.'

Mitar clicked open his cigarette case and helped himself to a cigarette. There was the sound of a match striking and then the smell of tobacco burning.

'It was Staka,' he said.

Chapter Five

I had known Staka Raditch, a young Yugoslav refugee girl, for about two years. We had met when she had been living at the camp at El Arish and I had been stationed there. Before long, we had started seeing each other regularly. The six months spent together at El Arish had been fun, strolling under the desert moon, kissing and holding hands. On my part, however, there had been no serious feelings, no love. I had promised Staka nothing, nor given her any reason to think that she might have a future with me. Despite that, she had – to my own disquiet – broken off her engagement to a Yugoslav soldier stationed in Italy. At her instigation, we had then discussed the possibility of marriage but nothing had been agreed.

When Staka and the rest of the refugees had been moved to El Shatt and I had been posted with my unit to perform guard duties at El Kantara, I had continued to visit her. It had been a surprise, however, when, on my first weekend pass to El Shatt, Zenka Yovanovitch, her friend, had suggested that I spend the night with Staka. Coyly, she had whispered that Staka wanted to sleep with me – and was waiting for me.

I had known I was spending the night at the camp, but not with Staka, and I had gone to her tent against my better judgement. Unlike many soldiers stationed so far from home, I had not jumped at the opportunity of a night of free love with a woman without any thought of the consequences. The reason, however, had not been that I was in any way more virtuous, considerate, careful or cautious. It was simply that I was ill at ease because I had known that, once I had slept with Staka, she would regard me as her own, that, like all Yugoslav girls at that time, she would expect marriage as her right.

As it turned out, Staka's night of love had proved to be a disappointment to us both. When I had entered the tent, I had been mortified to find that Staka was not alone, that I was expected to spend the night in the same tent as seven other couples, separated only by hanging blankets draped from the top to form individual cubicles. Zenka and her boyfriend had lain by our side and I had known that every word of love I whispered into Staka's ear would be overheard by seven other couples, that they would be listening to each intimate sound of our love-making and we to theirs. The whole situation – of sixteen people crowded together in the same tent – had proved to be so overwhelmingly inhibiting for me that I had been totally unable to concentrate on pleasing Staka or even on enjoying the experience myself. I was not a virgin, but neither was I used to making love in such unromantic and public surroundings and, on that occasion, I had failed.

Surprisingly, perhaps, the humiliating experience had not discouraged me totally and I had returned on my next weekend pass. Staka had been ready for me that second time. Zenka had gone to another tent, to share another bed, leaving Staka and me alone, the double bed to ourselves. The bed had been prepared, the mosquito net draped over it. The bed, and Staka, were waiting for me.

Although Zenka had gone, however, the others had been there, just like the first time. They had lain in the darkness, listening to our grunting, giggling at our moaning. I had made love to Staka, made love to her once, and I could make love no more, not with the others listening like that. Staka had been unimpressed by my performance, and her observations on it afterwards had been less than complimentary. Zenka, she had said, had told her that men could make love six times in one night, and I had made love only once. I had been glad that the darkness had hidden the humiliation that I felt. Maybe men could make love six times in one night. Maybe I could – but not that night.

It had been the following day, on my way back to El Kantara, that the first doubts had arisen. I had cursed myself for being such a fool, for allowing myself to fall into the trap and to be seduced. The two girls had had everything planned, all worked out between them. The result of my foolishness had been that everyone in the tent knew that Staka and I were lovers, and, as a consequence, expected us to marry. I had realised that marriage was important to Staka, more important than to most women. Only by marrying could she have escaped from the camp. Only by marrying would she no longer be a refugee. She could always have returned to Yugoslavia, of course, but Staka and her family were Royalists and to have returned under the Communists would have been unthinkable. Marriage to another refugee would have been pointless, a certain sentence to hopeless years in the camps. Marriage to me would have meant an escape, a passport to a new life away from the camps, the prospect of a bright future in Turkey.

I had felt sorry for Staka, sorry for the future that lay ahead for her if she did not marry me, sorry for the desolation, the sadness, the depression, the despair that she and the other refugees must have felt. They had no paid jobs, there was nothing for them to do except odd work around the camp, and they had nowhere to go. They were simply waiting, waiting. I was sorry that such people, any people, should be so drained of their self-respect, sorry that the emptiness of living should be so chillingly reflected in their eyes. Nevertheless, I had not wanted to marry. I was only twenty-one at the time and too young to settle down. My whole life had lain before me. I had not wanted to commit myself, not wanted to be trapped into marriage without having a chance to think seriously about it. I had needed time to think. Why had I not heeded the warnings of my conscience? Why had I not refused when Staka had offered herself to me? Why had I not resisted temptation?

Those had been the first doubts, those and the ones brought on by the hurt Staka had caused me by her humiliating words about my prowess as a lover. It had been an incident at the Arab-owned café, half-an-hour's walk from El Shatt, however, that had caused me to think more deeply about Staka and me, to question our relationship, to ask myself whether this was really the girl with whom I wanted to spend the rest of my life. It had been a trivial incident, more trivial than any of the others that had caused me to doubt my feelings for Staka, but, somehow, one that had made a deeper impression. Three cakes had remained on the plate on the café table after we had eaten as many as we had wanted and, as we had been about to leave, she had opened up her handkerchief and put the cakes inside, to take with her back to the camp. I had been unable to understand the reason for her action, whether she had taken them because she was likely to be hungry, or whether it was pure greed. When I had remonstrated with her, she had refused to put them back and had stubbornly insisted on keeping them. I had known that perhaps the quarrel had been my fault for not being more understanding, that perhaps I should have realised that three cakes meant more to a refugee girl than they did to me. What Staka had done, however, was bad manners in my view, bad manners according to the way I had been brought up, at least. Staka had shamed and humiliated me. She had disappointed me and, from that moment on, had irritated me.

Even so, I had not rejected her, nor jilted her, nor even ended our relationship. I had returned to El Shatt yet again, taking

with me a gift for her, a pair of shoes. It had been clear, however, that she sensed my ardour had cooled, that my feelings for
her were no longer the same. My attitude must have become
even more clear when I had not stayed the night.

Then, on Sunday, three days previously, Staka had seen me
at El Shatt on my way back from the café – with Vinka.

Despite the background of my relationship with Staka, the
story unfolded by Mitar and Milan as they sat at my bedside
was one that filled me with growing incredulity.

While I had been talking in Vinka's family tent, Staka had
crept up quietly outside and had thrown the liquid at me
through the tent window, or ventilator, the flap of which had
been rolled up because of the heat. It had hit the strips of canvas
across the window and had splashed about in all directions. The
woman sitting next to me on the bed had been splashed on the
back of the neck but was not seriously hurt. As well as causing
serious damage to my face, eyes, chest and arm, the liquid had
corroded my cap badge, webbing belt, shirt and watch.

'And Vinka?' I asked anxiously.

'She's all right,' said Mitar. 'It missed the others.'

The shock that resulted from the realisation that what had
happened to me had not been an accident, as I had vaguely
imagined, but a calculated attack, and that my attacker had been
Staka, was heightened by the information that what had been
thrown at me was vitriol. I had read about vitriol in books but
knew virtually nothing about it. All I knew was that it had been
used by jealous lovers in days gone by to destroy a person's
looks. The very mention of the word, however, sent a distinct
chill through me.

I reached for my cigarette packet on the bedside locker, took
one out and lit it. I felt Mitar and Milan watching the gap
between my lips into which the cigarette fitted with so little
room to spare.

According to Mitar, the liquid thrown at me had been caustic
soda mixed with oil – the caustic soda to cause the burns and the
oil to make it stick to my skin. Even if I had tried to wash it off
I would still have been burned. The water would have run off
the oil without diluting the caustic solution.

'She thought of everything,' said Milan grimly.

The irony of the situation was that the mixture had not
originally been intended for me. Staka and Zenka had prepared
it with the intention that Zenka should use it in an attack on a
fellow soldier from my unit, Sergeant Dubrovnic, a boyfriend

who had jilted her. Zenka had been expecting him at the camp that Sunday but, fortunately for him, he never arrived. Unfortunately for me, the two girls decided that, rather than waste their carefully prepared mixture, Staka should use it on me. Being a civilian, Staka had not come under the jurisdiction of the military police and, instead of being detained by them, had been arrested by the Egyptian civil police and taken to Cairo jail.

I found it impossible to understand why Staka had done it, how love could turn into a hatred so intense that she could do such a thing to me, even if the mixture had really been intended for Sergeant Dubrovnic and I had become the victim only as an afterthought. It was inconceivable how anyone, even a jealous woman, could – in a supposedly civilised age – throw vitriol into a man's face in order to destroy it. If only I had never met Staka. If only, when Staka and the other refugees had been moved to El Shatt and I to El Kantara, I had allowed distance to end our friendship.

I asked Mitar if he would write to my father to tell him what had happened to me. Back home in Istanbul, Mitar and my father had met at one of the regular parties given by the Yugoslav consulate for Yugoslavs living in Turkey. They had been friends ever since.

'It will be better coming from you,' I said.

'I promise,' said Mitar. 'Goodbye.'

It was only later that I discovered that Mitar's description of the mixture thrown at me as 'vitriol' – dictionary definition 'Sulphuric acid or any of its salts (throw vitriol i.e. into person's face to blind or disfigure)' – was incorrect. The caustic soda (sodium hydroxide) – the dictionary definition of caustic is 'That which burns or corrodes organic tissue' – was not an acid but an alkali. It had proved every bit as corrosive, however, and, by an opposite chemical process, had achieved exactly the same result. It had proved a most devastating weapon in a classic *crime passionelle.*

After two weeks in hospital, it became clear to me that not only was there something seriously wrong with my eyes, but with my face as well. It was not that the doctors had said anything, nor sister, nor even any of the nurses. They had not. Nor was it the pain. That had gone after three or four days. It was the smell, the smell that came from under the bandages, seemingly from the region of my nose, and which seemed worse when I sniffed. It brought back to mind a day in Yeŝil Köy so many years before, when I had been playing in the fields with my sisters and we had stumbled across a dead cat, its decomposing body open to the flies, its gaping belly crawling with maggots. There had been a smell of rotting flesh and stinking bones. I tried to dismiss the very real fear that my flesh was putrifying by telling myself not to be ridiculous, by reminding myself that, as a boy, I had constantly been falling and gashing my arms and legs and that pink, new skin had always formed when the time had been right for the scabs to come off. In the same way as when I had been a boy, Nature would heal my face, mend the burns, replace the damaged tissues with smooth, pink skin.

By that time, I was bored. The daily routine was always exactly the same – wake up, wash hands and body, injection, tidy up the bed, breakfast, drops in my eyes, a doze, more drops, lunch, more drops, a visit from the eye specialist, *Carry on with the same treatment, Sister,* more drops, tea, a visit from one of the English officers from the other single rooms, more drops, supper, another injection, more drops. I had lain there in the darkness for two weeks, swathed in bandages, sweltering under the mosquito net. I longed for the day when they would take off my bandages and let me out of bed, let me go to the lavatory by myself and let me read a book. Staka had a lot to answer for.

I was concerned that the bandages were still on my face and that the doctors had told me nothing. Although the pain had gone, my face still felt tight and the hole between my lips was no bigger. I could still insert nothing larger than a teaspoon when I ate and, worse, I was unable to clean my teeth.

There was, however, occasional relief from the boredom and the worry. Two weeks after I had entered hospital, my room door opened and sister walked in. I could tell, from the rapid swish of skirts and the staccato clatter of footsteps, that she was in a hurry. When she spoke, her voice was pitched distinctly higher than usual and the words came out hurriedly, as if she were short of breath.

'I am sorry to tell you,' she said, 'that there has been a terrible mistake.'

The 'terrible mistake' to which sister referred had occurred on my admission a fortnight before. Although I had been an acting staff sergeant at Saida, I had, like everyone else, reverted to my substantive rank of corporal when the regiment had disintegrated. On my admission to hospital, one of the staff had misread the documents sent with me in the ambulance from El

Shatt. The abbreviation for corporal had been taken to be the abbreviation for captain – it had been read as 'Cpt' instead of 'Cpl' – and I had been entered as such in the official records. My khaki shirt with the two stripes on the arm would have avoided the confusion but it had been left behind at El Shatt when they had taken it off in Pavlo's tent. Since my arrival, everyone had been suffering from the delusion that I was an officer. Sister had discovered the truth only five minutes before. The reason for her disquiet was that, because of my exalted rank, I had been put into a private room in the officers' quarters when, in reality, I should have been in a ward with the other ranks.

I realised that the 'terrible mistake' was the reason I had been treated so well, why the nurses had called me 'Sir' and had politely inquired what I would like to eat, why sister and the doctors had treated me with such respect, certainly more respect than I was used to in the army and more than a corporal was entitled to expect. I realised, too, that that was the reason the other patients, the British officers, had been so friendly, calling to see me in my room, sitting down and having long, cheerful chats. All the time, in my innocence, I had thought that the private room, the concern, the attention, the respect, the friendliness, the fussing, had been because of my condition, because they felt sorry for me, because I was in bandages and had my eyes covered up.

'You can't stay here, of course,' said sister, unable to keep the agitation out of her voice. 'The orderlies will be coming for you in a few minutes.'

There was no time for any goodbyes, not to the nurses, not to sister, not even to my friends, the British officers. My demotion was even more rapid than my unexpected, and unannounced, promotion had been. My feet, as they used to say in the army, had not touched the ground. Sister was right. It had been a *terrible* mistake.

Soon after my arrival in the other ranks' ward, I was visited by an occupational therapist from the Red Cross who introduced herself as Sister Grayson. She explained that she thought it would be a good idea if I had something to occupy my mind and suggested that she should teach me to make ladies' belts. She started to show me how to plait together three coloured strings and then finish them off with a buckle to produce what she called a very smart ladies' belt for wearing round the waist with a frock. Her occupational therapy lesson in making ladies' belts had a far from therapeutic effect on me, however. My reaction was that plaiting coloured strings was girls' work and blind men's work, that and making cane baskets, and I told her so in no uncertain terms. Did she think I was blind just because my eyes were covered? Did she not know that I would be able to see again soon? How dare she give me work fit only for blind men? If I were to do any work at all, it had to be men's work.

My angry over-reaction was due to the understandable, but unspoken, fear that once I started doing blind men's work I would be doing blind men's work forever. She tried to persuade me that she had suggested the work not because she thought I was blind but because it would be good for my morale. If I occupied my mind I would forget my troubles, she said. It was all part of the healing process, all part of the treatment to get me well again. I would hear none of it, however.

'No thank you,' I told her angrily.

She sighed.

'I'll see you tomorrow,' she said.

By the next day, my temper had cooled and I had begun to think that perhaps, after all, she had been right, that I had been hasty, jumped to the wrong conclusions, not listened to what she was saying and not thought enough about it. Perhaps she had been telling the truth when she had said it was all quite normal. Perhaps it really did help when people's minds were occupied. Certainly, none of the other patients had reacted like I had. I had listened to them as she had gone from bed to bed, three to the right of mine and four opposite, and they had laughed and joked as they had plaited the pieces of string together after she had gone. They had whistled and sung, too. I began to think that, perhaps, I was the odd one out, that if the others were making belts, and enjoying it, and did not regard it as girls' work or blind men's work, then I might enjoy it, too.

I worried in case she would not come back like she had promised, in case she would not bother with me again after the disagreement of the previous day. I knew I had been rude, very rude, and I had meant to be. I could scarcely blame her if she did not try again.

My fears, however, proved groundless. When she returned, she had found out my first name and called me by it, and when she asked if I would like to try some therapy I was only too ready to agree. She showed me once more how to make the belts and then placed three strings into my hands. I ran my fingers over them, their full length, and laid them side by side across my knees. My fingers twisted the strings, over and over, nimbly, just like I had done at school as a small boy all those years before.

'Oh, fine!' she said. 'You don't need me to show you. Well done!'

She asked Harry, the patient from the next bed, to keep an eye on me, to make sure I did not get stuck and to show me what to do when I came to the end. A chair was drawn up and Harry sat down beside me.

'Carry on, Kosta,' he said. 'You're doing all right.'

Maybe I did not have my sight, not for the moment, at least, but when it came to making ladies' belts I was as good as any man in the ward.

The following day, I was listening to a record request programme on the hospital radio station when the announcer's voice crackled from the loudspeaker above the door, just to the left of my bed.

'And the next request is for Corporal Kosta in Ward Two,' he announced. 'It comes from Sister Grayson of Occupational Therapy and she asks for Bing Crosby and The Andrews Sisters singing *Down In The Valley* and *Don't Fence Me In*.'

A rousing cheer echoed round the ward, drowning the first few lines of *Down In The Valley*. I lay back on my pillow, listening to the voices on the record. The valleys back home in Turkey would be beautiful at that time of the year, the rich green of the hills slipping down to the plains below, the plains golden and heavy with wheat and maize, the sunflower crops glowing and shining in the warm sunlight.

The record ended and the second one began. *Give me land, lots of land, and the starry sky above.* I wondered when I would see a starry sky again, when I would walk in the cool of an Egyptian evening and see the million shimmering stars against the black velvet backdrop of the silent desert, when I would see the silently-moving ships reflected in the moonlight on the Suez Canal or the minarets of Alexandria silhouetted against that starry sky. *Don't fence me in.* It was three weeks since I had arrived in hospital, three weeks swathed in bandages, caged between brick walls without a single breath of fresh air, and I was certainly beginning to get that fenced in feeling.

Within minutes of the second record ending, Sister Grayson was at my bedside.

'I hope you didn't mind,' she said. 'Did you like it?'

'Yes, thank you, Sister,' I told her. 'I enjoyed it.'

She said she had noticed that I seemed to enjoy listening to the radio and wondered if I liked classical music. I told her that I was not an expert but that I did like it, particularly Chopin and Mozart. She asked if I would like to go to one of the record concerts held each week in the recreation room and I readily agreed.

The experience was one that made a tremendous impression on me and one that made me realise, for the first time, something that I had never believed possible – that there were, indeed, certain advantages in not being able to see. What I had told Sister Grayson was true. I was no expert on classical music. As a boy, I had liked opera and had often listened to my mother's record collection but, despite my father's encouragement, I had not learned to play the piano like my twin sister. Since then, my preference had been for popular music and Sister Grayson's choice of Bing Crosby and the Andrews Sisters had been perfect for me.

At the record concert, however, sunk in a deep armchair with Sister Grayson beside me and classical music-lovers all round me, the appeal of the records in the ward suddenly seemed to diminish. In the ward, there was a continual noise of matches being struck, patients talking, nurses going about their work, making it difficult, if not impossible, to concentrate.

In the recreation room, however, there was complete silence from the audience, each member of it engrossed in the music. To my surprise and exhilaration, the bandages over my eyes seemed to heighten what was already a tremendously exciting experience. There was nothing – no orchestra, no conductor, no heads in front of me – to detract from the exquisite sounds, just blackness in my eyes and the music in my ears. I was lost in a dream world of aria and arpeggio, chord and concerto, sonata and symphony, of Borodin and Brahms, Rachmaninov and Ravel, Strauss and Stravinsky. I was soothed, satisfied, warmed, comforted, floating, dreaming, enveloped by happiness. Could I ever be as happy again?

Despite my long-time desire for the bandages to be removed, when the day finally came I was not prepared for it. My immediate reaction was that, without them, I would not be able to face the other patients, not looking the way that, by then, I suspected I must look. I knew my face was burned and the skin still felt tight and drawn, as if stretched over my cheekbones and forehead from ear to ear. My lips were still sealed together and my head was shaved – and I knew what I looked like without any hair. Once, back at El Kantara, I had shaved my head as a joke to play in a football match and, without my thick, black hair, I had looked like a Japanese war-lord, with two bumps I did not know I possessed protruding from the top of my head like a pair of horns. The damage to my face, I knew, must have made my appearance even more grotesque and, without my mask of bandages, I felt naked.

I turned over on to my left side, my face against the wall, seeking to hide myself, ashamed to expose my face to view. The wall offered some protection, but not enough. I wanted to find out how I looked by feeling my face with my fingers but I knew that that would only draw attention to my face, make them realise I was self-conscious about it, make them stare at it even more.

'Hello, Kosta,' said Harry's voice. 'I see you've got your bandages off.'

Why did not Harry go away? Why did he not go back to his own bed and leave me alone? I turned to face him. There was no sudden intake of breath, no exclamation of shock, no swear word, no whistle of surprise, not even an expression of sympathy – but I knew, knew from the breathless silence, from the momentary pause before he spoke again and from the hesitancy in his voice when he spoke, that he was shocked.

'Give me a hand to the toilet, Harry,' I said.

That was where I wanted to be, in the toilet, with the door locked, on my own, away from them all. I bolted the door and sat down on the lavatory seat. Gently, tenderly, I smoothed my fingers over my face, exploring every tiny crevice, trying to see my misfortune through my finger-tips.

The right side of my face seemed almost untouched. There was a scab on the eyebrow but not a big one and the eyebrow itself and the eyelashes were still there. The eyelid appeared to be uninjured and the eyeball moved freely underneath. I could not see any images but I could see colours and I could tell that it was daylight.

I could see light with my left eye, too, although the light was an unnatural red. My fingers moved across to the left side. The top of my head, forehead, nose, mouth, neck and chin, virtually the whole of the left side, appeared to be a continuous mass of hard, scaly scabs. A discharge from the sores, hardened and crystallised, was matted and congealed with three weeks' growth of beard, unaffected by the damp cloth with which sister had

dabbed my face, refreshed but not washed it for fear of opening
the eruptions. The surface felt more like the contours of a relief
map than those of a human face. My lips, as I knew, were sealed.
A hole had appeared to the left of my nose.

Round my left eye, loose skin was hanging, loose skin that, at
the same time, felt stiff and tight. My eyebrow and eyelashes
had disappeared. The flesh underneath my eyeball was no longer
there, nor was the right-hand half of my eyelid. The piece of
eyelid that remained was shrivelled and burned like meat that
had been left in the oven for far too long. The burned flesh was
fused to my eyeball, so that when my right eyeball moved my
left one did not move with it or, if it did, there was no sensation
of it doing so.

My left eyeball itself seemed to have sunk right in, almost as
if there were no eyeball there at all, and, in the corner of my
eye-socket was a hole, a huge hole into which my finger disappeared with frightening and chilling ease.

Chapter Six

The discovery of the full, frightening effects upon me of the attack by Staka was one that reduced me to an immediate state of panic and, when the initial waves of panic had passed, to a state of shock. I remained rooted to the lavatory seat, numbed by the news that my probing fingers had communicated to my consciousness, transfixed by the shock brought on by the sudden realisation of its significance. For three weeks, ever since the day of the attack, I had succeeded in convincing myself – despite occasional and natural doubts – that all would be well, that the burns to my face would mend, that the skin I knew had been snipped off and cut away would be replaced by new, pink skin, that the body's normal healing processes would repair the damage, that the scars would fade and that soon there would be no trace of my injuries at all. Now, however, I knew the truth. I knew that the flesh to the left of my nose would not heal, because the flesh was no longer there. I knew that the flesh under my left eye and on the eyelid itself would not heal, because the flesh was no longer there. I knew that the flesh in the corner of my left eye would not heal, because the flesh was no longer there, only a hole big enough for my finger to fit comfortably in. I knew that I was disfigured and that, judging by what my fingers had found, the disfigurement would be permanent. For the first time, I knew the real extent of the damage to my face and, as a result, I was overwhelmed by feelings of horror and fear, of despondency and self-consciousness. I dreaded the inevitable return of Harry to the lavatory to help me back to the ward. I dreaded the inevitability of being forced to face the other patients.

Back on my bed, I attempted frantically to think of a way in which my desperate desire to hide my face from the world once more could be achieved. My opportunity came when I heard sister's footsteps.

'Sister,' I said. 'I've just been to the toilet and the light hurt my eyes. I need my bandages on.'

It was an excuse, a pretence, a pathetic plea for the cause of my self-consciousness to be covered up again.

'Oh, no,' she said severely. 'Doctor gave instructions that your bandages were to be left off.'

'But I need them, Sister. The light hurts my eyes.'

'Your face will heal more quickly exposed to the air.'

'Please, Sister!'

'I can't.'

'Please!'

The pleading in my voice seemed to have a softening effect upon her original adamant attitude. She paused. I could tell that she was thinking, perhaps realising that my story was a sham and considering what was the real reason behind my request for the bandages.

'I can't let you have the bandages on,' she said at last. 'But I could let you have some dark glasses.'

'That would be fine, Sister. Thank you.'

She returned with the glasses a few minutes later and fitted them over my eyes.

'How's that?' she asked.

'Much better, Sister. Thank you very much.'

I lay back on the bed and, for the first time since leaving the lavatory, began to relax. Gradually, my feelings of anxiety and shame about my appearance began to diminish. Soon I was no longer ashamed of my face, of what the other patients might think about it, because I knew they could no longer see it. Thanks to sister, I had my mask once again. Perhaps the bandages would have been better, perhaps they would have covered more of the ravaged face, but the dark glasses were almost as successful in hiding me from the world. Perhaps they did not completely cover the damage to my face but, at least, they obscured the damage round my eyes. Nobody, I knew, would be able to see through them and the knowledge of that fact provided an immensely satisfying sense of security and reassurance. Behind them I felt comforted and much more at ease.

From that moment on, I was continually on my guard to ensure that my face was never exposed to any of the other patients. Not one of them ever saw me again without my mask. Previously, when my head had been bandaged, I had slept soundly in the mornings, wakening sometimes long after the other patients, being roused only when one of the nurses brought me a cup of tea. Without my bandages, I willed myself to waken up each morning early, before the others, so that my protective mask would be in place by the time they awoke. The time mechanisms in my brain, carefully instructed each night before I went to sleep, regularly and dutifully carried out their orders to rouse me each day when the ward was still quiet with slumber. Each day, my first action was to reach out to my bed-side locker, feel for the glasses and put them on. Only then was I ready to face the day, to bid the other patients a good morning and to drink a cup of tea. Each day, the glasses remained in position from early morning until after lights out. Only when the ward was dark did I remove them and place them on my locker once more. Nobody but nurses and doctors saw my face without them.

Comforting though it was to be behind my dark glasses, however, the comfort and confidence they provided was by no means sufficient for me to present to the world the sort of personality I had presented before the attack. I was a frightened young man, frightened to venture far from my bed for fear of bumping into something or someone and hurting myself, frightened of what lay ahead for me in the future. I withdrew into myself. I became quiet and introspective. I spent long hours where I most wanted to be, where I was least unhappy, alone on my bed, hiding myself in the corner of the ward. The other patients tried hard to help me overcome my fears and anxieties. They talked to me, took me for walks in the hospital grounds, escorted me to the NAAFI canteen for cups of tea and tried to persuade me that, once I reached England – where I was hoping to be sent – for hospitalisation, the surgeons would soon restore my sight. The staff kept me busy with occupational therapy and by taking me to concerts. I agreed to it all and took part in it all without protest or complaint but also without enthusiasm or even interest. It mattered not one iota to me whether I went to the canteen or a concert or for a walk or occupied my fingers or simply lay alone on my bed with my thoughts. I was not aggressive, nor was I disagreeable, rude, nasty or difficult. It was simply that I was devoid of any feelings that could be remotely described as happy ones. I was melancholy, despondent and filled with despair. I had lost my *joie de vivre*.

Two incidents that occurred during that time, however, partially recaptured the interest in life that had deserted me and restored my hopes for the future. One evening, while walking in the ward, I suddenly saw a flash of colour with my right eye. It took only a few seconds for me to decide what it was.

'I can see a blue blanket!' I told nobody in particular, trying to keep the excitement out of my voice. There was a delighted murmur from the rest of the ward.

'Kosta can see the blue blanket!'

'Well done, Kosta!'

Not long afterwards, when the hubbub had died down, I asked Harry, the patient from the next bed, to take me outside to the lavatory. As we were returning, I looked up and saw a whitish glow, again with my right eye. At first, I thought it was the light from one of the roadway lamp standards or from one of the hospital rooms. Then, suddenly, I realised that it was neither.

'I can see the moon, Harry!' I cried triumphantly. 'I can see the moon!'

In fact, I could not see the outline. I could not tell what shape it was, whether it was a new moon, a half-moon or a full-moon, but I could see a white-coloured glow in the sky and I could tell that it was the moon. The excitement, when Harry and I returned to the ward, was even more intense.

'Kosta can see the moon!' Harry announced.

'That's marvellous, Kosta!' someone said.

'It proves you're getting better,' said someone else.

'Just wait till you get to England, Kosta,' said Harry. 'You'll be able to see all right then!'

Six weeks after my arrival at the 13th General Hospital at Suez, sister announced that it had been decided to transfer me to another British military hospital, the 63rd General at Almaza, near Cairo. The reason, she said, was that the 63rd General had a top eye specialist on its staff and a second opinion on my condition was wanted from him. The following morning, Harry helped me to pack and Sister Grayson gave me a letter to be handed to the Red Cross welfare officer at the new hospital, explaining to her the type of occupational therapy I had been engaged in. After breakfast, I said my farewells and, feeling decidedly apprehensive at having to start completely afresh with new doctors at a new hospital and new patients in a new ward, set off by ambulance on the six-hour journey to Almaza.

On arrival, I was taken to a ward which, judging by its noise, was a big one. It was lunch time. There was a tremendous clattering of plates and dishes, the clanging of cutlery being dropped on the floor, the babble of non-stop conversation and raucous voices shouting from one side of the ward to the other. Often, back in the eight-bed ward at the 13th General, I had longed for quiet but, compared with the cacophony of my new ward, it seemed I might almost have spent the past six weeks on an uninhabited desert island. Harry and his pals might almost have been bound by a vow of silence.

The ward sister guided me to her office and asked a few routine questions. Did I have pain in my eyes? Did I sleep well? Were my bowels open? A nurse showed me to my bed and left me sitting on a chair. I felt completely lost. I gazed, unseeing, around me, hoping that someone would speak to me. It seemed a long time before anyone did.

'Hello,' said a voice at last. 'Where have you come from?'

It was the patient in the next bed. I told him a little about myself and, from him, discovered that I was in a 60-bed ward, that it was a good hospital, with friendly staff and patients, and that the chief eye specialist I had come to see was a Major Gillan. I unpacked my kit and put it in my bedside locker. Immediately after the evening meal, I went to bed. After the long journey from Suez, I was in need of an early night and I fell asleep almost at once, wondering what the following day would bring, whether the specialist's verdict on my eyes would be good news or bad news.

I awoke full of hope. I washed, shaved and enjoyed breakfast, longing for 11 o'clock, the time Major Gillan always carried out his rounds, to arrive. After what seemed an eternity, it did.

'This is the new patient, Major,' said sister. 'Corporal Fettel.'

'I won't see him now, sister,' he replied. 'Bring him to the dark room when I've finished my rounds.'

I tried to listen to his conversation with the other patients, to judge from his words and from the tone of his voice what sort of man he was. He seemed to offer everyone words of comfort and encouragement and, even though I could not see him, I concluded that he was a kind and friendly person.

In the dark room, I was seated on a chair and Major Gillan flashed lights into my eyes. He instructed me to look up, look down, look to the right and to the left and asked me if I could see anything when I did so. I could not. At the end of his examination, he told me that the cornea of my right eye was badly burned and that he could see little of my left eye because it was covered with burned tissue: he could not give an opinion on the condition of that eye until he had cleared away the tissue. He patted me encouragingly on the shoulder and told sister to take me back to the ward.

The following day, Major Gillan returned to my bedside and gave me news that I had not dared to hope for. Because of my condition, he had decided to send me to England, where corneal grafts were carried out and where I would have a better chance of successfully regaining my sight than in Egypt.

'You will be flown to England at the first opportunity,' he said. 'On the first available plane.'

Not unnaturally, I was delighted. So, too, for my sake, were the other patients. As soon as Major Gillan had left, they crowded round my bed, patting me on the shoulder and congratulating me.

'You'll be all right in England, Kosta!'

'You'll soon be able to see once you get there!'

The hospital's Red Cross welfare officer called on her rounds. She introduced herself as Sister Freeland and I handed her the letter I had brought with me from Sister Grayson. She read it, asked me how my injuries had occurred and promised to come to see me after her rounds. When she returned, we talked for a long time and, during the conversation, discovered we shared a common interest in the French language.

'From now on,' she said brightly, 'you and I will speak together in French. The practice will be good for me.'

The following day, Sister Freeland brought me a loom and showed me how to operate it to make a scarf. True to her word, she spoke in French, except for difficult translations that forced her to revert to English, and I replied in French. From that day on, whenever we met, we used English as little as possible.

In the weeks that followed, Sister Freeland and I discovered that we had much more in common than simply a love of French. Somehow, from that first meeting, we seemed to take an immediate liking to each other, to be totally compatible and, before long, it seemed only natural that she should no longer be Sister Freeland to me, but Lois. Whether purely because of her liking for me or because of sympathy for me, or perhaps both, Lois made a decided point of befriending me. She taught me to touch-type on a borrowed typewriter, spending hours showing me the correct positions to hold my hands, helping me to memorise where the individual letters, numbers, full stops and commas were. Within three weeks, she had attained the object she had set out to achieve – to give me the ability to type my own letters home, instead of having to rely on other people to write them out for me. So confident was she of my newly-acquired skill that she did not feel it necessary to check my letters, only the addresses I typed on the envelopes.

Soon after our first meeting, she took me outside the ward for the first time, for a walk in the hospital grounds. As we strolled arm-in-arm, she described the scene for me, the large, modern building, three- and four-storeys high, the chapel that stood in the gardens, the layout of the gardens themselves, the positions of the paths, lawns and flower-beds and the varieties and colours of the flowers.

'Bend down, Kosta,' she urged. 'Smell this.'

She positioned my nose over a cluster of flowers and I sniffed in their scent. She told me what variety they were and described them for me and, as we walked, repeated the procedure at each flower-bed we came to.

Doctors and nurses passed us as they moved from one hospital building to another. Lois introduced me to those with whom she was particularly friendly.

A new sound came to my ears. I stopped.

'I can hear a hissing noise,' I told Lois.

'It's water,' she explained. 'There's a spray watering the garden.'

It was a new experience for me to be guided on an outdoors walk by an intelligent woman like Lois, one who described everything to me in an interesting way, and, with her help, I was able to visualise the scene almost as clearly as I could have done through my own eyes – perhaps more so, for I was also aware of the varied fragrances of the different flowers, something of which I would certainly not have been aware in normal circumstances. Had I been able to see, it would certainly never have occurred to me, on a walk round a garden, to have stopped at each flower-bed to smell, and to attempt to distinguish between, the aromas of the many different varieties. It was clear to me that Lois was trying to make me feel at ease, feel at home, and, in that objective, she succeeded completely. I felt at ease and at home because she was with me and because she was such a kind and friendly person.

As part of her plan to keep me occupied and interested, Lois persuaded me, each week, to push her trolley for her on her regular tour of the wards, distributing one free issue of a round tin of fifty Player's cigarettes to each patient and selling sweets, chocolate and tobacco. It seemed that she knew almost every patient by name and that she introduced me to all of them.

'This is Kosta – he can't see,' she told them.

The patients joked with me and teased me about going around with such a beautiful girl as Lois. It was the first indication that I had had that Lois was pretty and, as a result, I was secretly proud to be seen in her company, delighted that she had chosen me as her special patient and strangely self-satisfied at the thought that the other patients might be even faintly jealous. In addition, I was pleased that, although I could not see, I was able to be of use to someone, even if it was only pushing a trolley.

No sooner had life begun to assume a new interest for me than my spirits were dashed by the first of many disappointments. Perhaps because of the good relationship I had with Lois, the task of breaking the news to me fell to her. Because I was a Royalist Yugoslav and because the Allied Powers had recognised the Communists under Marshal Tito in Yugoslavia, it had been decided that I could not be allowed to enter Britain. Officially, I was classed as a stateless person and, were I to be allowed into the country, I would be a political embarrassment to the Government.

The news was a bitter disappointment. I felt that everything was lost. I had heard so many wonderful forecasts from the other patients, and from Lois herself, that, once I was in England, my sight would be restored. Major Gillan, I knew, did not want to operate in Egypt. Now there seemed to be no chance of an operation to restore my sight.

Lois tried to coax me out of my despondency by encouraging me to be optimistic.

'Don't give up hope,' she urged, without much conviction. 'We'll try to do something through the Red Cross.'

Almost before my attempts to regain my sight had started, my hopes of ever being able to see again had been ended, not by a human failing or a medical inadequacy, both of which I could have understood and accepted, but by a political issue, which I could not.

In an attempt to counteract the effect upon me of the distressing news from England, Lois began to spend even more time in my company, to take me for walks every day, instead of every few days, round the hospital to visit the many friends whom, by that time, I had made, and to stroll in the fragrance-filled gardens. As the days passed, my mood of depression began to lift, I began to accept my blindness and my outlook became more cheerful. One English patient, a former boxer, taught me the rudiments of the noble art of self-defence, how to hold up my hands to defend myself and how to lead with a classic English straight left. To the delight of the other patients, the two of us used to hold good-humoured boxing matches, bobbing and weaving, playfully tapping each other with carefully-pulled punches, falling into clinches and collapsing with uncontrolled laughter as the spectators shouted and cheered.

Despite my improved mental attitude, however, the words of Major Gillan – that when I went to England I would see – were always in my mind. It was a further disappointment, therefore, to learn from Lois a few weeks later that Major Gillan was being posted back to Britain while I remained in Egypt with no hope of following him and that, as a result, I would no longer be his patient. Instead, a new eye specialist, a Captain Spinks, was taking over my case. My first meeting with Captain Spinks came soon afterwards. I had been to church one Sunday morning with some of the other patients when an orderly told me the new eye specialist wanted to see me in the dark room. His examination was brief. Immediately it was over, Captain Spinks told me gravely that he must operate on my right eye. The cornea, apparently, was dangerously thin and, if he did not operate, the eye would collapse.

Two days later, I was given neither breakfast nor a morning cup of tea. A nurse administered an injection in my arm and, about fifteen minutes later, my entire body felt dried out, as if devoid of all fluids. By the time a trolley arrived to wheel me to the operation theatre, I felt totally relaxed, almost as though I did not belong to this world. In the theatre, anaesthetic was injected into my arm.

'Count to five and you will go to sleep,' said the anaesthetist. I followed his instructions and, before I had reached a count of six, darkness enveloped me.

I awoke, vomiting, back in the ward. I was vaguely aware of a woman's voice, a voice I did not recognise.

'Keep still,' it said. 'Don't move. Keep your head still. There's a bowl under your chin. Try not to move your head.'

For a whole week, I was made to lie flat on my back. It was a week that passed with agonising slowness, the boredom relieved only by being washed and fed, by sleeping, by visits from Lois and by dictating letters to her to be sent to my parents. Before the operation, I had written to my father and had told him about Lois and all her kindnesses to me. My father wrote beautiful English and Lois read to me a letter she had received from him, thanking her for looking after me so well. I was pleased, for my sake as well as Lois's, that he had taken the trouble to let her know how much both he and I appreciated her kindness. I tried to find out from Lois about the operation, what Captain Spinks had found and whether it had been successful. Lois seemed either to have little information, however, or to be distinctly unwilling to part with it.

'We'll have to wait and see when the bandages come off,' she said repeatedly.

The bandages were taken off a week after the operation. To me, it seemed that my right eye was exactly the same as before. I could still tell with both my eyes that there was light in the ward and the light I could see with my right eye was still red. Captain Spinks said nothing during his examination of the eye. Then he turned to sister.

'He can get up now,' he said. 'I want to see him in the dark room.'

'He'll be very weak walking.'

'Put him in a wheelchair.'

Captain Spinks did not say anything to me during the whole of his examination in the dark room and I did not dare to ask. By that time, I had learned that it was folly to ask too many questions, to show signs of impatience. That was a course destined only to anger them. My friends had impressed upon me that it might take a long time and had urged me to have patience and I heeded their words. In addition, there was not the same friendliness about Captain Spinks that there had been with Major Gillan. He sounded cool and aloof and, rightly or wrongly, I felt that, to him, I was a mere number, not a person. Questions, I decided, would definitely not be welcomed. I was wheeled back to the ward no wiser about my condition than when I had left it.

Half-an-hour later, I was lying on top of my bed when Lois sat down beside me on the bedside chair.

'Kosta,' she said in a matter-of-fact voice. 'I've just been talking to Captain Spinks. He's told me they won't be able to do anything for you. You will be blind all your life.'

Chapter Seven

The words that Lois had spoken to me were immediately both chilling and frightening. I could feel the colour draining from my face, my heart beginning to pound and my hands beginning to tremble. Not unnaturally, the verdict of Captain Spinks was one that not only horrified me but badly shocked me as well. I was twenty-two years of age, full of life, and to be condemned to a lifetime of blindness seemed to be a sentence too cruel to bear and one that was totally undeserved.

Within less than a minute, however, the symptoms of shock that had engulfed my body began to subside and were replaced by feelings of defiance and anger, defiance at the verdict itself and anger at the way in which it had been given to me. Immediately, in my mind, I defiantly rejected the pessimistic conclusions of Captain Spinks and, instead, clung to the optimistic forecasts of Major Gillan. The anger I felt was at the way Lois had broken the news to me, so blunt and direct, with no comforting words leading up to it, Lois, my best friend, who had taken me for walks and befriended me. Worse, the matter-of-fact tone of her voice seemed to me to be incredibly brutal and callous, cruel and unfeeling, almost as if she were gloating at my misfortune. Why had Lois done it? Why her? Why had she not let someone else break the news?

In that moment, I forgot all the kindnesses Lois had shown to me. I was convinced that her kindness, her friendliness, her helpfulness, had all been a sham. Now, at last, she had revealed herself as she really was – cold, callous and cruel. Only a cruel person could have come straight out with such news, news that she must have known was certain to hurt me dreadfully; only a callous person could have told me in such a gloating voice, not in a sad or sympathetic voice that one might have expected. I resented her, hated her and wanted nothing more to do with her. That one sentence – 'You will be blind all your life' – had completely turned me against her.

'I don't believe it,' I told her coldly. 'Major Gillan told me that when I went to England I would see.'

'I'm sorry,' she said. 'That's what Captain Spinks says.'

'Major Gillan told me I would have a corneal graft in England.'

'I know – but that was then,' she persisted. 'The condition of your eye must have changed.'

'It hasn't changed – it's just the same as it was then,' I told her bitterly. 'I should know – it's my eye.'

'But Captain Spinks has examined it and he says there's no hope.'

'Why should I believe a young captain?'

'Because he's an eye specialist – and a good one.'

'I prefer to believe Major Gillan.'

'You must accept it, Kosta. Nothing can be done.'

'I don't believe it.'

Not only did I not believe it, I did not want to believe it, nor did I want to accept it. The way in which Lois had defended Captain Spinks convinced me even more of her treachery, convinced me that the two of them must be working together. In my mood of cold fury, I not only resented Lois's actions but her very presence at my bedside, too. When she attempted to resume friendly relations, to cheer me up, I was not ready to be placated and I was nasty and bitter towards her.

'We'll still be able to go for walks together,' she said brightly, almost as if nothing had happened, as if nothing had been said.

'No, thank you,' I told her grimly.

'But you like it in the gardens.'

'I don't want to.'

'You'll still visit your friends?'

'No, thank you.'

'We'll still be friends?'

'I don't want your friendship any more.'

Lois ignored my remark and the bitterness that lay behind it and tried to pursue a new line of argument with me.

'You mustn't take it too badly,' she said. 'Blind people these days can be taught to lead independent lives.'

'I don't want to listen to your talk.'

'They can do everything that a sighted person can do.'

'Go away and leave me alone.'

She was silent for what seemed a long time before she spoke again.

'I'll see you again, Kosta,' she said.

'Don't bother,' I told her.

I lay alone on my bed and thought about what Lois had told me. I did not weep or show any emotion but I was unable to erase her words from my mind. 'You will be blind all your life.' What hurt me even more was the fact that she had left me with no hope. Even when I had protested and told her that I did not believe it, she had still insisted that there could now be no chance. It seemed almost as though she did not want me to have hope, as though she wanted me to accept my blindness.

The other patients – possibly in reality, although more likely in my imagination – seemed to become more friendly towards me, stopping to talk and joke even more than usual, and I was convinced that Lois must have told them that my blindness would be permanent.

'Hello, Kosta!' more than one of them said.

My reaction was invariably the same.

'Buzz off!'

Not infrequently, the language I used was considerably stronger.

'Fancy a walk to the canteen?' they asked.

'Go away – leave me in peace,' I replied.

I had always been religious. For as long as I could remember, I had prayed every evening, either before going to bed or when I was in bed, asking for God's blessings on my parents, my sisters and other relatives, and on those relatives who had died. For two days after Lois gave me Captain Spinks's verdict, however, I turned against God. I lay on my bed with closed eyes, distraught and mentally weary, and the prayers I said were not loving ones, Christian ones, for people who were dear to me but bitter ones full of introspection and self-pity.

'If you exist, Lord, why are you making me suffer like this?' I asked. 'I'm the only blind man in the ward. Why am I the only one suffering in this way? Why am I suffering at all? Why are You punishing me in such a dreadful way? Why give me such bad news at the age of twenty-two?'

By the time a day had passed from that unforgettable moment when I was told I would always be blind, I was beginning to feel uneasy about the embarrassing and self-pitying nature of my prayers and guilty about the fact that not only had I lost my faith in the Lord but had actually begun to doubt His existence. Full of remorse, I asked sister to send for the Roman Catholic padre, a young Englishman in his thirties whom I had met during my regular attendances at services in the hospital chapel. I had received communion from him twice or three times a fortnight since my arrival and he had become a regular twice-weekly visitor to my bedside for cheerful talks. Now, in my moment of need, when my faith was at its weakest, I needed the strength that both he and the taking of Holy Communion could provide.

The following morning, the nurses tidied my bed in preparation for the priest's visit. A table cloth was spread over my bedside locker and a glass of water placed upon it. A screen was placed round my bed. Suddenly, the noise and the clatter that was always present in a ward of sixty patients was stilled. In the total silence that followed, I could hear the padre's footsteps approaching my bed.

'Good morning, Kosta,' said the familiar voice.

'Good morning, Padre.'

'I hear you've had bad news.'

'I have, Father.'

'I was sorry to hear it.'

He placed a chalice on the locker and then sat on the edge of the bed. I knelt before him in my hospital uniform of white shirt and blue trousers.

'When were you last at Mass?' he asked.

'Last week, Father,' I told him.

'That's good.'

'Can I make my confession now, Father?'

'Yes, when you're ready.'

I made the sign of the cross.

'I've been thinking bad thoughts about people, Father. Particularly towards someone who was kind to me and was trying to help me. I know I shouldn't have done.'

'Don't take it to heart.'

'I felt weak when she brought me the bad news. I lost my faith in the Lord. I know I should have taken it in a better spirit, Father.'

'It was understandable. It was in a moment of desperation.'

'But I still feel weak, Father. I feel as though I'm losing my faith even now.'

'The Lord suffered. He put us in this world to face trials and tribulations and He suffered for us. You musn't lose faith, my son.'

'I'm trying not to, Father.'

'You must pray more and take the sacrament more often. That will give you strength.'

'I confess to despair, Father. I know that's a bad thing for a Christian.'

'Don't despair. If you truly believe you will never despair. Our Lord suffered without a murmur and, in the end, he was resurrected into glory. He said, "Forgive them, Father, for they know not what they do." You should try to be forgiving, too, my son, just like our Lord was.'

'I'll try, Father.'

'Always remember, my son, that this life is nothing. It passes. You suffer in this world but you will be rewarded in the next world. If you believe that, everything makes sense.'

'Thank you, Father. I'll remember that.'

'Have I heard all your confession now?'

'That's all, Father.'

'Will you make your act of contrition now, my son?'

I made my act of contrition, saying the set prayer silently to myself, asking God's forgiveness for my sins. The priest put his hand on my head.

'I absolve you from all your sins,' he said. 'For your penance, my son, you will say three Our Fathers and ten Ave Marias.'

At the end of the set prayers of the communion service that followed, the priest attempted to place the communion wafer on to my tongue but found he was unable to do so because the gap in my sealed lips was so small. Only when he broke the wafer into two pieces did he succeed. After the taking of the bread, I drank from the glass of water at my bedside. The service ended and the padre took his leave.

'Goodbye, Kosta,' he said.

'Goodbye, Father.'

I was grateful that, in the huge ward, patients and staff of different Christian denominations, of different religions and of no religion, had shown such thoughtfulness and reverence during the whole of the time I had been closeted with the priest. The total silence that had gripped the ward from the moment of his arrival had continued to be observed throughout the whole of his visit and was finally broken only when his footsteps could no longer be heard.

The words of the padre and the taking of Holy Communion had an immediate and profound effect upon me. Only the previous day, I had felt that everyone was my enemy – the other patients, the nurses, Captain Spinks and, particularly, Lois. Now, however, I felt that I had received renewed strength. Now I had the courage to face another day. I was calm, cool, encouraged, almost strong. I felt clean, cleansed of my sins, peaceful, mentally relaxed and at ease with my conscience. Lois, I knew now, had not been gloating when she broke the news.

Her matter-of-fact approach, her lack of sympathy, had been a deliberate attempt to keep the news clinical, a deliberate attempt to avoid commiseration and pity. Her insistence that there was no hope had been deliberate, too. She had been cruel to be kind, believing it to be better for me to accept the truth, the inevitable, from the start, rather than to be tormented by false hopes in months, perhaps years, to come. Once accepted, she must have believed, the inevitable would become bearable. Now, having talked to the padre and taken Holy Communion, I realised that, perhaps, she was right. I forgot my blindness, accepted it. I knew that God was surrounding me. I knew that I had to accept all the suffering that lay ahead of me in this world without fear, without complaint, without despair. I knew, too, that throughout it all Christ would be with me and that, despite everything, I would find happiness.

'Lord, give me strength,' I prayed. 'Give me courage. Give me patience. Lord, let the miracle happen so that I will see again one day.'

The events of the previous two days were forced to the back of my mind. I enjoyed my breakfast, put on a smile, was pleasant to the other patients and, to all outward appearances, was back to normal. Even sister, on her rounds, noticed the change.

'Good morning, Kosta,' she said. 'You're looking much happier today.'

'Good morning, Sister, I'm feeling much happier.'

By the time Lois arrived, I was prepared for her. I hoped she would not mention my eyes but, if she did, I was ready for it. To my relief, however, she did not.

'Have you had a good night?'

'Yes, thank you, Lois.'

'Would you like to go for a walk today?'

'Yes, please, Lois.'

'I shall have to teach you to walk by yourself.'

'That will be nice.'

'You'll soon be independent.'

'I hope so.'

'I'll come back for you this afternoon.'

'Thank you very much, Lois.'

Despite my apparent return to normal, however, I knew that what I felt was not really true normality. No matter how hard I tried not to think of it, the fact that I had just been told I would never see again kept creeping back into my consciousness and

I knew that, to some extent, I was playing a part, creating an impression, pretending to be the brave soldier, the brave patient, who could not care less, who could smile through adversity.

In the days that followed, however, I began to enjoy life once more. Lois began taking me out again, for walks, for picnics, to classical music record concerts or simply to sit in the hospital grounds and talk. On my own in the ward, I used to put out my hands in front of me so that I would not bump into anything. With Lois, however, I felt at ease and full of confidence simply walking with her arm through mine or with her hand in my hand. Lois told me about her home and her parents, how they always had a Bible on the table at home. During the war, she had been a member of the Women's Land Army and had driven a tractor. She described England to me and told me how green it was, with fields and hedgerows and trees and trout-filled rivers. My pleasure at having Lois for company was heightened by the effect it had on the other patients.

'You lucky old sod, Kosta,' they used to say. 'Not only going out – but having a pretty girl to take you. I wish it was me.'

For some reason, she had chosen me to befriend, to do a little extra for, and that made me feel wanted, made me feel important.

One day, without warning, she asked me if I would like to go to a dance.

'Where?'

'In Cairo,' she replied. 'At the YMCA club.'

'But how will I see?'

'Don't worry. I'll be your eyes.'

'I won't be able to dance.'

'Of course you will!'

'I'll trip over your feet.'

'Never mind.'

'I might ruin your shoes.'

'If you do you can buy me a new pair.'

The obvious reluctance with which I greeted Lois's suggestion did nothing to deter her from carrying it out. She was determined that I should be made to face the world, to begin to lead as near normal a life as possible. My natural apprehension at attending my first dance as a blind man increased even more as we arrived by taxi at the YMCA.

Inside, we sat at a table. Lois said there were lots of tables ringing a wooden dance floor. I could hear the movements of bodies dancing past to the sounds of a gramophone record. Lois introduced me to some people she knew. I had bandages over my eyes and, knowing that, I was at ease in meeting them. Lois left me to fetch food from the buffet and, when she had gone, I felt completely alone. I could hear the babble of voices from every corner of the dance floor, from every one of the tables round me. I was surrounded by people, yet I felt totally lost. The thought came into my mind that Lois would not come back, that I would be left on my own in this strange place, that I would never be able to find my way back to the hospital, and I began to panic at such a dreadful possibility. Her voice, when I heard it again, was as welcome as the shepherd's call to a lost sheep.

'It's only cucumber sandwiches and lemonade, I'm afraid,' she said. 'I'm sorry there's nothing stronger to drink – but they don't approve of booze here.'

'That will do fine, Lois,' I assured her, smiling, caring only that she was by my side once more.

'Do you want to dance?' she asked when we had eaten the sandwiches and drunk the lemonade.

Before I had joined the army, I had learned to dance at parties given at home by my sisters and me, though I was not a particularly good dancer. In normal circumstances, I would have been delighted to dance with Lois but now, because of my blindness, her invitation filled me with apprehension. I was frightened because I did not know how I would manage to dance without being able to see. I was overcome by dread at the possibility of my treading on her feet. Lois, however, appeared to have no qualms or, if she had, she did not reveal them. She sounded relaxed and the way she was talking to me, perfectly naturally, as if she waltzed round dance floors with blind men every day of her life, began to lessen my anxiety and put me at ease.

'If you tread on my feet it doesn't matter,' she said, reading my thoughts.

Another record started to play. It was a tango. The name of the tune was *Jealousy*. It was a non-vocal record, in strict tempo purely for dancing, but I had heard the sung version many times and I knew the first few lines of the lyric. *'Twas all over my jealousy, 'Twas all over my jealousy*, it began. I tried to stifle a cynical smile. It might almost have been written for me – and sung by Staka.

'Come on,' said Lois. 'Have a go and enjoy yourself.'

'How will I be able to guide you?'

'I've told you – I'll be your eyes.'

She took my hand and led me on to the dance floor. I could tell that it was crowded. The first few steps, however, made it clear that it was hopeless. Being unable to see, I guided her not away from people, into the open spaces, but into the other dancers. We bumped into several couples, I apologised profusely, our legs became entangled and I almost overbalanced and fell.

'It's no good, Lois,' I told her. 'We'll have to give up.'

'No we won't,' she replied firmly. 'I'll take the part of the man. I'll guide you.'

Lois began to move towards me, guiding me backwards, and I took my first faltering steps in the opposite direction from the one in which I had always danced. It was awkward and unnatural for me to be dancing the woman's steps but, at least, it was more successful than before. Lois, at least, could see where we were going, could avoid the more bone-shaking head-on collisions. Even so, my lack of sight still resulted in the occasional collision. Three more times during that one dance I had to turn my head and say 'Excuse me!' as we finally brushed past the couple into whom we had bumped.

'Relax!' Lois urged. 'You're like a lump of lead!'

'I'm trying my best to relax, Lois. I'm trying to be natural.'

'Try a bit harder. Just be yourself.'

'Is everyone looking at me?' I asked anxiously.

'Don't be silly,' she said. 'They're all far too busy dancing to look at you.'

By the time we had danced a slow foxtrot, my anxiety had begun to recede rapidly. By the time we had danced a quickstep, followed by an old-fashioned waltz, danced to the tune of *The Blue Danube*, it had gone completely. I no longer cared about anyone. Lois had given me confidence in myself and I was thoroughly enjoying the evening. I realised that Lois and I would never make our mark as contestants in the world ballroom dancing championships, nor ever provide serious competition for Ginger Rogers and Fred Astaire but, at least, we had managed to make our way round the dance floor. Perhaps our movements were slow and deliberate, perhaps the steps we danced were not always the correct ones, perhaps we were occasionally out of step and perhaps the rhythm was sometimes lost but, at least, we enjoyed ourselves. When our legs became entwined and we almost fell, we stopped dancing and collapsed with laughter into each other's arms. I knew that neither Ginger Rogers nor Fred Astaire would have obtained such fun from so appalling a Terpsichorean *faux pas*.

We went back to our table, had another drink of lemonade and then returned to the dance floor for the last waltz. I held Lois close to me. I could tell that she was not dressed in her usual outfit, the uniform of a Red Cross welfare officer, and I asked her what she was wearing. She was in civilian clothes, she said, a black skirt and a white blouse. I tried to visualise the girl I held in my arms. I knew, from what the other patients had told me, that she had an oval face, blue-green eyes and chestnut hair, and I knew that everyone said she was pretty. I knew, from the many occasions I had held her hand while out walking, that she had long, slender fingers. I could tell, from holding her close to me on the dance floor, that she was tall, about five-feet-nine-inches, that she was slim and had an attractive figure, the sort of figure most men, most soldiers, dream about, especially when incarcerated in hospital for weeks on end, with no female company but the professional company of nurses and no hope of a less clinical association with the opposite sex in the foreseeable future.

The dance ended and we stood to attention while a recording of *God Save the King* was played. It seemed only natural that, sitting together on the back seat of the taxi we had hailed to take us back to the hospital, Lois and I should hold hands.

'Did you enjoy yourself?' she asked.

'Yes, thank you, Lois. It was lovely.'

'I'll take you again,' she said. 'Are you happy?'

'Very happy.'

During the time I had been stationed in Egypt, in the days before I had lost my sight, I had visited Cairo several times and was familiar with many of its sights, sounds and smells. I had seen the women in old-fashioned black dresses and with long, black scarves draped over their heads, the elegance of the wide, tree-lined boulevards and palm-fringed embankments bordering the River Nile, the dozens of mosques and minarets looking exactly as they had done in days gone by, in the days of the sultans and caliphs, the narcissi, lilies, jasmine and other cultivated flowers in the gardens, the cypresses, eucalyptus, elms and willows in the parks, the hundreds of open stalls and tiny shops in the twisting maze of lanes that formed the Ali Baba world of the bazaars, the ancient-looking boats with their tattered sails on the Nile, and the *feluccas*, Mediterranean coastal vessels with oars or lateen sails, not only winding their way from the river mouth through the fields and sand-spits of the Nile Delta but also venturing up-river into the city itself. As the taxi sped through the darkening streets, Lois described to me some of the sights I had not seen before.

I sank into the padded upholstery. I felt relaxed, contented, full of *bonhomie*, pleasantly nostalgic. I thought of my parents, of the dance, of Lois, but my thoughts seemed almost far-away, as if in a dream. I was aware of the arousing fragrance of Lois's perfume and I was conscious of the pleasure I felt at having a lovely girl sitting next to me and at holding her hands. Yes, without doubt, I was a lucky man to be able to go out like that and enjoy myself so much.

Suddenly, Lois turned in her seat, leaned across my lap and fell into my arms.

'Kiss me, Kosta,' she whispered.

Chapter Eight

I could feel the warmth between us as Lois lay in my arms, not only the physical warmth caused by the closeness of our bodies but the spiritual warmth of our feelings for each other. In all the weeks, months by then, that I had known Lois, I had never once thought of kissing her. Had I thought of it, I would never have dared to kiss her, to try to kiss her, to ask her for a kiss even, for fear of what her reaction might have been. Warm though we were towards each other, close though our relationship had become, I was still conscious of the fact that she was a Red Cross welfare officer, while I was only a corporal, and that welfare officers were to be treated with a certain amount of respect by the other ranks, no matter how friendly they might become off-duty.

For my part, my feelings for Lois had been purely platonic. To me, she was a good and close friend, no more. The reason that I had not thought of her in romantic terms was not that I found her unattractive but simply that the possibility of a romantic relationship with her had not occurred to me. For me, there was still the barrier of the professional relationship, the welfare officer-patient relationship, even though I realised that I was, to her, a rather special patient. I had not considered that there could ever be anything more.

Now, however, when Lois was lying in my arms asking me to kiss her, when, for the first time, I was thinking of kissing her, when, for the first time, I wanted to kiss her, was longing to kiss her, I could not. I could think only of my face, of what I looked like, of how horribly disfigured I was. Bandages covered my eyes and encircled my head. My face was grotesquely scarred. My mouth was nothing but a little hole. My lips were sealed. I was repelled by my own appearance and the thought of a pretty girl like Lois being kissed by such a face filled me with repugnance. Why had she said it? How could such a pretty girl bear to be kissed by a face like that? Why should she want me to kiss her?

'I can't, Lois,' I told her at last.

'Why not?' she asked.

'How can I kiss a pretty girl like you with a face like mine?'

'I want you to.'

'No! Look at my face! My mouth is shut. I'm disfigured. How can you ask?'

I knew that, if I kissed Lois then, there was a distinct possibility that I would fall in love with her and that she would fall in love with me. That, I knew, would plunge both of us into an impossible and complicated situation. One day, perhaps sooner rather than later, Lois would be returning home to Britain. I would be left in Egypt, a stateless person, unable to go with her to Britain, or to follow her later, because of the political situation, because, as a Royalist, my entry into Britain would cause difficulties with the Communist régime in Yugoslavia. Even supposing I was eventually allowed into Britain, what could I possibly offer Lois in my present pathetic plight?

Suddenly, a new thought came into my mind, a disturbing thought, a thought that I did not even wish to consider but one that, I knew, I could not now put out of my head. Supposing, just supposing, the reason that Lois had asked me to kiss her was not because of any feelings of warmth for me, because she liked me, even because she loved me, but because she felt sorry for me. Supposing, just supposing, she had asked me to kiss her not because she was feeling loving towards me but because she pitied me. Supposing, just supposing, she had asked me to kiss her not because she wanted to be kissed, because she knew that to be kissed by me would give her pleasure, would make her heart beat faster, would make her long for more, but because she thought it would give me pleasure, make me feel wanted still, make me feel like a man still, make me feel that I was desirable still.

I considered the possibility that the reason was none of those, that Lois had simply been overcome by the warmth of the evening, by the romance of the East, by the exotic sights and sounds of old Cairo, by the scents of the lily, jasmine, narcissus, cypress and eucalyptus, by the seductive effects of her own perfume, by her own feelings of happiness. I longed for there to be a simple and natural explanation. I considered them all – and I rejected them all. Inexorably, I was drawn to the conclusion that Lois had been motivated by pity. I became convinced of it.

To this day, I do not know why Lois asked me to kiss her. I have often wondered why. At the time, so totally convinced was I that I knew the reason, that she had asked me to kiss her because she pitied me, that I did not ask her. Instead, I withdrew into myself, crawled back inside my protective shell, erected the barrier round me once more and allowed feelings of self-pity, self-doubt, resentment and bitterness to well up inside my breast. I released my left hand from that of Lois and withdrew my right arm from round her shoulders. Lois pushed herself up from my lap and resumed her seat, sitting rigidly and formally beside me. I moved away from her to the far side of the taxi seat and stayed there, leaning against the corner like a stiff and unbending wooden clothes-prop waiting to be called into use on wash day. Lois followed my example and slid across to the opposite end of the seat.

The warmth between us had disappeared. Everything had changed. So heavily-charged was the atmosphere that I doubted that even the proverbial knife could have cut it, not unless it was an unusually sharp one. The question of Lois's request for me to kiss her was never mentioned again. The rest of the journey was completed in total silence.

As the weeks passed, I began to think of my friends back at El Kantara, the British army base twenty-four miles due south of Port Said where I had been stationed before my first admission to hospital. The 1st Battalion Royal Yugoslav Guards were still carrying out guard duties there. Because, after six weeks, I had been moved from the 13th General Hospital at Suez, at the southern entrance to the canal, overlooked by the bare mountain peaks of the Sinai Peninsula and the barren Gulf of Suez coast-line, to the 63rd General Hospital at Almaza, near Cairo, the only friends from El Kantara I had spoken to since the day of Staka's attack had been Major Rapotec, Lieutenant Mitar Djuritch and Private Milan Milanovitch – and their visits had been during the first few days of my hospitalisation.

'I'd love to see the boys again,' I confessed to Lois one day. 'Back at El Kantara.' I thought about what I had said and realised that, even if I met them again, I would not actually see them. I amended my statement accordingly. 'I'd love to meet up with some of the boys to have a chat.'

'What's stopping you?' asked Lois.

'It's too far for them to come,' I said. 'I can't expect them to. Not all the way from El Kantara.'

'But you could go there.'

'How?'

'I'll take you.'

Within a few days, Lois had obtained permission from the doctors for me to be allowed a forty-eight hour pass and, somehow, had obtained a jeep to take us there. When we arrived, the warmth of the reception from my friends almost compensated for the long, hot journey through the dusty desert, through villages that had changed little over the years, with tumbledown houses built of mud and clay, Arabic signs over the shops, men riding ancient bicycles, women in long flowing robes and yashmaks, carrying enormous baskets on their heads, all vividly described to me by Lois.

So delighted were my friends to see me, so sincere was the spontaneity of their greeting, that I was convinced that, through the centuries, through history, nobody could have received a more rapturous reception upon his return except, perhaps, the prodigal son, and that was only a parable. Everyone crowded round me, clapped me on the back and demanded to know how I was.

The delirium of the first half-hour was followed by an excited tour of the camp. I was taken to the tents of various friends with whom, so far, I had not been reunited and who had not been told of my arrival.

'Here's Kosta!'

'Come in, Kosta!'

'Have a drink, Kosta!'

As the wine flowed and as its effects both upon my friends and upon me became imperceptibly apparent, I began to harbour my first doubts about the wisdom of my visit. There was too much kindness from them, too much sentimentality, too much sympathy. It poured from their lips and from their hearts. It flowed over me, enveloped me, suffocated me, and the more of it there was in which to wallow the more upset, irritated and angry I became.

'Poor old Kosta!'

'What a dreadful thing to have happened!'

'It's destroyed your whole life!'

'Poor you!'

I was upset that I had to be guided from tent to tent in a camp that I knew so well and that, once inside each tent, its occupants seemed almost to be competing to see which of them could bestow the most attention upon me. No sooner had I entered the first tent and exchanged greetings with my friends than one of them took hold of my arm to guide me to a seat. No sooner had he done so than others jumped up to take hold of my other arm.

'Be careful, Kosta!'

'Mind you don't fall!'

'Look out – don't hurt him!'

Together, they walked me to a convenient chair and settled me down. They fussed round me, chattering, asking questions, inquiring whether there was anything I wanted. Increasingly, their none-too-welcome attentions reminded me of those of a flock of over-anxious, over-protective mother hens.

'Have a glass of wine, Kosta!'

One of my friends poured me a drink. Another passed it to me with detailed warnings about the location of the glass in relation to my hand. A third grasped my right hand and wound my fingers round the glass. The rest clucked sympathetically.

'Here you are, Kosta – it's just in front of your right hand.'

'Just about two inches away.'

'Got it?'

'Be careful!'

'Are you sure you've got it?'

'Mind you don't spill it!'

'Don't fall with a glass in your hand!'

Their actions and reactions were repeated, almost identically, in each tent at which I called. Everyone wanted to help. I realised that everyone thought he was doing his best but, un-fortunately, their attentions left me limp and lonely, feeling as lost as a sheep that has wandered far from the flock, as helpless as a new-born baby.

The get-together in one tent included most of the battalion football team, of which I was a leading member and captain. Also there was one of the battalion officers, a major, who made an observation which, in the general hubbub of conversation, I was doubtless not meant to hear but which, unfortunately, I did.

'We used to call him the Sherman Tank,' he said. 'When he walked, the earth used to tremble. And look at him now . . .'

I knew exactly what he meant. I had earned the nickname of the Sherman Tank because of my displays on the football field. I was virtually six feet tall and weighed thirteen stone. I had broad shoulders, a barrel-like chest, powerful neck muscles for heading the ball and bulging thighs and calves. Not only did I drive my players to the point of exhaustion, I drove myself, too, usually from the centre-half or left-back positions. I was famous for my ferocious tackling, powerful shooting and stampeding runs up field, shoulder-charging the opposition from my path, forcing my way past defensive tackles, bursting through the middle like a big, unstoppable power-house of a bulldozer. It was because of that that I had become known as the Sherman Tank.

'And look at him now . . . ' Now I was covered in bandages, unable to see a football, let alone kick one, having to be led around the camp like a little dog. The major's remark was hardly tactful, to say the least. A person with tact would scarcely have tried to draw attention to, and compare, what once I was and what I had become. At first, I was consoled by, and prepared to forgive him because of, the thought that it had been said in sorrow, uttered out of sympathy. Then I remembered that the major came from the same village as Staka. Although he and Staka were not related, they came from the same stock and, because of that, I began to doubt his motives, to wonder if the remark was not a sympathetic one, but a sarcastic one. I was sensitive about my blindness, easily hurt. I became convinced that he was cynically comparing my former self with my present self, letting everyone know that here was a man who was once so active, who had once taught him physical training – as, indeed, I had in my capacity as a physical training instructor – who once had been captain of the football team, and pointing out the pathetic shambles I had become, moving around like a robot, zombie-like, having to be pointed in the correct direction, having to receive instructions for almost everything I did. What a change in a man! 'And look at him now . . . '

I was hurt by the major's words and I was still thinking about them, and suffering from them, when Lois and I, together with both the officers and men of the battalion, sat down to a meal, specially prepared in our honour, and served on tables for which crisp, linen table-cloths had even been found. The hurt was quickly replaced by acute embarrassment, however, as Lois and I, as principal guests, faced the assembled gathering. The first course of soup, which I could manage to drink easily with a spoon, was followed by a main course of meat, potatoes and salad, which I was not then adept enough to eat with a knife and fork. I could feel one hundred and fifty pairs of eyes upon me, burning into me through my bandages, as I tried to eat the food with a small spoon. Lois was forced to help me find the various morsels. She took my hand and guided it round the plate, locating the food for me and implanting the locations in my memory with the aid of an imaginary clock.

'Here's the meat at twelve o'clock,' she said. 'Here's the salad at three o'clock. The potatoes are at six o'clock and there's a piece of lettuce at nine o'clock.'

'She's an angel,' they said to me in Yugoslav.

'You lucky man to have such a woman looking after you!'

The eyes burned into me with even greater intensity, watching, astonished, moved, horror-stricken, as the small spoon bearing the food slipped into my mouth through the gap in my sealed lips. I could feel my face reddening with embarrassment, feel the blood coursing through my body and flushing my features, and I was glad that they were not able to see all of my face, that the bandages round my eyes and head partly obscured my discomfiture. The conversation during the meal was forced, stilted, difficult, and I was relieved when it was finished. I drank the Egyptian wine that was served with it but left the final few pieces of food.

'There's some more left on your plate,' Lois pointed out, telling me something I already knew.

'I'm not hungry,' I lied.

I could not tell Lois the real reason, not with the others listening. The last few pieces of food were always the most difficult to capture. It was always necessary to go hunting for them, searching, feeling with the spoon all over the almost-empty plate and, even then, it was frequently nothing but fresh air that was scooped up.

Only when the meal had ended and the plates had been cleared away did I begin to feel at ease. Still sitting at the tables where we had eaten, we were treated to a concert performed in our honour by the men. Yugoslav songs were sung. Someone played the drums. A small choir sang. The audience joined in a sing-song. And, all the time, I was happy in the knowledge that everyone was watching the singers, the drummer, the choir, and not watching me.

When the time came to go to bed, however, my lack of confidence returned. Lois left me with my friends while someone else showed her to her own quarters. Without her, I was lost. She was my right arm, my eyes, my strength. I had drunk quite a considerable amount of wine during the day, on our arrival, during our tour of the tents, at dinner and during the concert, but not enough to shed my inhibitions. In order to make me feel more at home, it had been arranged that my quarters for the night should be the same tent in which I had previously slept. Even my old bed had been provided for me. The soldier who had taken my place in the tent had moved out, into another tent, vacating my former bed so that I would be sleeping in the same position in the tent and would know exactly where everything was. It was a considerate gesture that was greatly appreciated by me and one that, together with the fact that all the other occupants were the friends with whom I had previously shared the tent, did much to put me at my ease.

One problem arose almost immediately, however. Before going to bed, I needed to visit the lavatory. The camp was an isolated one, out in the desert, and the latrines were five minutes' walk away from where the tent was situated. Even a sighted man could have lost his way in the dark, let alone a blind man, and I knew that I could never find my way to the lavatories on my own. It was an embarrassment having to ask one of my old comrades, Pavlo Ivanovitch, to take me there and, after we had struggled through the soft sand, almost stumbling as our feet sank into it, it was even more of an embarrassment to have to ask him to show me where the toilet paper was. My discomfiture was increased by the knowledge that, as I sat in one of the cubicles, one of a row, all open to the sky, Pavlo was standing outside, waiting for me. The lavatory seats consisted of squares of wood with holes cut into them and, underneath the row of cubicles, a huge pit had been dug in the sand. Normally, at that time of night, I would have been grateful for the fact that there were few flies about, not the inevitable swarms that crawled and flew and seemed to fill the lavatories during the day-time, but I could hear Pavlo whistling outside and I felt I had to hurry before he became too impatient.

'Are you all right?' he called. He was becoming impatient already and I cursed the fact that I was so totally dependent on other people, even when going to the lavatory.

Back at the tent, I sat at a table with three of my friends. The other two sat on the beds. The wine flowed. We talked. I could feel their pity. They tried to comfort me.

'What did the doctor say?' they asked.

'Do you have any pain?'

'You'll see a good specialist if you get to England.'

'Don't worry. You'll be able to see.'

They asked about Lois – a lovely person, they said – and I told them how I spent my time at the hospital.

Despite the fact that I had spent six months in the tent, I was unable to find my way around. I was humiliated at having to be assisted to my bed, to be guided to it in case I fell over the beds or bumped into the tent pole, and the humiliation was increased when, as I began to undress, my friends tried to help me unfasten my clothing.

'It's all right. I can undress myself,' I told them, trying to keep the irritability out of my voice. 'All I need is a chair to put my clothes on nice and neatly, in the correct order, so that I know exactly where to find them in the morning.'

The oil lamp was extinguished. The hard army mattress was scarcely adequate cushioning from the wooden, plank-like base of the bed and the coarse blankets next to my skin were a poor substitute for the clean, white sheets at the hospital. I thought of changes that had occurred in my life since the last time I had slept in that tent, in that bed.

Only a few weeks before, I was one of the lads, running, playing football, playing volley-ball. It was at El Kantara that, as a joke, I had shaved my head, completely bald, to play in a football match. It was at El Kantara that my prowess at volley-ball, first learned at school, had won me many wagers. Sometimes, I had bet my friends that I could take on and beat as many as six of them at the same time. The sweat had poured off me as I smashed the ball over the net to score the points and, more often than not, I had won. I was good at all sports and, because of it, I was popular not only with the men but with the officers, too.

Only a few weeks before, I had carried out guard duties, had paraded on the square, had visited the camp cinema to see Bing Crosby, to see Walter Pidgeon and Greer Garson in *Mrs Miniver*, to see the British comedian George Formby singing and playing his ukelele, to see Tom Mix, Ken Maynard and Gene Autry in American cowboy films.

Now, I could no longer do any of those things. I was no longer a sportsman, no longer a soldier, not even fit to sit in a cinema audience. I was a complete wreck, completely lost, like a little child being led by the hand from place to place.

Only a few weeks before, I could see my friends. Now, I was completely in the dark.

Even my relationship with them was no longer the same. For them, for the other five in the tent, life had continued exactly as before. For me, everything was different – and the atmosphere between us was different, too. My every movement was watched. They were too kind, too fussy. I could feel their pity and I felt that I could not breathe. I felt apart from them. I was among friends I had known for years and yet I was among strangers. I was longing for the following day to come, so that I could return to the safety of the hospital. The sooner I left El Kantara the happier I would be.

Next morning, they led me to the ablutions, where I washed and shaved in cold water. My feelings of unease were not dispelled, however, until ten o'clock, when Lois called for me at the tent and I heard her voice for the first time since the evening before.

'So this is where you used to live, Kosta,' she said. 'I thought I'd come to have a look.'

'Ah, my guardian angel – you've arrived!'

My guide, my protector, my shepherd, my friend, had returned – and I was happy once more. They had made a fuss of her because she was my friend, spoiled her, she said. We breakfasted on toast and coffee. Lizards scuttled from under our feet as we toured the tents to say goodbye. We walked towards the jeep. Had I been able to run from the place, I would have done so. The longer I stayed there, the more disappointed, the more dispirited, I had become.

'Were you happy to see your friends?' Lois asked during the drive back.

'The first half-hour was lovely – but then I felt I was among strangers,' I confessed. 'Now all I want is to get back to the hospital.'

'You shouldn't try to hide,' she chided. 'It's good for you to meet people.'

Perhaps she was right. I did not know. All I knew was that I longed to be back in my familiar ward where I knew where everything was, where my toothpaste was, where my razor was, and where I did not need to be taken to the lavatory.

Chapter Nine

The security I felt in my familiar ward, and with Lois, was not to last, however. One morning in February 1947, when I had spent six months at the 63rd General Hospital at Almaza, sister told me that all the patients and staff were to be transferred to other hospitals. The British had apparently made an agreement with the Egyptian government to evacuate areas where there were large populations, which included cities such as Cairo and Alexandria, and withdraw to the Canal Zone. The 63rd General was to be either closed down or handed over to the Egyptian civilian authorities. It had been decided to send me to the 27th General, a big garrison hospital at Tell el Kebîr, near Ismailia, not far from the northern end of the canal.

Lois was being posted to Cyprus and came to say goodbye to me on the day before I was due to leave.

'We must keep in touch,' she said. 'I'll write to you from Cyprus giving you my new address. Then you can let me know all your news.'

I could detect no hint of emotion in her voice but my own feelings were of overwhelming sadness to be losing Lois. Except for that one moment when she had told me I would always be blind – and I had long ago forgiven her for that – she had provided me with enormous strength and confidence. She saw the look of despondency on my face and tried to cheer me up.

'When I take some leave in Cyprus I'll come to see you at Tell el Kebîr,' she promised. My forlorn expression did not improve. 'One day, when you come to England, I'll take you to see my parents.'

She had told me about her life back home in England, in a small country town called Woking, in Surrey, just to the south of London. Her father, a stonemason who chiselled the inscriptions on gravestones, was a very religious man who would not permit a wireless, which he regarded as an apparatus of the devil, into the house. He was a passionate devotee of the Holy Bible and, as Lois's mother was equally religious, Lois had had a remarkably cloistered upbringing, enlivened – if that is the appropriate word – only by the family's regular readings from the scriptures. Lois had never said that she was unhappy at home but I had always sensed that she was. Army life had always seemed to suit her and I guessed that, in the Red Cross, she had found an escape from the confined atmosphere and restrictions of her home.

'Goodbye, Kosta,' she said.

We shook hands. She went away. I was alone.

The four-hour journey to Tell el Kebîr was completed by ambulance. I did not relish the prospect of starting all over again at the new hospital. It was difficult, especially as I was newly-blind, to adjust to new voices, new people, new routines, new buildings. This time, without Lois, it was even more difficult to readjust.

Somehow, the hospital itself did not seem to have the same friendly atmosphere as the 63rd General had had. The buildings seemed more like barrack-blocks than hospital wards. My own ward, however, was intimate, even if it had little else to commend it. There were only four beds, each occupying a corner position in the small room. Sister introduced me to the other three patients, who showed me the way, down a corridor, to the outside lavatory.

A few days later, sister announced that a badly-injured soldier had been admitted and that a blood donor was urgently needed. Were there any volunteers? I stepped forward. To my surprise, she declined my offer. Not only was I surprised, I was affronted – and I demanded to know the reason why.

'Because you're blind,' she said. 'You need all your blood.'

It seemed a pathetically lame excuse. In my sensitive state, I became convinced that the real reason was not that I needed my blood but that, because I was blind, I was not suitable as a donor; because they regarded me as being physically handicapped and, therefore, physically unfit, my blood was thought not good enough. The rejection was not simply that of my blood but of me as well. They could not accept my blindness. They were rejecting me as a person and it was that that hurt. My three room-mates tried to reassure me, to convince me that my offer had been declined simply because they did not want to disturb me, but I could not be coaxed out of the mood of sullen despair and dejection into which I had lapsed.

The temporary resentment I felt towards sister rapidly evaporated, however, when she revealed to me that she spoke French and, as the letters sent to me by my father were always written in French – the language we always spoke in the family – offered to read them to me. Her kind gesture was one of which I took full advantage. On one occasion, however, my inadequate knowledge of colloquial English caused considerable embarrassment both to sister and to myself.

I knocked on the door of her office, anxious to know the news contained in the two letters from my father, both of which had arrived at the same time.

'Good morning, Sister!' I said breezily. 'I have two French letters for you today!'

There was a gasp, followed by a long, shocked silence. When she spoke, there was a definite, frosty edge to her voice.

'I beg your pardon!' she said, in a tone that suggested she did not know what the world was coming to.

'I have two French letters for you,' I blundered on. When the resumed silence showed no signs of being broken, I added, 'From my father – for you to read to me.'

The distinct sigh of relief puzzled me. I could not understand what could possibly be disconcerting her. After all, it was not the first time I had handed her a French letter.

'Oh!' she said vaguely. 'I thought you meant something else . . . '

It was only later, when I recounted the story to my three friends in the ward, that I learned that the peculiarities of the English language are not always what they seem.

Whether I had knocked my arm while asleep I never knew. When I awoke, however, my right wrist was swollen and painful. An X-ray revealed a fracture. A plaster cast was put on the arm from the fingers to the elbow, leaving only the ends of the fingers and thumb uncovered. The arm was placed in a sling across my chest.

To my chagrin, I could no longer wash myself or shave myself. The little independence I had gained had gone.

Two days later, my right hand became more painful. Then it began to throb.

'If you move your fingers to exercise them,' said the doctor called by sister, 'it will be all right.'

It was not. On the contrary, the pain became worse and worse until, eventually, I was complaining bitterly almost every five minutes. Pain-killing tablets did little or nothing to ease my discomfort.

'My hand is getting worse!' I shouted from time to time. 'I can't stand it!'

Nobody took any notice. Possibly because I was not only blind but foreign as well, the nursing staff decided that I was making a fuss over nothing. After three days, three days in which I had suffered increasingly severe pain, even my friends in the ward apparently became convinced that I was a professional moaner and attention-seeker.

At first, they treated my complaints as a joke but, when they continued despite sister's assurances, their humour turned to irritation.

'Why are you making such a fuss?' one of them asked testily. 'There's nothing wrong with you. They've told you you're all right.'

It was too much. We were in the middle of lunch and, with my good left hand, I snatched up the dish of tapioca pudding with which I had just been served, took careful aim in the direction of his voice, and hurled it with all the strength I could summon, with all the fury I felt after three days of unheeded complaints, with all the anger I had confined inside me at the way in which I had been ignored. It missed him and crashed against the wall. The shattered fragments of the dish flew like shrapnel all over the room. Tapioca clung to the wall and slid down on to the floor.

'Shut up!' I shouted. 'Just you bloody shut up!'

The commotion brought sister hurrying into the ward.

'You musn't lose your temper like that!' she scolded, when she discovered what had happened. 'Other people have to clean up the mess, Kosta!'

'I'm in pain and nobody does a thing to help!' I shouted.

'Doctor says to move your fingers and it will be all right!'

'I move my fingers – but the pain just gets worse and worse!'

'You're a naughty boy to throw that dish!'

'Buzz off!'

Four days after the pain had first started, I could no longer feel my fingers or thumb. They were so swollen that they looked like beef sausages. The pain in my hand and arm, though, was agonising. I knew that something was wrong, seriously wrong, and I knew that, in view of the indifference with which I was being met by both staff and patients, it was vital that I acted quickly to make them realise the gravity of my situation.

Thoughts of suicide passed through my mind. The fingers of my left hand were free. I could pick up a razor blade, slash the veins of my right wrist, and end it all – but did I have the courage? The Lord giveth, the Lord taketh away. Perhaps it might be better to inflict a superficial wound, just enough to draw attention to my plight, just enough to let them know how desperate I was. I opened my locker and took out my razor. Stealthily, I removed the blade and hid it under my blankets.

There was a shout. One of the other patients had seen me. Sister came hurrying in. There was a whispered conversation. She stalked over to my bed.

'What are you trying to do, you naughty boy?' she demanded. 'Why have you got a razor blade in your blankets?'

She took the blade away. I said nothing. She knew, or thought she knew, that I was planning to kill myself.

In a low voice that I was not intended to hear, she asked the other patients to watch me and to report any untoward incident. Soon afterwards, she decided that further precautions were necessary. A male nurse positioned himself on a chair at my bedside. I could tell that, at lights out, the light over my bed remained on. I was under observation. Thankfully, a strong draught of foul-tasting medicine sent me to sleep and, gratefully, the sleep banished the pain.

The following day, I found I was no longer allowed a knife and fork. Only a spoon was provided with which to eat my meals. The cutlery I always used had disappeared from my locker. So, too, had my razor blades. The night-and-day observation continued. The light above my bed was left on all night once more.

On the eighth day after I had fractured my wrist and the sixth day after the more severe pain had started, the agony in my right arm became excruciating. I was frightened. The whole of my arm was swollen. My thumb felt like an enormous balloon. I had been in continual and increasing pain for eight days, the sweat had rolled from me, I was exhausted by both the physical and the mental torture, and I could bear it no longer. I was still not sure of my real intentions when I had concealed the razor blade under my blankets but there was nothing uncertain about my new resolve. Tortured the way I was, there was no point in going on living. I did not want to live.

My opportunity came that evening when the male nurse left my bedside and my room for a few moments. Maddened by the pain, driven to distraction by the relentless throbbing in my arm, I jumped out of bed and groped my way across the ward. I had always been taken to the outside lavatories by the nurses or by the other patients and I tried to visualise in my mind the way to go. Barefoot, and wearing only pyjamas, I felt my way along the corridor, into the open air and into the latrines.

I stumbled into the first cubicle, locked the door behind me, stepped up on to the seat and removed the cord from my pyjama trousers, determined to hang myself to put an end to my misery.

Chapter Ten

I could hear shouts coming from the direction of the ward, followed by the sound of footsteps, hurrying, running, becoming louder all the time. The outer door of the latrines burst open and fists hammered on the door of the cubicle.

'Open up!' bellowed a man's voice.

'No!'

'Unlock the door!' I recognised the voice as that of the male nurse who had been sitting at my bedside.

'Go away!'

Sister, alerted by the other patients, arrived on the scene.

'Open this door at once, Kosta!'

'Leave me alone!'

More fists battered at the door, then bodies were hurled against it. Something heavy thudded repeatedly at the wood-work, smashing it, splintering it.

I was still standing on the lavatory seat, my pyjama trousers in a crumpled heap round my ankles, where they had fallen when I removed the cord, feeling frantically above my head with my one good arm, searching for somewhere to tie the cord, feeling for a secure anchor to which I could attach the instrument of my death, when the door burst open and crashed into the wall behind it. Several pairs of hands grabbed me and dragged me down from the seat. At least three male nurses ushered me, half-carried me, struggling, back to the ward.

'Leave me alone!'

'Don't be daft!'

'Let me go!'

'Take it easy!'

I could hear sister, following behind us, ordering someone to fetch the doctor. I was put into bed. Two male nurses stayed with me. The doctor arrived, gave me an injection and I fell asleep almost at once.

When I awoke the following day, the pain in my arm was worse than ever. Again I complained to the nurse who was still sitting at my bedside. Again he took no notice.

'You don't understand! I can't take any more!'

'Doctor says to move your fingers and it will be all right.'

'I've heard it all before!' I raged. 'You're all bloody stupid!'
'How are you, Kosta?' asked sister.
'Go to hell!'
'Why did you do it?'
'Because it's driving me mad!'
In the afternoon, the doctor came.
'How are you, old chap?'
'Bloody awful!'
'Hmmm!'

Not long afterwards, an orderly informed me that I was being
transferred to yet another hospital, the 19th General at Fâyid,
on the Great Bitter Lake stretch of the Suez Canal, eighteen
miles south of Ismailia. I was being sent there to see an eye
specialist, to make me better, he said. They washed and dressed
me. A male nurse travelled with me in the ambulance.

It was night when we arrived. The nurse held me by the arm
on the short walk from the ambulance to the hospital entrance. I
was puzzled by what sounded like the rattling of keys. There
was the sound of a key turning in the lock of the entrance door.
We passed through. Then there was the same sound again as the
door was locked behind us.

A staff nurse on night duty in the office recorded my details,
asked a few questions and inquired about my arm. He sent for a
doctor.

'What we will have to do,' said the doctor after he had
examined it, 'is to cut the plaster away a little.'

I could hear the sound of the instrument cutting its way
through the plaster right up to the wrist. The doctor peeled back
the part that was covering my hand. He said nothing.

'It's very painful,' I told him. He still said nothing.

I was led to a ward, nurses helped me to undress and then put
me to bed. From the distance we had walked in the ward and
from the distance I judged my bed was from the end wall, I
guessed there were about twenty beds, ten on either side. I was
given strong medication to ensure that I slept right through the
night.

Before my eyes closed, however, before I slipped into a heavy,
drugged sleep, I lay in bed listening to the sounds around me. It
seemed a strange place, somehow oddly quiet, much more quiet
than the previous three hospitals I had been in, even at night.
Every so often, however, the silence was broken by strange
noises, weird noises, moaning and groaning, almost like animal
noises, not a bit like in my previous wards. In the other wards,

there had often been patients who were seriously ill, or badly injured, but, no matter how sick they had been, I had never heard them make noises like the patients in this ward.

Eveything seemed somehow different. The whole atmosphere of the place was different. The patients were different. Even the male nurses were different. I could not understand why, each time a nurse walked past, I could hear the rattling of keys, why each nurse seemed to have a big bunch of keys dangling from his belt, why the doors were kept locked, why they were opened only to let people in and out, and I went to sleep vaguely uneasy.

The following morning, my disquiet continued as I lay listening to the sounds of the ward beginning to start upon its daily routine. Unlike every other hospital I had been in, there were no women nurses, only male orderlies, and I could not help but wonder why. In addition, the orderlies were speaking to the patients in a way I had never heard before, roughly, gruffly, with a distinct air of authority in their voices, ordering the patients around.

'Come on!'

'Get up from that bed at once!'

'Come on, get up!'

'Go and get washed!'

'If you don't get up, we'll shut you in the side room!'

Not one of the patients said anything in reply. Not one of them complained at their treatment. Not one of them objected. Instead, they were mumbling, mumbling in a strange, incoherent way, mumbling like men who had been out on an all-night drinking spree and had drunk themselves into a helpless stupor, mumbling like a lot of madmen.

It was only then, as the words flashed into my thoughts, that I realised with a shock where I was. I was in a lunatic asylum.

Chapter Eleven

It was eleven o'clock before the orderlies managed to give me any attention. Until then, nobody had spoken to me. They washed me, fed me my breakfast with a spoon and then left me on my own once again.

Within minutes of their departure, as I was lying there considering my predicament, I sensed someone approaching my bed and standing by the side of it. Suddenly, without warning, a blow came out of the darkness and crashed into my stomach. I cried out in surprise and with the pain. Within seconds I was gasping for breath. The blow had completely winded me. I curled up in the bed, my knees drawn up tightly to my chest, writhing in agony and fighting to regain my breath.

'Matseeki!' somebody shouted angrily. 'You black bastard!'

There were more shouts and I could hear running footsteps. 'He hit that new chap,' somebody shouted. 'The blind one.'

A scuffle seemed to be taking place only a few feet from my bed. It appeared to develop into a tremendous fight. Beds were pushed out of line as bodies crashed into them. At least one bed was overturned. Finally, the fighting subsided and I could hear somebody being dragged along the floor. A key turned in the lock of the ward door. People passed through and the door was locked again. The raised voices grew more faint. There was the sound of keys jangling as another door, further down the outside corridor, was opened. The door slammed. A key was turned in the lock.

'Sorry about that,' said one of the orderlies apologetically when he returned to my bedside. 'It was a black chap we have in here. He's a bit of a nutter is Blackie.'

I could not help but agree. If anything, the orderly's assessment was something of an understatement. A normal person would scarcely have attacked a man who was blind, who was lying helplessly in bed, whose right arm was in plaster and in a sling across his chest, and whose hand and arm were puffed up like a balloon.

'What made him hit me?'

'He must have been jealous of the attention we were giving you.'

'Is this a nut house?'

'It's just a hospital.'

'Why am I in here?'

'For your own good.'

'I'm not mental, you know.'

'I didn't say you were.'

'I'm blind and I have a bad hand – there's nothing else wrong with me.'

'We're going to try to cure you.'

'Of what?'

'You'll get treatment.'

'For my eyes? For my hand? Or because you think I'm mental?'

'Don't worry. We'll cure your eyes and arm.'

He had not committed himself either way about my mental condition. I realised that I was in a state of acute depression and that attempted suicide was regarded as not only an extremely serious action, especially in the army, but also a crime. They reasoned that no normal person would ever try to do such a thing and anyone who did must obviously have taken leave of his senses. In my case, however, I knew that I had been driven to attempt suicide by the excruciating pain in my arm, by my failure to persuade the doctors to heed my pleas for help, and, because of that, I was upset that they had put me in a mental hospital.

One of the patients introduced himself as Adolph, a Pole who had been living in Egypt and who was now serving in the British Army. He sounded perfectly normal, not in the least like the patients I had heard making strange and weird noises, and I wondered why he was in a mental ward. He spoke good English and Italian but, when I told him that I was a Yugoslav from Turkey and that I spoke French, he decided that, from then on, we should always converse in French, which he spoke perfectly.

'If we do that, nobody else will be able to understand what we're talking about,' he whispered. He said it in a conspiratorial tone that made me doubt the correctness of my initial diagnosis of his sanity.

Adolph told me that I was in the psychiatric wing of the 19th General Hospital. The ward was a long one, he said, with no tables or chairs, only beds, and at least one orderly was always watching the patients. Matseeki, the patient who had attacked me, was an African and completely mad.

'What did he hit me with?' I asked.

'His fist,' said Adolph. 'There's nothing else. Nothing he could have used as a weapon. They take away everything here – knives, forks, razors. There's nothing.'

I asked him how long patients usually stayed there.

'It all depends how people behave,' he said. 'They let me out once – but they brought me back because I got into a fight. The psychiatrist himself is a nut-case. You'll see when you meet him. He's a madman.'

Three doctors arrived to examine my arm. I could tell, by his accent, that one of them was German – a fact that, in a British Army hospital, surprised me. It was only later that I discovered that he was a prisoner-of-war and that, back in Germany, he had been a leading specialist in fractures.

'Let me have a look at your arm,' he said in fluent English.

I was lying flat on my back with my arm removed from the sling and resting on the pillow.

'I am going to pick it up,' he warned. 'I shall try not to hurt you.'

He took hold of my arm and lifted it. My wrist and hand were grotesquely swollen and neither seemed to have any strength in them. Fierce pain shot through my entire arm. I gasped.

'Don't worry,' he said. 'See if you can move it.'

He was silent for what seemed a long time.

'I am afraid we will have to take you for an immediate operation,' he said.

Chapter Twelve

Within fifteen minutes, I had been placed on a stretcher, lifted on to a trolley, carried into an ambulance and transferred to the hospital's surgical wing. In the operating theatre, the plaster was cut from my arm and the whole of the arm was shaved. An injection put me to sleep.

I awoke to find myself in a peaceful room. An orderly was standing beside me.

'Where am I?' I asked drowsily.

'In a room on your own in the surgical wing,' he replied. 'I'm standing here to keep you company, seeing as you're by yourself.'

I knew that he was lying and that the real reason he was there was to ensure that I did not try to commit suicide again.

'Is it all over?'

'Yes, they've operated,' he said. 'It was gangrene.'

He said it in a matter-of-fact way but I knew that gangrene was an extremely serious condition and that he was undoubtedly trying to minimise the danger in order not to worry me.

Under further questioning, however, the truth emerged. The plaster on my arm had been too tight. The blood supply had been restricted and, as a result, gangrene had set in. The German doctor had made an incision at the base of my thumb to drain the dead tissue and pus. He had fought to save my arm – and, hopefully, had succeeded. It had been extremely close, however. Had treatment been delayed for another two days, my arm would have had to be amputated from the elbow. Even then, my life might not have been saved.

'Will I have to return to that place again, that mental ward?' I asked.

'I don't know,' he said. 'I think you may still have to be kept under observation.'

'Why will I have to return?' I protested. 'I'm not mad. It was only the plaster that drove me mad. Nobody took any notice. It would have driven anybody mad!'

I stayed in the private room for five days, the male nursing staff washing me, changing me, checking on the condition of my hand, guarding me. Then an English doctor called.

'We've managed to save your arm,' he told me. 'But now that you are all right again we'll have to transfer you back to the psychiatric wing.'

I did not reply. My face, undoubtedly, made my feelings very clear.

It was not until I returned to the psychiatric wing that the dressing on my hand was changed for the first time.

'There's a big hole in your hand,' Adolph told me afterwards. 'You could put your finger in it.'

Each day, when the dressings were changed, I had to sit for five minutes with my hand immersed in a bowl of liquid. What it contained I did not know. Each day, after I had immersed my hand, the hole was tightly packed with gauze and the hand and arm bandaged. I could tell, from the amount of gauze that was packed in, that the incision made by the German doctor between the base of my thumb and forefinger was a large one and that Adolph was undoubtedly right when he said a man's finger would fit inside. I could not yet move my fingers. They were stiff and sore. It was extremely painful when the gauze was packed into the hole but the unbearable throbbing and agonising pain had gone and for that I could not have been more thankful.

A few days later, when I was allowed out of bed, I was told that I was wanted for interview by the hospital psychiatrist, an English colonel.

'How are you feeling now?' he asked as I sat in front of his desk.

'I'm feeling all right.'

'You haven't been all right.'

'I've been all right except for my hand.'

'Was that all?'

There was something about his manner, his tone of voice, that I did not like. There was a sarcastic quality about his questions and the way he spoke.

'Certainly that was all.'

'Why do you think you're here?'

'That's what I want to know,' I said irritably. 'I don't know why I'm here.'

'Don't you?'

'Of course, I don't,' I replied angrily. 'You tell me.'

'It's for your own good.'

'How long are you going to keep me in this place?'

'We won't keep you long, corporal. Maybe a few days.'

'Why are you keeping me at all when I'm normal?'

'Are you normal?'

'Of course, I'm normal!'

'Are you sure?'

'Of course, I'm sure!'

'Then why did you try to kill yourself?'

'Because I was in agony with my arm and nobody would take any notice,' I shouted. 'I was proved right, too. It was gangrene. I could have lost my arm!'

'But normal people still don't do that,' he said calmly. 'They don't try to kill themselves.'

His questioning, his attitude, his sarcasm, his calmness, were all just too much. I completely lost my temper.

'How the bloody hell do you know?' I raged at him. 'It wasn't you who was suffering! You don't know the pain I was in!'

'Thank you, corporal,' he said. 'That will be all.'

I was still fuming when the nurses returned me to the ward. Adolph laughed.

'He was doing it on purpose,' he chuckled. 'He was trying to goad you into losing your temper, trying to see if you were able to control yourself, to see if your self-control had returned. He does that with all the patients. I told you he was a nut-case!'

Too late, I realised that Adolph was right. The psychiatrist had set a trap for me and I had fallen straight into it. I had thought that he had no sympathy for me, no understanding, and, all the time, he was deliberately baiting me to discover whether I had recovered sufficient composure to return to normal life. He had been trying to annoy me and he had succeeded completely. Now, as a result, I would be staying in the psychiatric ward. For how long, I did not know.

'A few days did he say?' asked Adolph. 'He says that to all the patients. It will be more than a few days – especially now.' He said it gleefully, obviously enjoying the joke, amused that I had acted like a simpleton in falling into the colonel's trap.

Three days later, my mood of depression began to lift. I began walking around the ward with Adolph. We were allowed to go for walks in the gardens and to the recreation room, where the other patients played table-tennis and I was able to listen to gramophone records. I began to go to occupational therapy. I started laughing and joking with the orderlies. Mary Keenleyside, the occupational therapist, was a great help. When she learned I was able to type, she loaned me a typewriter from her office and I wrote to Lois and to my parents. Each day, I was taken to the physiotherapy department, where I was made to exercise my hand by squeezing a piece of apparatus with a strong spring in it. I started to shave myself. My bad temper had gone. I was happy. I had almost returned to my old self.

My mental condition was so much improved that it came as no surprise when I was called to see the psychiatrist once more and was told that I was to be transferred to one of the open wards of the psychiatric wing. There were eight patients in the ward including myself, most of them suffering from depression but none of them dangerous. We passed the days visiting the canteen and strolling around the hospital.

Four weeks after I had been transferred to the open ward, we were standing by our beds awaiting the arrival of the junior psychiatrist, an RAF doctor, on his regular morning round. Sister Blair, a Scot, was with him and I could tell that she was excited. Indeed, the news that the doctor had to give me was certainly something about which to be elated. At last, it had been decided that I should be allowed to enter Britain. My papers had come through and I was to sail from Port Said in three days' time.

Not unnaturally, I was overjoyed. At last, at long last, my dreams were to be fulfilled. After the bitter disappointment of the original refusal to allow me into Britain, I had almost lost hope that I would ever get there. Now, at last, I was to sail to Britain and, once there, I would be able to have a corneal graft, just as Major Gillan had said, and, at last, I would be able to see again.

The euphoria lasted for exactly three days. Then, on the very day I was due to depart for Britain, my hopes were shattered once more. Whether a mistake had occurred over my papers I did not discover. Whether it was a case of confusion over identity I did not know. The result, however, was that I was not sailing for Britain after all. It was not I who had been allocated a passage but someone else.

After the way in which my hopes had been so dramatically raised, I found it impossible to be calm, to be stoical, to simply shrug off the news that had so suddenly and cruelly dashed them once more. The bitter disappointment was too much. For the first time since I had been blinded, I broke down completely and burst into tears. Five minutes later, the flow of tears stopped. My feelings of abject misery and dismay were replaced by feelings of blazing anger and resentment. My temper snapped. I flew into an uncontrollable rage.

'That's a dirty trick to play on me!' I shouted. 'One day you say one thing, next day you say another! You raise my hopes and then dash them!'

They called the doctor, the junior RAF psychiatrist. He listened to their tale of what had happened, the news that had just been broken to me, and my unpredictable reaction to it.

'Kosta, you are going back to the locked ward for your own protection,' he told me.

Chapter Thirteen

They escorted me back to the locked ward. Jock, a Scots male nurse, greeted me and tried to comfort me.

'You won't be here long, Kosta,' he said. 'It's just that you're depressed. They've just sent you here as a precaution.'

Adolph was still there. So were all the other patients I had previously come to know. I did not stay in the main ward. Instead, they put me into a small side room into which Adolph had moved. There were only two beds and I would be company for Adolph, they said.

Within two days, I had calmed down and had returned to normal. Within three days, I had started taking part once more in occupational therapy in the locked ward. Within ten days, I was allowed to return to the open ward of the psychiatric wing. They knew I was not mad and, after three weeks there, I was moved out of the psychiatric wing altogether and back into the surgical wing. I had a black patch like Lord Nelson over my left eye but my hand had recovered completely, my hair had grown and I was among friends.

Some weeks afterwards, I was asked by sister if I would act as interpreter to help the medical staff with a case in the ATS ward. A Yugoslav girl had been admitted with suspected appendicitis but, because she could not speak English, the doctors and nurses were experiencing difficulty in treating her. I readily agreed, secretly pleased that, even though I was blind, I was still of use to somebody.

I made my way to the ATS ward, knocked on the door of the office and told sister the reason for my visit. By that time, as a result of being the only blind patient in the hospital, I was well-known to most of the staff and many of the patients in all the wards and the sister in the ATS ward was no exception. She led me into the ward and to one of the beds.

'This is the Yugoslav girl,' she said.

'Good morning,' I said in Yugoslav. 'How are you?'

'Not too bad, thank you, Kosta,' said the patient.

The voice was immediately familiar, not only familiar but very well-known. For a moment, however, the surprise of hearing my name spoken by someone I had thought a complete stranger caused a temporary inability to think clearly and I could not place the voice. Then, with a shock, I realised who it was.

'Vinka!' I cried. 'What are you doing here?'

'They think it's my appendix.'

'Where have you come from?'

'From El Shatt. We're all still there.'

She told me the news from El Shatt, what had happened since the last time we had met on the day of the attack, about her parents, and the lack of any firm decisions about their futures. I told her about my eyes, the doctors' verdicts, and the events that had occurred in the various hospitals to which I had been admitted.

The doctor arrived and our talk became professional.

'Will you ask her where the pain is, please?' he said. I translated the question into Yugoslav, Vinka told me and I translated her reply into English. The doctor asked several more questions, thanked me and then, knowing that my blindness would not allow me to intrude upon Vinka's privacy, examined her abdomen without asking me to leave the bedside.

'That was very good of you, Kosta,' sister said when the doctor had gone. 'You must come again to keep her company. Every day if you like.'

The following day, I returned to the ATS ward with one of my friends. Sister gave her permission for both of us to go inside. I introduced him to Vinka. Then he left us alone and went to talk to the other patients.

'There's a girl called Dorothy who wants to meet you the next time we come,' my friend told me when we had left the ward.

The following day, he introduced me. Her name was Dorothy Hall. She was a London girl. I sat on her bed and we talked about nothing in particular. Then, once again, my knowledge of French helped to cement a friendship for me.

'I'd love you to teach me French,' she said.

'I will do,' I promised.

Dorothy told me about her life in London before the war and about her life since joining the ATS. There was something about her voice that attracted me and, on each daily visit after that, I found I was anxiously hoping to be able to move away from Vinka's bedside without appearing impolite, just as soon as I had exchanged a few words with her, so that I could speak with Dorothy.

During one of our talks, I felt Dorothy's hand reach out of

the darkness and, without warning and for no apparent reason, touch me gently on the right side of my face.

'You're very good-looking,' she said quietly.

Until then, ever since Staka's attack upon me, I had had a deep inferiority complex in my relationships with women. No matter how hard I tried, I could not rid myself of the sort of feelings I had had on the evening Lois had asked me to kiss her, of the conviction that no pretty girl could possibly be interested in me and that, if she were, it could be only out of pity. Now, however, I knew that what Dorothy had said to me had not been said out of sympathy. I was no longer miserable, depressed, introspective. I was cheerful, happy, laughing and joking. The left side of my face was still the same, still disfigured, and, with my black patch, I knew it was not an attractive sight. The right side of my face, however, was unmarked, undamaged, and it was the right side of my face that Dorothy had touched. I knew that her words had not been uttered out of pity. There was no longer anything to pity me for.

Knowing that, her words gave me the confidence I so badly needed. For a young woman, any woman, especially one in whose company I had been on only a few occasions, to tell me that I was very good looking, and to mean it, was the most pleasing, exciting, exhilarating event that could possibly have happened to me. It was a turning point. My attitude towards women changed. It gave me back my confidence, my self-respect. I was no longer ashamed of my appearance. I could now face women on equal terms.

I started to teach French to Dorothy, just as I had promised, first of all sitting at her bedside, then, when she was allowed out of bed, at a table in the ward and, finally, when she was allowed outside, sitting in the lovely, sweet-smelling gardens of the hospital.

Dorothy was not the only woman to help me lose my acute sensitiveness and self-consciousness and regain my confidence and self-respect. Mary, another patient in the ATS ward, had serious eye trouble. She had been in complete darkness for two weeks, both eyes being heavily bandaged, and, during that time, she had heard me coming into the ward each day, talking to Vinka and Dorothy, laughing and joking. When her bandages were finally removed and she was able to see again, her own experience of being in the dark seemed to create a bond between us. The darkness was something we both knew, both shared, something none of the others could share with us.

'You're very brave, Kosta,' she said in a voice so sweet that she sounded like an angel. 'You can't see – and yet you're so happy. I know what it's like. I've experienced it for a fortnight. For you, it has been so much longer.'

It was true that I was happy. Dorothy and Mary and all the other women patients had been the cause. Dorothy's words about how good-looking I was, Mary's unstinting admiration of the way I was facing up to my blindness, the increasing amount of interpreting work I was doing in the hospital, the fact that I was teaching French to Dorothy, all combined to give me renewed hope, renewed interest, in life and in the future. I was no longer totally useless, as I had thought. I was useful to other people, a useful man to have in the hospital when there were so many patients speaking so many different languages, a useful friend who could teach foreign languages to others. In addition, I knew that, despite my disfigurement, women still found me a pleasant and interesting personality and that Dorothy, at least, still found me attractive to look at.

Every day, life became more sweet. I looked forward to the start of each day and to my visits to the ATS ward. I began to take more pride in my appearance, more care of the way I looked, to make certain that I had a good shave, that my hair was carefully brushed and combed.

Dorothy and Mary started taking me for walks outside the hospital. Half-an-hour's walk away was a sea-water lido on the Great Bitter Lake, part of the Suez Canal, and, one day, they took me there. Not unnaturally, I was not looking forward to the prospect of my first swim since losing my sight. I was a good swimmer but they told me the water was deep and I worried in case I began to panic when I found myself out of my depth and unable to see the shore. I worried in case, in my panic, I lost my sense of direction and swam the wrong way, out into the vast, sea-water lake, fourteen miles long and eight miles wide, into even deeper water. Dorothy and Mary, however, were re-assuring.

'Don't worry,' they said. 'Just follow the sound of our voices and you can't go wrong.'

We sat at tables under a verandah and had a drink. Then they led me down five steps, across soft sand and into what they said looked like the open sea, so vast was the stretch of water. Stan, an English soldier friend, and three of the other girls from the ward were also there.

'Don't leave me alone!' I shouted nervously.

'We won't,' they shouted back. 'Just follow our voices.'

We swam to a raft about fifty yards from the beach. I climbed aboard and lay there in the warm sunshine. The feel of the water on my skin, the pleasure of using my muscles, the movement of my body through the water, had all been an exciting, satisfying experience. My confidence returned immediately. I plunged back into the water and swam happily for a long time, always taking care to follow their voices, to listen to their directions, enjoying it as much as I had before being blinded.

The visit to the lido was the first of many. It was during those long, relaxed afternoons in the company of the girls that I began to appreciate the qualities of English women, to realise the difference between them and other girls. The girls I had known, mainly Turkish, Yugoslav and Greek, had narrow minds, narrow outlooks, narrow attitudes. Their sheltered upbringing had turned them into timid, shy, backward creatures whose personalities now seemed to me to be incredibly dull. The English girls, on the other hand, were frank, open, broad-minded, easy to talk to. They were keen on sports, good conversationalists, free of inhibitions. They laughed and joked, could take a joke against themselves, did not become offended by saucy remarks, were totally happy and extrovert and unafraid to display their emotions, their feelings.

For the first time, I realised that I was happier in the company of English girls than in that of Vinka or of anyone else.

A Yugoslav captain, whom I had known before losing my sight, was brought into hospital with a broken leg and, as he could not speak a word of English, I was asked to act as interpreter. When he was able to move around on crutches, he called to see me in my ward. We sat talking and I commented on the pleasant smell of his pipe tobacco.

'Why don't you buy one?' he asked. 'It would be very nice for you.'

I had never smoked a pipe but it seemed a good idea. We went to the NAAFI together and selected an inexpensive, curved briar and a tin of Four Square tobacco. My career as a pipe-smoker was about to begin.

'Jesus! It's Sherlock Holmes!' they chortled on my return to the ward.

The aroma of the burning tobacco seemed beautiful to me, like the fragrance of a wood fire on an autumn day, like an exotic incense drifting tantalisingly over the heads of a church congregation. With the pipe alternately clenched manfully between my teeth and clutched determinedly in my hand, I felt no end of a man, a real toff, almost like the traditional English country gentleman I had read about.

The rugged, masculine, purposeful image I presented – or imagined I presented – was not to last, however. Clouds of thick, grey smoke enveloped my head. I coughed and spluttered, blew when I should have sucked, and, in a matter of minutes, felt decidedly queasy. Within ten minutes, I felt distinctly ill.

Sympathy, however, was not forthcoming, either from my fellow patients or from the nurses. For some inexplicable reason, they appeared to find my attempts to become a pipe-smoker highly amusing. The ward exploded into shrieks of helpless and unrestrained hilarity. I suspected that I was not the only one with tears in my eyes, although for a different reason.

Surrender, however, was a word I did not understand. I had thought that smoking a pipe would be as easy as boiling an egg and I had discovered that it was not. Because of that, I was determined to master the not inconsiderable art.

My career as a pipe-smoker was short-lived, however, not because of any failure on my part to master the intricacies of packing the pipe properly – the tobacco eased in not too tightly, not too loosely – of keeping the stem clean, of preventing the bowl becoming too wet with saliva, or even of blowing and sucking at the correct times. I mastered them all with considerable success. Nor was it short-lived because of any failure on my part to become accustomed to the habit. It is a fact that the human body is capable of becoming accustomed to almost anything and, amazingly, mine became accustomed to smoking a pipe. It was short-lived because of sister.

So delighted was I with my new-found pastime, with my newly-acquired accomplishment, that I was not content to smoke my pipe only when outside or when sitting in an easy chair in the ward. It was necessary for me to light up my beloved briar while in bed, too.

Unfortunately, because of my blindness, I was not always aware of the exact location of the ash-trays and, more often than not, the ash went everywhere but where it was intended to go. When, one day, I knocked out my pipe and the ash went into the bed, sister could bear my habits no longer.

'You're a naughty boy, Kosta!' she scolded. 'We put clean sheets on your bed every day – and now we're having to change them twice a day because of your blessed pipe. You'll burn the hospital down if you go on like this!'

When my mentor, the Yugoslav captain, next came to see me, I broke the news to him that my career as a pipe-smoker looked like drawing to an unexpectedly early conclusion. If I did not curtail it, I was sure that sister would.

'Just don't empty your pipe all over the bed,' he urged.

'I can't help it,' I told him. 'It's no good being shouted at all the time. I'm going to give it up. She's right, anyway. I might set fire to the place.'

We walked to the NAAFI together and I bought a packet of twenty Player's Navy Cut cigarettes for a shilling. I was a pipe-smoker no longer but, at least, sister would be happy, the laundry would have fewer sheets to wash and the hospital buildings were likely to have a less insecure future.

Not long after Lois Freeland had left for her new base in Cyprus, to which she had been posted from the 63rd General Hospital at Almaza, she arrived on a visit, just as she had promised.

I was sitting on my bed, immediately after lunch, when she walked into the ward and greeted me. Although I was not expecting her, I recognised her voice at once.

'Lois! How nice!'

'How are you? You're looking much better.'

I told her about my experiences in the psychiatric ward and about everything else that had happened to me. She told me about Cyprus, how much she liked the climate and the people, and said that, in about six months' time, she expected to be posted back to Britain.

'I hope by then you'll be in England yourself,' she said.

We went for a walk. She took me to the lido. We drank lemonade. I told her that I regularly swam in the lake.

'You're opening your wings quite a bit, Kosta,' she said, surprised. 'You're a completely different person. More at ease. Relaxed. Happier.'

Lois had come only for the afternoon and, after five hours, she left to return to Cyprus.

'It was a lovely surprise, Lois,' I told her. 'Thank you for coming.'

Although I meant it, I was no longer sad to see her go, not like the previous time we had parted, at the 63rd General. Now, I had friends, I was useful as an interpreter and as a French teacher, I was enjoying swimming in the lake. My life had changed completely.

I was no longer lost without Lois. I was no longer totally reliant upon her. At last, I was independent. I could stand on my own feet.

Chapter Fourteen

My continued presence in the hospital as an in-patient became something of an embarrassment to the British authorities. I was no longer sick. My hand had healed. I was not receiving treatment. In normal circumstances, I would have been discharged weeks before. Because I was blind, however, I could not be returned to my army unit, the 1st Battalion Royal Yugoslav Guards. Nor could I be simply discharged from the army and left to my own devices in Egypt. The army had a duty to resettle me. Nor could I be sent to Britain for discharge because an entry visa for Britain had been refused. In an attempt to find a solution to the problem posed by my presence, the commanding officer of the hospital, a doctor, sent for me to attend an interview in his office. He greeted me warmly and seated me in front of his desk.

'Now, Corporal Fettel,' he began. 'You know there has been some difficulty about your going to England? Because of your nationality?'

'Yes.'

'Well, I understand your parents are in Turkey.'

'That's right.'

'How would you like to see them again?'

'I'd like that very much.'

'So how about going there? We will pay all your expenses. You can fly to Turkey any time you want.'

A danger signal began to ring in my brain. I was suspicious of the way the conversation was going and, the more I thought about it, the more convinced I became that the commanding officer was trying to get rid of me. Once before, at El Arish, near the northern coast of the Sinai Peninsula, not far from the border with Palestine, when I was fit and well and had my eyesight, I had made inquiries about leaving the army and returning to Turkey and had been told that it was not possible. Then, when I had tried to do it the right way, the straightforward way, they had refused to allow me to return home. The only way I could have returned would have been by deserting. Some Yugoslavs from Turkey had done so and had gone to the Communist Yugoslav embassy in Cairo, where they had been provided with passports that had enabled them to return to Turkey. I had resisted the temptation to join them, believing that it was better to act in a correct manner, that if it were not possible to leave the army in an honourable way then, rather than leave it in a dishonourable way, it would be better to remain.

Now, however, now that I was blind and of no further use to them, the British wanted nothing more to do with me, were trying to get rid of me.

'So how about going to Turkey?' the commanding officer repeated, breaking the silence that had followed his earlier, similar question.

'I'm longing to see my mother and father and sisters and all my family,' I told him. 'It would be wonderful. But not now. Not while I'm still blind. I'll go to my family when I can see.'

'But you could go to your family and then get treatment.'

'There would be no specialist treatment in Turkey. Nothing. I'll stick it out here.'

'But all your links are with Turkey. All your roots.'

'Yes, but right now I'm attached to the British forces.'

'We know that.'

'I was blinded in the army and I want to finish my treatment in the army. It's the army's duty to finish my treatment.'

'But perhaps you will have to stay on in Egypt by yourself and become a refugee. Don't forget that.'

At the time I had decided to stay in the army until I could leave in an honourable way, I had sought not only the advice of my father but also that of Captain Moir, a Scot who was liaison officer between the British forces and the Yugoslav battalion attached to them at El Arish. He was an enthusiastic footballer and, through our common interest in the game, we had become friends. I had explained to him that I wanted to go home to Turkey but did not wish to become involved in politics between Royalist Yugoslavs in exile, the Communist government in Yugoslavia, Turkey and Britain. His advice had been the same as that of my father. Stay, he had said. The political situation could change.

Now, sitting in the commanding officer's office, faced with his dire warning of the possibility that I might end up as a refugee condemned to remain in Egypt for ever, I thought about Captain Moir's words. If the political situation could change to enable me to leave the army and return to Turkey without any problems, so, too, could the political situation that was preventing me from entering Britain.

'I'll take that chance,' I told the CO. 'I shall stay here until I have eyes. Then I will go home. I will go to my parents when I am all right.'

I did not want to return home as a blind man. At the 63rd General Hospital at Almaza, Captain Spinks had said that I would never see again. Major Gillan, however, had said that I would be able to see when I went to England and, still, I believed Major Gillan. I was an optimist. I was determined. I knew that they could not force me to go and I was determined to stay.

To my surprise, after not receiving any treatment for so long, I was summoned to attend an examination by one of the hospital eye specialists. After he had examined me, he announced that he would like to operate upon my left eye.

In view of what Major Gillan had told me, I was not over-anxious to undergo any operations until I was in England, when I hoped a corneal graft could be performed.

'But I'm still hoping to go to England,' I told him. 'Major Gillan said he wouldn't operate until I went there.'

'Yes, we know that,' he said. 'But, in the meantime, we want to do a little work on the eye to find out exactly what the situation is.'

I was still reluctant to permit any operation to restore my sight in Egypt but, when he explained that it would not involve the eye itself and would simply be some plastic surgery to the tissue surrounding the eyeball, I decided to agree. Before any attempt could be made to restore my sight, he said, the eyeball itself had to be moving freely and be exposed. At the moment, mine was fused to the surrounding eyelids. The operation would be simply to improve the skin and tissue around the eye. At least, it would be a step forward, even though it was one I was not keen to take before reaching England.

My head was partly shaved, at the back, where they were planning to take some skin to graft on to my eye in what the specialist called a building-up process. I awoke to find my black patch had been replaced by bandages, swathed round my head and eyes.

A week after the operation, sister and the specialist arrived at my bedside. The bandages were removed. The doctor asked for a swab. He wiped my left eye, gently, tenderly. He examined the graft.

'Could I have some scissors, please.'

Sister passed the scissors to him and I could tell that he was cutting something with them. There was no pain, just the noise of the scissors cutting, snipping, as if they were cutting their way through a piece of cloth. Little pieces of skin and flesh were falling on to my face.

'Necrosis,' said the doctor.

'Yes,' said sister.

'Scar tissue, blood vessels,' said the doctor. 'Very bad things, these burns.'

He cut away the skin all round the eye and placed a piece of gauze over it. Neither he nor sister told me what they had found and I did not ask. I had long since learned that the fewer questions asked the better they liked it.

In any case, I did not need to ask. I did not, at that time, know the English word *necrosis*, meaning the mortification of a piece of bone or tissue, but I could speak Greek and I knew the Greek word *nekros*, meaning corpse, and realised that, without doubt, the English word must have been derived from that.

They did not need to tell me that the skin was dead. The graft had failed.

Chapter Fifteen

Early in 1948, I was required to give evidence at the Cairo trial of Staka. A Yugoslav friend accompanied me. Dressed in civilian clothes – military regulations forbade the wearing of uniform in Cairo at that time – we booked a room and breakfast at a pension in an unfashionable part of the city. I had stayed there on previous occasions when I had spent leaves in Cairo before losing my sight and I was well-known to the Yugoslav woman who ran it. When she saw me, blind and disfigured, she wept noisily.

The following day, my friend guided me up seemingly never-ending steps and into the court building, a mausoleum of a place with high ceilings and stone pillars, which echoed to the sounds of footsteps and hushed voices. I was extremely nervous. Before I was taken into the court-room itself, it was explained to me that the trial proceedings would be in French. Because of my knowledge of the language, an interpreter would not be needed for me.

I was led into the court and shown to a seat. The trial began. A lawyer outlined the prosecution case. Then my name was called.

'Constantine Fettel!' The usher's call seemed to be bellowed almost in my ear.

Hands guided me. I did not know where I was going but I guessed that it would be into the witness-box. I was left standing in what appeared to be a wooden box with a brass rail in front of me. I gripped the rail hard, removing my right hand only to grasp the Holy Bible while taking the oath. Weeks before, when the date of the trial had first become known, friends of Staka had urged me to be compassionate, to accept my blindness, not to be vindictive, not to make my evidence as unfavourable as possible, not to damn her, when I attended the trial. I had told them then that I felt no nastiness towards Staka, no animosity, and that my intention was simply to tell the court what had happened. Now that I was in the witness-box, that was still the way I felt. I would tell the truth, the whole truth and nothing but the truth. No more and no less.

The prosecutor asked me a number of questions, about where

and how Staka and I had first met, how long we had known each other, what our relationship had been and how many times, and where, we had made love. Then he turned his attention to the day of the attack.

'Would you tell the court what happened on the evening of the twenty-first of July, nineteen-forty-six?'

Eighteen months had passed since that fateful day but its events were indelibly etched on my memory. The prosecutor asked many questions and, by the time my evidence had been completed, the day was almost at an end and it was time for the court to adjourn.

On the second day of the trial, it was the turn of the defence. I was recalled to the witness-box to be cross-examined. To my surprise, the cross-examination was fierce, severe, antagonistic towards me. By his questioning, it was clear that the defence lawyer was trying to present a picture of Staka as a poor, un-educated, young, helpless refugee girl with little or no future except in the camps, who had been courted and pursued by me, a soldier experienced in life and the ways of the world, who had finally succumbed to my seductions only when I had promised to marry her, a promise I had subsequently failed to keep. The attack upon me had been a *crime passionelle*, carried out in a mad moment of despair and jealousy. I agreed that we had vaguely discussed the possibility of marriage but denied that I had promised to marry her or had taken advantage of her in any way. I vehemently denied that I had set out to seduce her. On the contrary, I told the court, it had been Staka who had planned that we should sleep together. Her friend had urged me to go to the tent, where Staka was waiting for me. On the second occasion, too, it had been Staka who had planned it all. The bed, the mosquito net, everything had been ready and waiting for me. I told the truth but, the more I protested my innocence, the more I had an uneasy feeling that few people believed me.

My cross-examination ended and I was briefly re-examined by the prosecutor. Then I stepped down from the witness-box and resumed my seat in the body of the court.

A British doctor was called to give medical evidence. He produced the case-notes and testified as to the various opinions expressed on my condition. These included the verdict of Major Gillan. The major had recorded that he had examined my eyes and that, in his opinion, when I went to England and had a corneal graft, I would be able to see.

The defence case began. Staka was called to the witness-box. She was unable to speak French and gave her evidence through an interpreter. Her testimony followed the pattern set by her lawyer in his cross-examination of me. I had promised marriage to her, she claimed, she had agreed to sleep with me because of that and then I had not kept my promise. Contrary to what the prosecution had claimed, her attack upon me had not been premeditated. She had not had time to think about what she was doing. It was a spur-of-the-moment decision. She herself had not prepared the mixture she threw at me. It had been prepared by her friend and she had been encouraged by her friend to use it on me when the man for whom it had been intended had not arrived at the camp as expected. She was sorry for what she had done. She had not intended to blind me, only to disfigure me. At the moment she had carried out the attack, she had not known what she was doing.

Hearing Staka's voice for the first time in eighteen months, for the first time since she had blinded me, had no profound effect upon me. I felt nothing, no animosity, no hatred, no sorrow, no sympathy, no feelings of any kind. I was completely cold, unmoved, immovable. I was, however, struck by the fact that her voice seemed to have changed. Somehow, it sounded incredibly hard and cruel, not in the least like I remembered it. She had been in jail for eighteen months, which, perhaps, could account for the change in her voice, for the embittered tone, for the harsh, abrasive sound.

In his final speech, the defence lawyer was quite explicit in expressing his opinion of me. He was unsparing in his condemnation. I realised that he was simply doing his job, that he was being paid to present me in as unfavourable a light as possible and to present Staka, his client, in as favourable a light as possible. Even so, even knowing that, it was still highly disturbing, embarrassing and annoying for me to be forced to sit there and listen to him trying to convince the court that I was a heel, a cad, who had taken advantage of an innocent girl by proposing marriage and had then let her down, had jilted her.

The cases for the prosecution and defence ended, the court went into recess and, when it reassembled, I could hear a man's voice giving judgement. It had been a very wicked act, he told Staka, to ruin a young man's life in such a way. However, in view of the medical evidence that, when he went to England, he would be able to receive treatment that would restore his sight, the court had decided to be lenient. She would be sentenced to five years' imprisonment, with the eighteen months she had already served in jail counting as part of the five years.

My feelings were neither of sorrow nor gratification, of pleasure nor displeasure, of remorse nor revenge. I did, however, consider five years in jail to be an insufficient punishment for what Staka had done to me. The medical evidence, that with treatment I could regain my sight, had undoubtedly influenced the court in its decision to be lenient.

I left court with the friend who had accompanied me to Cairo and with the Yugoslav woman who owned the pension where we were staying, both of whom had sat through the entire trial.

'Five years?' said the woman incredulously. 'It should have been fifteen.'

Back at the 19th General Hospital, the eye specialist who had carried out the first, unsuccessful skin graft decided to attempt another one. Like the first operation, however, it failed. Undeterred, he tried a third time. Yet again, the graft failed to take and the skin died. The reason, he explained, was that there was too much thick scar tissue surrounding the eye.

The disappointment that resulted from those failures, however, was relieved by the news that behind-the-scenes moves were being made in a bid to obtain permission for me to enter England. The Red Cross, prompted initially by Lois Freeland, had taken up my case and were putting pressure on the British government. The Red Cross had discovered that I had a cousin in England, a Yugoslav girl from Turkey, like I was, who was married to an Englishman. They had not only agreed to stand as guarantors for me if I was allowed into Britain but had also offered to provide a home for me.

The news about these exciting developments was brought to my bedside by a relation of my cousin Rita, a British army captain who was married to her husband's sister and who happened to be stationed in Egypt not far away. He had brought with him a letter from my cousin in which she confirmed that they would stand as guarantor, would give me a home, and would continue the fight to obtain permission for me to enter the country. She also revealed that she and John, her husband, had visited the Home Office in London to state my case.

Not long after the army captain's visit, a message arrived at the hospital stating that, finally, it had been agreed by the Home Office that I should be permitted to enter Britain.

I was going to England at last.

Chapter Sixteen

Two more disappointments awaited me before I finally set sail for England. Twice I was given sailing dates. Twice they were cancelled at the last moment. Even though I had visited the British consulate in Suez, had sworn an oath that the details I had provided about myself were correct and had been given my entry papers, still, it seemed, final clearance for my departure had not been obtained. For some reason, not all the necessary papers were ready.

At last, however, sixteen months after my arrival at the 19th General Hospital, the day of my departure arrived. The ward buzzed with excitement. Many of the patients from the 19th General, as well as from other hospitals, were leaving for Blighty, as they called it, at the same time, including Arthur Parker, one of the patients in my ward, and Dorothy Hall, from the ATS ward.

I had not been discharged from the army for the simple reason that there was nobody to discharge me. As a Royalist Yugoslav, I was not recognised by the Allies and, therefore, it was not possible for them to discharge someone whose very existence they did not acknowledge. If I had any status at all, it was that of a stateless person with a special permit to enter Britain. For the duration of the voyage, I was technically still under army command. As soon as I stepped ashore in England, however, I would become a civilian. For that reason, all of my kit was left behind at the hospital. I set off on the journey to Britain wearing civilian clothes bought from the NAAFI – a sports jacket, grey trousers, shirt, tie, underpants, socks and shoes – and all my other worldly possessions in one suitcase. They included one of the scarves I had made in occupational therapy classes and which I had saved as a gift for my cousin, Rita.

It was seven o'clock in the morning. The sun was shining. Even at such early hour, it was very warm. Ambulances ferried us to the railway station at Fâyid. A special train transported us to Port Said, Egypt's famous seaport at the northern end of the Suez Canal, where it enters the Mediterranean Sea. My friends described the view to me but I was too excited, too busy with my own thoughts, to take much notice. I could not believe it, that at last it was really happening, that a new life was about to start for me, that I was on my way to England. Yet it was true. I was looking forward to meeting my cousin for the first time since 1941. She would be the first relative I would have spoken to for seven years. I wondered how she liked England. I had heard so much about the country from Lois, from the doctors and from the other patients. Although I was excited and deliriously happy, I was, at the same time, slightly apprehensive. England, for me, was a foreign country. I was going into the unknown. Much as I liked the sound of it, I hoped that my stay would be a short one. All I wanted was to go into hospital, have a corneal graft, have my sight restored like Major Gillan had said, and then return home to my family in Turkey. Now the miracle had begun to happen.

At Port Said, I could hear porters shouting, patients bellowing. My friends led me up the gangway of the hospital ship, *El Nil* (The Nile), formerly the luxury yacht of King Farouk of Egypt, which had been converted by the British into a floating hospital. Our quarters seemed similar to a large hospital ward, except for the bunk beds, one on top of the other. Because of my blindness, I was allocated a bottom bunk near a washbasin.

Four hours had passed by the time everyone was aboard and all the cargo had been loaded. It was a thrilling moment for me when the ship finally began to leave the quayside. Ships' sirens were sounded. Hooters were blown. People on the quayside and hundreds of passengers lining the rails were shouting and cheering and waving.

I clutched the ship's rail, successfully imagining the scene described to me by my friends. They clapped me on the back.

'You made it, Kosta!' one of them said.

'Now you'll soon be able to see!' said another.

It was two years and eight days since Staka's attack upon me.

I was not sorry to be leaving the land of the Pharaohs. I had enjoyed my visits to Cairo, the cosmopolitan capital, strolling along the palm-lined Nile Corniche, hunting for bargains in the souvenir shops of the bazaars, and to Alexandria, the second city, on the north coast, near the western mouth of the Nile, once the great commercial centre of the Mediterranean, where Cleopatra reigned supreme. I had enjoyed the fascination of the desert villages, where the way of life had scarcely altered through the centuries, and the sight of the wayside acacia trees, the thorn tree of antiquity. I had even enjoyed life in the numerous army camps at which I had been stationed and the hospitals in which I had been a patient. Egypt, however, also held many unhappy memories for me and I was glad to be away. My only thought was to get to England, have my sight restored and return home to Turkey.

The voyage from Port Said to Southampton took eleven days, including an eight-hour re-fuelling stop at Valetta, Malta. It passed pleasantly. We strolled round the decks after breakfast, chatted over cups of tea and cigarettes in the canteen, sipped lemonade to keep cool in the heat of the day, took siestas in the afternoons, attended film shows in the evenings. One film I particularly enjoyed was *The Bells of St Mary's*, in which Bing Crosby played the part of an American Roman Catholic priest.

The ship entered the Solent on 9 August 1948. Tugs took us in tow. I lined the rail with the rest of the passengers as the ship moved up Southampton Water and into the port itself.

A sudden jolt told me that the ship had docked, slightly bumping the quayside. At last I was in England. My new life was about to begin. The gangway went down. Everyone surged forward. Hundreds of passengers were pushing and shoving, all converging on the gangway.

'You'll find the green countryside of England completely different from Egypt, Kosta.'

'It won't be long now till I'm seeing my mam and dad and sister, Kosta.'

I was happy for my friends, happy because they themselves were so happy, because I knew how wonderful it must be for them. In a few days, two days, perhaps, they would be able to leave hospital and go home to their families. For me, however, it would be an uphill struggle. I had a long way to go before I could return home to my mother and father and sisters.

I was ushered through customs. I had nothing to declare. I showed my entry papers to the immigration officials. Then came the moment when my friends had to leave me.

'Goodbye, Kosta!'

'You've got my address. Don't forget to write.'

'Best of British luck!'

I stood there, lost and alone in a foreign country, unable to see, unable to tell what was going on around me. John, my cousin's husband, was supposed to be coming to meet me. We had never met before. We were complete strangers to each other. I worried in case he could not find me, did not see me, and, even if he did, would not recognise me.

'Hello!' said a voice at my elbow. 'Welcome to England. I'm John. Rita's husband.' He took my right hand and shook it. He was a stranger to me but he sounded friendly.

'I thought you might not find me.'

'I had a description of you from my brother-in-law.'

'It was good of him to come to see me in hospital.'

'We wanted to let you know we were still trying to get you to England.'

He took my suitcase and led me to his car. Rita and her mother-in-law were away on a visit to relatives in Turkey. Because there was nobody at John's home to look after me, he drove me to Camberley, in Surrey, to the home of his sister and her husband, the army captain who had visited me in Egypt, where I was to stay until Rita returned. It was my first home in England.

Two weeks after my arrival, John accompanied me to St Luke's Hospital at Guildford, in Surrey, where an out-patients' appointment had been arranged with an ophthalmic surgeon, Mr Boxill.* He was friendly but said little. He examined my eyes with bright lights and then, while I rested my chin on some sort of apparatus, sat directly opposite me, looking first into my left eye and then into the right eye. I could hear the rustle of the sister's starched uniform as, at Mr Boxill's request, she passed him various instruments. The examination ended. Breathlessly, I awaited his verdict. Yes, my eyes were, indeed, very badly damaged, he said. However, he would be able to help me and would arrange for me to be admitted for an operation.

A week later, three weeks after my arrival in England, I was admitted to Shepherd Ward, one of the hospital's surgical wards, to which four beds for eye patients had been allocated. I was not in the least apprehensive. My feelings were only of elation that, at last, something was going to be done. At last, I was about to have my first operation in England.

Mr Boxill explained that the operation would be to separate the left eyeball from the burned tissue that was adhering to it and to insert a glass shield between the eyeball and what remained of the destroyed eyelids, in order to prevent the two

---

* William Michael de Courcy Boxill, MRCS Eng., LRCP Lond. 1943, DOMS Eng. 1946. Then ophthalmic surgeon, St Luke's Hospital, Guildford. Later, consultant ophthalmic surgeon, Guildford Hospital Group.

from fusing together again. Although the left side of my face was the side that had suffered most in the attack, it appeared that the condition of my left eye was better than that of my right eye. Mr Boxill could see the cornea but, before any attempt could be made to graft a new cornea on to the eye, it would be necessary to clear away the scar tissue and to try to form new eyelids by plastic surgery. At the same time, he would also separate my sealed lips.

For two days, I was prepared for the operation. Blood tests were carried out and X-rays were taken. Then, on the morning of the operation, I was placed on a stretcher, and because there was no lift, was carried down a stone staircase to a waiting theatre trolley. It was the only disconcerting moment. Being carried on a stretcher down steep steps, at an angle, expecting to slide off or to be tipped off at any moment, was not an experience I was anxious to repeat.

I awoke to find bandages round my eyes once more. I could feel no pain in my eyes. My lips were sore, however, and I could tell that they had been parted, that my mouth could now open. My lips felt prickly and I could feel the prickles with my tongue. It was the stitches, a nurse explained. They would be removed in a few days. Not surprisingly, after being sealed together for two years, my lips had lost their elasticity. They felt tight. At least, however, I was able to open my mouth and that, after so long, was a decided pleasure.

Mr Boxill visited my bedside and seemed quite pleased with his handiwork.

'That's a good job I've done,' he said proudly. 'Now you will be able to eat properly.'

Four days later, he removed the bandages and told me that he had to take out the shield. It would be painful, he said, and it was important that I did not move my head. He pressed with his fingers and thumb underneath my eye and squeezed the shield out. He was right. It was painful and my eye felt sore after it had been removed. He burned off some more scar tissue round the eye with a silver nitrate stick, washed out the eye with a saline solution, replaced the shield – like a giant-sized contact lens, big enough to cover the whole eyeball – covered my eye with a Vaseline gauze pad and re-bandaged my head.

One evening, soon after I had finished dinner and the nurse who had fed me had cleared away the dishes, I was lying in bed listening to the sounds of the other patients' visitors arriving. I was not expecting any visitors myself but, to my surprise, I heard footsteps stop at my bedside.

'Hello, Nino,' said a woman's voice. A hand touched my arm, gently, tenderly, lovingly.

A chill draught seemed to find its way down my back, causing me to shiver. My scalp tingled. My eyes, severely damaged and totally sightless, were still capable of tears and I swallowed hard to stop the tears from spilling out. For seven years, the name I had answered to was Kosta, the shortened version of Constantine. It was the name used by all my friends in the Yugoslav army, at each camp I had been stationed at, by the refugees, by girl friends, by the British soldiers, by the nurses and doctors, by Lois. Not for seven years had I heard anyone call me Nino, my family name, a diminutive of Constantine that denoted more intimacy, more familiarity, than Kosta, and I was momentarily overcome with emotion at the sound of it.

'Hello, Rita,' I said.

My cousin sat at my bedside and held my hand. John, her husband, chatted for a few minutes and then left us together. She had just returned from her visit to Turkey and had hurried to the hospital to see me. She had seen my parents, my sisters, my other relatives and had told them that, at last, I had been given permission to enter England. She gave me messages from my family, all the news from Turkey, asked me about my treatment and what the doctors intended to do.

As she talked, I could hear the tremor in her voice, a constant quavering, and I knew that she was crying. She was crying at the sight of me, lying there in bed, blind, helpless, terribly disfigured, at the memory of what I once was, of what I had been on the last occasion she had seen me, and I could also tell that she was trying hard to stem her tears, to keep me from knowing that she was weeping for me.

The thirty minutes allowed for visiting sped past. The bell rang. Visitors began to leave.

'I'll come to see you again,' said Rita. She hurried away, anxious to be out of the ward, anxious to let her tears flow, anxious to rid her body of the emotion that was wracking it.

My thoughts that night were of my family back home in Turkey. I wondered what their feelings were, how they felt about what had happened to me. They were happy, Rita had said, that I had gone to England so that I could have some treatment.

When, finally, I fell asleep, I was still fighting back the tears. Rita was the first relative I had met for seven years.

A second operation, two weeks after the first, was carried out to remove more scar tissue. Two weeks after that, Mr Boxill decided that I could go home for a rest before returning for further operations.

John collected me from the hospital and, as Rita had returned from Turkey, drove me to their bungalow at Farnborough, only about ten miles from my first home at Camberley, but over the border in Hampshire, the next county.

Both Rita and John made me feel very welcome, wanted, one of the family.

I played with Norman, their two-year-old son, was shown to my room and settled in happily.

Only one minor worry clouded the pleasure of my first few hours with them. At one of our previous meetings, Rita had confessed to me that, while I had been staying with John's sister and her husband at Camberley, I had urinated on the lavatory floor. For seven years, in the army, I had been used to men's urinals of the stand-up type, with several stalls in a row, and, even after I had lost my sight, so adequate was the area of white ceramic wall at which I had to aim that even the most serious error of judgement was not sufficient to cause a catastrophe. At the home of John's sister, however, where the lavatory was of the sit-down type, the dimensions of the basin were such that the slightest misdirection could be calamitous. My aim had been at fault on only one occasion but the urine had soaked the wall, ruining the wall-paper, and had seeped through the floor, leaving a distinct mark on the ceiling of the room beneath. I had been extremely upset when Rita had told me, saddened to think that I had ruined the decorations, especially as John's sister and her husband had been so kind. At Rita's house, I was worried in case my aim proved faulty yet again, in case I angered Rita, in case I humiliated myself. I need not have been concerned. I was relieved to find – if relieved is the right word – that Rita's toilet was tiled, so that the damage to the walls, at least, would be negligible. However, even though the tiles provided an un-doubted protection, I decided that I would not take any chances. Like a man who wears a belt as well as braces, I deter-mined to be ultra-cautious, to be doubly-sure. The solution to my problem, I decided, was simply to sit down on the seat every time. That way, I would have required the inaccuracy of a novice artilleryman on the-morning-after-the-night-before in order to miss my target. It was effeminate but effective.

I was sensitive about my helplessness and was determined to make myself as independent as possible. After a few days, I began to help with some of the household chores. Rita did the cooking, John washed up the crockery and cutlery and I dried them.

The bungalow was L-shaped and I began to familiarise myself with its layout. I felt my way around, following the walls, and soon I had the plan of the entire bungalow memorised. Starting at the front door, there was a small hallway. On the right was the bedroom that Rita and John shared. On the left was the sitting-room. A passage led off the end of the hall. At opposite ends of the passage were Norman's bedroom, to the left, and the kitchen. Between them were my bedroom and the bathroom.

When Rita saw how capable I was, how well I could find my way around the bungalow, she was impressed, so impressed that she began to entrust young Norman to my care. I became a baby-sitter, looking after Norman while Rita and John spent an occasional evening out enjoying themselves.

My rehabilitation, my integration into the normal life of a typical family, a typical household, continued successfully. When I was not working, not trying to make myself useful around the house, not playing with Norman or looking after him, I liked to sit in my chair and listen to the radio. I particularly enjoyed comedy programmes and sporting events. My favourite comedy characters were Tommy Handley, Ted Ray and Vic Oliver. My favourite comedy show was ITMA, a famous British radio programme, featuring comedian Tommy Handley.

Then, however, my progress received a set-back. Usually, before sitting down in my armchair, I gripped the arms to make certain that I knew where it was, then turned round, felt for the arms again and lowered myself on to the seat. For some reason, on one particular occasion, I failed to carry out my normal safety procedure. Perhaps I had become over-confident. Perhaps I was momentarily forgetful. Whatever the reason, I made to sit down in my chair without first ensuring that it was exactly where I thought it was.

Not only was it not precisely where I thought it was, it was not there at all. I missed the chair completely, crashed heavily on to the floor and banged my head, hard.

Rita screamed. She rushed to my aid and cradled my head in her arm. I was dazed but I was vaguely aware of her presence. Within a short time, my head began to clear. I was not badly hurt. Soon I had fully recovered. Fortunately, my head had missed the sharp corners of the surrounding furniture and had crashed against the wall, which was not sufficiently hard to cause permanent damage. I had a headache and a large, bruised lump, but nothing worse.

Although I soon recovered from the physical ill-effects of the fall, I was left with a certain amount of mental scarring. The confidence that I had gained was lost. I began to feel my way around with less certainty. I became more anxious about the possibility of stumbling and of falling.

The demoralising effect of the fall upon me, however, was minor compared with that upon Rita. Not only had my fall severely shocked her at the time but its after-effects resulted in considerable loss of confidence on her part in my ability to cope. More and more, she began to fuss round me, to want to help me, to put chairs into position for me, to assist me around the house. The more attention she tried to give me, the more irritated I became by it.

I realised that Rita was acting from the best of intentions, that she was not used to having a blind man in the house, that she did not know what to expect, that she knew nothing of the actions and reactions of the blind, that she was apprehensive because of her lack of experience of such a situation, but she was more nervous than I was of the dangers involved and, even though I knew she was afraid for my sake, her over-protectiveness began to suffocate me.

Her kindly attentions were not, I knew, appreciated as they should have been. Instead of showing gratitude, as I knew I should have done, I resented her aid, her helpfulness, because of the obvious inference that I was helpless and in need of aid. I longed to return to hospital where the nurses, being more used to blind patients than Rita was, were inclined to permit far more freedom of action, to allow patients to help themselves, without anxiety about the possible consequences. My resolve to regain my sight and, with it, my independence, was strengthened by Rita's good-intentioned fussing.

It was a relief when, eight weeks after I had moved into Rita's home, I was recalled to St Luke's Hospital at Guildford for a further series of building-up operations. I was admitted to Poyle

Ward, a medical ward in which four beds were allocated to Mr Boxill's patients.

During that period, my relationship with Mr Boxill became cemented. Not only did I like him personally, I respected him and admired him. He inspired in me tremendous confidence. I trusted him. Such was his personality that I came to regard him almost as a god. Certainly, the respect that he received when he conducted his rounds suggested that he was regarded as a god by the staff at St Luke's. A sudden and prolonged silence from both patients and staff greeted his arrival in the ward each day. Sister and the junior doctors hurried behind him, always maintaining a respectful distance between them and him. His footsteps echoed across the parquet flooring like the brisk clip-clop of a horse's hooves on the cobblestones of a deserted street. I heard the sound of running water as he washed his hands in the wall wash-basin before addressing me in his deep, confidence-giving voice. The glass shield in my eye and the burning of the scar tissue with the silver nitrate stick had become increasingly painful but, no matter how uncomfortable, I did not consider complaining.

'Kosta,' he said to me one day, while waiting for sister to return with an instrument he had requested and which was not on her tray, 'I would rather give you your sight than have someone give me a million pounds. You and I together will win the battle.'

If, until then, my trust in him had been anything less than total, it became complete from that moment. I placed myself entirely in his hands. He could do whatever he liked with me and I would accept it without question.

'You're the boss, Mr Boxill,' I told him. 'You do what you want.'

As I settled into the hospital routine, life became almost pleasant. In between operations, I was not confined to bed and, each morning, I was the first to fling back the bedclothes and make my way to the bathroom for my morning bath and shave, always ensuring that I was back in the ward in time for breakfast. Even better than being able to bath and shave myself was being able to go to the lavatory by myself, thus dispensing with the need for bedpans and bottles. My days were spent wandering in the ward from bed to bed, talking with the other patients, and typing letters home on a typewriter provided for me by Sister Dorothy Parfitt, the ward sister, who showed great kindness to me. Because her desk in the ward was next to my bed, it was not difficult for me to engage her in what must have sometimes seemed to her to be endless conversation and, as a result of our frequent discussions, we became good friends.

Only occasionally did my somewhat exuberant presence threaten the harmony of the ward. Sometimes, during periods when I was feeling not only energetic but creative as well, the typewriter on the table across my bed would scarcely be still from morning until night. Understandably, perhaps, the non-stop clatter, the never-ending clickety-click, began to scrape the raw nerves of some of the patients, particularly those whose beds were near to mine and those who were feeling particularly unwell. Their protests were good-natured but I knew that I was expected to take the hint and, invariably, I ended my literary efforts for the day.

Good-natured, too, but also carrying a half-serious message, were the protests of Victor and the other porters. Because there was no lift, whenever I was needed in the operating theatre or in some other department of the hospital, Victor and his colleagues had the unenviable task of carrying me down the stairs and, later, back up again. It was a task that required considerable physical strength and one that Victor obviously regarded as being almost beyond the call of duty. So heavy did my thirteen stones seem to them that Victor and his porter friends were constantly complaining of the danger to their manhood and threatening to sue for damages over the double hernias they felt were inevitable.

Though many of the events in my day-to-day life were light-hearted, there was, inevitably in a hospital full of sick people, a more serious side, however. Even more likely than Victor's double rupture was the inevitability of death and it was during that period in hospital that I became acquainted with it.

An old man had been admitted two days previously suffering from pneumonia. He had been put in the next bed to me, on my right. I knew that he was seriously ill because, when I stretched out my hand, I could feel the screens that had been placed round his bed. In addition, by that time, my hearing had become extremely acute – Nature's way of compensating for the loss of one sense by increasing the efficiency of another – and I could hear sister informing staff as they came on duty that he was very sick.

Then, suddenly, the noise and the bustle of the ward were stilled. An eerie and respectful silence hung over the entire room and I knew that he was dead. It was almost as if news of the old

man's moment of dying had been flashed telepathically round
every patient, round every nurse, and, for the first time, I knew
what was meant by a deathly silence.

The silence was broken by movement next to me, by the
sound of a trolley being wheeled to the old man's bedside, by
the sound of water splashing as his body was sponged down, by
the sound of scissors cutting his finger nails and toe nails as his
body was laid out in the ward before being wheeled away to the
mortuary.

That first experience of death was one that made a deep
impression on me. It was one that was to be repeated on
numerous occasions. Many of the patients suffered from heart
disease and many of them died. One night, two patients died
almost simultaneously, both of them in beds next to mine, one
on either side. By then, however, the deaths of other patients no
longer produced in me the same sobering effects as they originally had done. A continual close acquaintance with death had
diminished the awe that I had at first felt and was replaced with
an almost matter-of-fact acceptance of it. Like other long-stay
patients for whom hospitals had become virtually a way of life,
I had become reconciled to death, immune to it, able to treat it
with a certain disrespectful levity.

'It must be my turn next!' I joked with the nurses, within
hours of the first ominous silence, the removal of the body to the
morgue and the clean, crisp sheets and pillow-cases, ready for
the next patient, appearing on the deserted bed.

Chapter Seventeen

By September 1949 I had undergone a number of building-up operations and skin grafts, some successful and others unsuccessful, and was back in hospital for yet another one. The thirteen months since I had arrived in England had been spent entirely either in hospital or at Rita's home, alternating regularly between the two. Frequent spells in hospital for operations had been followed by my being discharged to Rita's care and attending out-patients' clinics while awaiting recall to hospital for the next one.

As the night staff came on duty one autumn evening, I heard a voice that was unfamiliar to me. Although, if my eyes had been suddenly opened, I would not have recognised the regular nursing staff by their faces, their voices were indelibly printed on my memory and, within seconds of hearing each one, I knew exactly which of the staff was speaking to me. One of the two nurses who had just come on duty, however, was definitely not one of the regulars. I could hear the two of them moving from bed to bed, settling the patients down for the night, but it was the one who came to my bed, the one with the rubber-soled shoes that squeaked when she walked, whose voice I did not recognise.

'Good evening, Kosta.'

'Good evening, nurse.'

She passed on to the next bed and I listened as she greeted each patient in turn. Her voice was soft, sweet, melodious, kindly, like that of an angel. Even though I did not recognise it, even though I knew that she was not one of the regular staff, her voice did not seem totally unfamiliar, however. Somehow, I felt that I had heard it before and the fact that she had called me by my first name suggested that she knew me.

Suddenly, I remembered. Some months before, probably six, I had been taken to Pymhurst, the nurses' home about a mile from the hospital, by Maureen Keen, one of the ward nursing staff, who lived there. By that time, I was a gay, happy-go-lucky, young man, full of fun, always laughing and joking, popular with the nurses. Depression and pessimism were in the past. My trust, my hopes, were placed in Mr Boxill and in God and I was confident that, one day, I would see. My optimism, my sunny outlook on life, my cheerfulness, appeared to be infectious and, to my surprise, I had found that I had begun to have more success with the opposite sex than I had had before being blinded. When I had my sight, my main interest in life had been sport. I had had little time for girls. When my sporting interests could no longer be pursued, however, I had found a new interest in the opposite sex and, in hospital, the opposite sex meant nurses. Maureen Keen was one of them and she had become my girl-friend.

On that evening at the nurses' home, six months before, Maureen had called to one of the other residents of the home.

'Come and meet Kosta!' she had said. 'Kosta, this is Nurse Argyle.'

I had given no thought to what impression my appearance must give, with my black hair, scarred face and pink glasses.

'How do you do, Miss Argyle!'

Even then, at that first meeting, she had sounded a nice girl, a sweet girl. She had not stayed to talk. Instead, she had hurried away.

'How do you do,' she had said. 'Please excuse me, but I must rush off to my music lesson.'

Three weeks later I had met her again. I had been waiting for more than an hour in Mr Boxill's out-patients' clinic, waiting for my turn to come, when I had felt someone sit down beside me.

'Do you remember me?' that same, sweet voice had said. 'I'm the nurse who was introduced to you at Pymhurst, when you were with Maureen, and I was rushing off to my music lesson.'

'Of course, I remember. You're Nurse Argyle.'

'I thought I'd sit with you to keep you company. You looked so lonely sitting there on your own.'

The brief conversation had ended when my name had been called to enter the consulting room. I had time only to ask a favour of her.

'Could you get me a taxi?' I had asked. 'I'm going round to Maureen's place. I'll only be a few minutes with Mr Boxill.'

She had done so and, in the intervening months, we had not met again. Now, however, as I lay in bed listening to her voice, I vowed to try to know her better, to think of a plan to bring her to my bedside.

At lights out, I deliberately kept myself awake. I waited until I was certain that the other patients were asleep. Then, when next I heard the squeak of her shoes as she came out of the kitchen and into the ward, I made my first move.

'Nurse!' I whispered.

'Yes, Kosta?'

'I'm thirsty!' I lied. 'Would you be kind enough to bring me a glass of water, please?'

She brought the water and partly leaned over me as she bent to hand me the glass. As she did so, I felt two tapes touching my arm and realised that she was still wearing her cloak and that the tapes that tied it were dangling down. I clutched the tapes in both hands and pulled her towards me.

'Sit and talk to me,' I said.

'You'll spill the water.'

'I'm lonely.'

'Then go to sleep.'

'I don't want to sleep.'

'What do you want to do?'

'I want to chat.'

'It's against the rules.'

'Be a sport.'

'You'll get me into trouble.'

I tried to stifle a smile. It was obvious that she had uttered the words in all innocence, that she was totally unaware of the obvious double-meaning, and I knew I would be wise not to enlighten her, or to make a facetious comment.

'Have a heart. I can't see. I need you to cheer me up.'

'Why me?'

'I like your voice.'

She sighed, paused, gave another sigh, a resigned one, and sat down on the edge of the bed.

'It's against the rules to sit on patients' beds,' she said. 'But it's rather uncomfortable bending down with you holding on to my tapes.'

'That's better, Nurse Argyle.'

'Student Nurse Argyle.'

'Student? How long have you been nursing?'

'I'm in my first year.'

'Do you like it?'

'Very much.'

'Will you stay on this ward?'

'For three months. They send student nurses to a new ward after that. I shall be on nights the whole time. Then I shall be moved on.'

'Tell me about yourself.'

'I can't. I must go.'

'What do you like?'

'Somebody will see me.'

'Tell me.'

'It's against the rules, sitting here like this.'

'Tell me.'

'Animals. Riding. Music. I was going to my music lesson when you met me at the nurses' home.'

'Do you live there?'

'Yes.'

'Where is your home? Your parents' house?'

'At Elvetham, near Hartley Wintney, in Hampshire. About twenty miles from here.'

'What does your father do?'

'He's the rector there.'

'Rector?'

'A clergyman. Church of England.'

'Ah! A priest!'

'I must go now before somebody sees me.'

She stood up and started to move away but I grabbed the tapes again and gently pulled her back.

'Not yet,' I said.

I told her about my own father, about my own home, my mother and my sisters, but I could tell that she was only half-listening, that she was worried in case the charge nurse walked in from the kitchen and found her breaking the rules by sitting on my bed.

'Have you any brothers or sisters?' I asked.

'A sister three years older than me, a brother two years younger and a sister four years younger. Now I really must go. The charge nurse might want me.'

'Nobody wants you. Only me.'

Not wishing to cause her further anxiety, I released my hold on the tapes. She plumped up my pillows, straightened my blankets and settled me down for the night. So anxious was she to get away that she had not even asked me how I had been blinded.

'Goodnight,' she said.

'Goodnight, nurse. I'll see you tomorrow.'

I listened until the last faint squeak of her shoes faded behind the kitchen door. The silence of the ward was disturbed only by the occasional grunt, the odd snore and, every now and again, a low moan.

Since losing my sight, I had grown to like the opposite sex. Ever since the day that Dorothy Hall had touched my face and told me that I was good-looking, I had lost my inhibitions, my feelings of inferiority, of insecurity. Dorothy had changed everything. I was cheeky, forward, bold, without a trace of shyness. I was on good terms with many of the nurses. I went out regularly with Maureen Keen. I made regular forays into the kitchen to tease the staff, to help with the washing-up, to laugh, to joke. I flirted outrageously with the nurses and they with me. Once, as I was regaining consciousness from an operation, I had a wet dream and the nurses, realising what had happened, laughed uproariously, teased me unmercifully, and passed comments that were far from ladylike. I took advantage of the fact that I was blind. Because of it, I was allowed to behave more flippantly, more exuberantly, more boisterously, than I would otherwise have been.

'Kosta, behave yourself!' sister sometimes said. 'The nurses have their work to do!' It was, however, only an occasional and good-natured rebuke.

Student Nurse Argyle, I could tell, was not like the other nurses. Something about her, I knew, was different. She had an attractive voice but so, too, had some of the others. Nurse Argyle's, however, had more. It was beautiful, melodious, clear, educated. Not only did she seem to have had a better education than some of her colleagues, but, to my surprise, she appeared to be hesitant and shy, almost reserved, qualities that I had not previously experienced in my encounters with other nurses, all of whom, without exception, I had found to be as uninhibited, boisterous, saucy and impudent as I. Nurse Argyle seemed to be serious, cultured, well brought up, eminently respectable. She had youth, innocence, freshness. All my instincts had warned me not to flirt too outrageously with her at our first real meeting, not to say, as I often said, 'Kiss me goodnight before I go to sleep, nurse!' All my instincts had warned me that to attempt to kiss her, a girl who had obviously had such a sheltered upbringing, or to put a hand on her thigh, as I might have done with some of the others, would be fatal, a certain way to end a friendship that I hoped was just beginning.

The following evening, I ensured that I was comfortably installed in the ward kitchen long before Nurse Argyle arrived at eight o'clock to begin her night-shift. I knew that, after settling down the patients for the night, her duties would bring her to the kitchen, where she would have to help with the preparation of the following morning's breakfast.

I was tapping at my typewriter, on the kitchen table, when she walked in.

'Good evening, Kosta,' she said quietly.

'Ah! Nurse Argyle! Good evening!'

'What are you typing?'

'A letter to my father.'

'In Turkey?'

'Yes. Istanbul.'

'But it's in French. I'm sorry. I couldn't help noticing.'

'We always write to each other in French. I went to a French college and we always speak French in the family.'

'I wish I could speak it properly.'

'You speak some?'

'Not very well.'

'Would you like me to teach you properly?'

'Yes, please!'

'Then we'll have to have a little chat in the evenings. You'll soon improve.'

'I'll look forward to it. But you must have patience.'

My interest in improving the linguistic ability of Nurse Argyle was less than my interest in Nurse Argyle herself. Sometimes, it seemed to me that the sole purpose for which I had been sent into the world must be to increase the knowledge of the French language among the entire female population. Both in Egypt and in England, my own knowledge of the language had proved an immediate point of interest, had provided an immediate introduction, in my encounters with the opposite sex, and my unselfish offers of tuition, received with warmth and gratitude, had led to the cementing of many a friendship. It had never failed. A sound knowledge of French and a willingness to teach it, I was convinced, should have been the first lesson of any manual on how to win friends and influence people, particularly female. In the case of Nurse Argyle, it had provided an excuse to bring her to my bedside each evening.

I could hear a rasping sound.

'What are you doing?' I asked.

'Cutting bread,' she said. 'Ready for breakfast. We butter it and then cover it with a damp cloth to keep it fresh. Then we have to spoon out portions of marmalade and lay trays.'

Mr Bubb, the charge nurse, walked in.

'Mr Jones is asking for a bed-pan, nurse,' he said. 'Could you get him one, please?'

She put down the breadknife.

'I won't be long,' she said.

When she returned, she told me of her great love of music, that she played the organ at her father's church and that, for a long time, she had suffered agonies of indecision over whether she should pursue a career in nursing or in music. Finally, nursing had won. Now, because of her nursing studies, she was unable to devote as many hours as she would have liked to her piano practice.

'Nurse Argyle,' said Mr Bubb. 'Would you help me to change the sheets on Mr Brown's bed, please?'

'I'll be back as soon as I can,' she whispered.

'Bloody nuisance!' I muttered, in the direction of Mr Bubb.

I longed to hear the squeak of her shoes, for the squeak to tell me that she had returned to the kitchen, and, by the time she did, I had thought of another excuse to engage her attention.

'Could you tell me the last word I've typed, Nurse Argyle? I can't remember what I've written with all these interruptions.' The way in which I delivered the words was full of meaning and I trusted that the obvious point I was making would not be wasted on Mr Bubb.

Some people, however, are extraordinarily reluctant to take even the most unsubtle hint and Mr Bubb, it seemed, was one of them.

'Come on, Kosta,' he said. 'I'll take you back to bed. It's time for the nurses' break.'

'No,' I said. 'Nurse Argyle will take me.'

'Nurse Argyle is busy cutting bread.'

'She's finished.'

'No, she hasn't.'

By that time I was becoming desperate.

'Have you finished cutting the bread, Nurse Argyle?' I called to her.

Before she could reply, however, Mr Bubb took charge of the situation.

'Nurse Argyle is wanted in the female ward when she's finished cutting the bread,' he said firmly, taking me by the arm and leading me back to bed.

For the second night in succession, I willed myself to stay awake. When Mr Bubb had gone for his supper, I heard the squeak of her shoes and called her over.

'You must have another name, Student Nurse Argyle,' I said. 'What is it?'

'Ena,' she said. 'But you mustn't let anyone hear you calling me that. It's against the rules.'

'I like it. It's a nice name.'

'It isn't!'

Although our first real conversation had been only the previous evening, although I scarcely knew her, I decided that the old saying – faint heart never won fair lady – was a true one, and I plunged straight in.

'Would you ask sister if you can take me for a walk?'

'Maureen takes you for walks and to church,' she said.

'I want you to take me.'

'Won't Maureen be jealous?'

'I don't know. We'll have to see.'

'I don't think I would be allowed to take you out, anyway,' she said. 'Not while I'm on night duty. I'm supposed to be in bed by ten o'clock each morning.'

'Later in the afternoon then, when you've had a sleep.'

'It's my first time on night duty. I don't want to break any rules.'

'Ask.'

'I know they won't let me, not when I have to be on duty all night.'

'Ask them.'

She was silent for a moment and I sensed that she was thinking.

'I might be able to take you on my day off,' she said quietly.

Chapter Eighteen

At the end of her first week on night duty, Nurse Argyle was due two free days. Undoubtedly, her break was well-deserved but, unfortunately, for me at least, she spent them at her father's country rectory at Elvetham. I was in the ward kitchen when she returned. She seemed surprised at the welcome I gave her.

'What have you been doing?' I asked.

'Writing. Playing the organ. Looking after my goats. Milking them, brushing them down. I take them out for walks.'

'Good idea,' I said. It seemed a suitable, non-commital comment to make to someone who appeared not to regard taking goats walking as being even a little unusual.

'A dreadful thing happened while I was home, though.'

'Tell me.'

'Well, I was running around the garden with Nanny, one of my goats, and I just thought I would see if she would go into the house. She followed me to the door and then, before I could stop her, ran into the house and straight through the open door into the drawingroom. Unfortunately, Mummy was in there holding a meeting of the Mothers' Union. It was a very genteel gathering. All the ladies of the parish were sitting there, delicately nibbling their cucumber sandwiches and sipping tea out of china cups, when in rushed Nanny and made straight for them. At first, they all cooed over her but she was after the sandwiches on the plates on their laps, of course. No sooner had Mummy introduced me to them – "This is my student-nurse daughter" – than Nanny stuck her nose into the sandwiches, into their laps, into their bosoms, everywhere, and started munching away like mad. It didn't take her long to polish them off and when she'd finished she started on the sandwiches Mummy had left on a plate for the ladies to help themselves. You can imagine the effect it all had on the ladies of the Mothers' Union! They all started shouting and screaming. "Mrs Argyle!" they were shrieking. "Get this dreadful creature away from me!" There were cucumber sandwiches scattered all over the place and tea slopped into saucers and spilled all over the carpet. Oh, it was dreadful!'

She paused for a moment and then giggled.

'You'll never guess what happened next,' she said, unable to keep a smile out of her voice.

'What?'

'Well, poor Nanny was frightened to death with all the noise that was going on,' she said. 'What do you expect? She was terrified out of her wits. All the old dears shouting and screaming . . . '

'What did she do?'

'Well, she was so scared that she lifted up her tail and . . . '

'You don't mean . . . ?'

'Yes, it all came out . . . '

By that time I was helpless with uncontrollable laughter.

'You mean . . . ?'

'She did marbles all over the carpet!'

I was not familiar with the English word *marbles* used in the sense that Nurse Argyle intended but I was under no illusion as to what she meant.

'Marbles!' I gasped, the tears streaming down my face. 'That's a new one on me!'

'They were, too,' she said. 'Just like marbles.'

'What did they do?'

'All the old dears were shocked, naturally. Anybody would be, I suppose. My mother started screaming at me hysterically, "Ena! Get that goat out of here!" and all the old ladies began to beat a hasty retreat.'

'That's the funniest story I've heard in a long time!'

'I haven't finished yet.'

'There's more?'

'Much more.'

'I can't take any more!'

'With all that noise going on, poor Nanny just wanted to get as far away from them all as possible. It's a big rambling mansion, the rectory, and the first escape exit Nanny saw was the staircase.'

'Oh, no!'

'Off she went like a shot from a gun, clattering up the bare, oak staircase, sliding all over the place on the beautiful polished wood, galloping along the landing, scattering expensive Persian carpets everywhere. I've never heard such a noise as her hooves made clattering over the bare boards. Of course, Mummy was furious. She made me go and apologise to all the old girls.'

It was a very funny story. I had not laughed so much for many years. She was eighteen and the innocence and freshness of her tender years had been reflected in the way she had told the story. I began to look forward more than ever to the time when she came on duty. Each day, she seemed to have something interesting to tell me, something new, something different. She was my window on the outside world.

She told me that she liked to ride through the woods, galloping flat out, with the wind blowing through her hair. Her mount was a polo pony, owned by a wealthy lady parishioner of her father's, which she had been asked to exercise and which she was glad to do.

When she was at home, she played the organ at her father's church services. The church did not have a regular organist and, when she was on duty at the hospital, the congregation had to struggle along singing the hymns unaccompanied.

'He's a brilliant preacher, my father,' she told me. 'Unfortunately, he's sometimes rather forgetful. The other week, in the middle of the service, he announced the wrong hymn. I'm afraid I'm not proficient enough at the organ to sight-read if I haven't played a piece before. I have to practise the hymns like mad beforehand, so that I know them off by heart. I'd been practising *Love Divine All Loves Excelling* and, blow me, if Daddy didn't announce *Onward Christian Soldiers*! As it turned out, the next hymn listed on the hymn-board was neither of them. You can imagine how I felt!'

'What did you do?' I asked.

'Well, I didn't know whether to play the hymn that Daddy had announced, the hymn that I'd rehearsed or the hymn that was listed on the hymn-board.'

'Tell me. What did you do?'

'I started to play the hymn that was listed on the board but, after I'd played the first three bars, I realised that some of the congregation were following me, some were singing *Love Divine All Loves Excelling,* and some were following Daddy, who was lustily singing *Onward Christian Soldiers.*'

'And then?' I asked, wiping the tears from my eyes.

'I realised it was hopeless trying to play on when most of them were singing something else, so I stopped playing, looked down at Daddy from my seat in the organ loft and said in the loudest stage whisper you've ever heard, "Excuse me, but I'm afraid you have announced the wrong hymn." I didn't know whether to add Reverend or Daddy or what.'

'What did he do?'

He carried it off very well, poor Daddy. By that time, the

voices of all the rival factions in the congregation had trailed away. I think they had decided to call it an honourable draw. They were all staring open-mouthed, absolutely amazed, some of them staring at Daddy and the rest of them at me. Daddy cleared his throat and made an announcement with all the aplomb he usually reserves for an advance announcement of a forthcoming jumble sale. "I am sorry," he told the congregation. "I should have announced the last hymn number on the board." The sea of faces turned back to their hymn books, Daddy turned back to leading the singing – in the correct hymn this time – and I turned bright red. It was awful! I didn't know where to put myself.'

'I can imagine!'

'I don't know what to do with him. I have to plead with him to remember the hymn numbers.'

The *faux pas* over the hymns was not the only embarrassing moment suffered by Nurse Argyle in the service of her father's church.

Once, during a sermon of such brilliance that it had surpassed even his own high standards, her father had been making a particularly dramatic point while recounting the Old Testament story of the walls of Jericho falling down.

To illustrate the climax of the story, he had been quoting verbatim from the Book of Joshua, Chapter 6, Verse 20: 'So the people shouted when the priests blew with the trumpets: and it came to pass, when the people heard the sound of the trumpet, and the people shouted with a great shout, that the wall fell down flat, so that the people went up into the city, every man straight before him, and they took the city.'

Up in the organ loft, the rector's daughter, who realised that the sermon, too, had reached its climax and would soon be ended, had begun to prepare the organ for the next hymn, pushing in some stops, pulling out other stops, switching on the organ engine. Unfortunately, in doing so, she dislodged her hymn book, a huge tome containing hundreds of hymns set to organ music, that she had placed on a shelf on the organ.

'As Daddy reached the bit about the people hearing the sound of the trumpet and everyone shouting with a great shout and the walls falling with an almighty crash, he stopped dramatically, as he always does in his sermons when he wants to make a telling point,' she continued. 'Just then, just when a great silence hung over the entire church, my huge hymn book toppled off the shelf and fell down on to the organ keys with an almighty crash.

You've never heard anything like it! The whole church was filled with this awful discord, this almighty roar of the most dreadful organ sounds, reverberating round and round! Of course, everybody turned to look at me. I was so nervous I just snatched the book off the keys and shouted down at them, "So sorry!" as if it were an everyday occurrence. I could have died!'

'Never mind, it could have been worse!' I chuckled.

'Worse! How worse?'

'The church could have fallen down!'

I laughed at her stories until my sides ached. Each time she arrived on duty she seemed to have something new to tell me. I knew that I was beginning to like her more and more each time I talked to her. I wanted to be near her, to be with her, all the time.

It was only to be expected, therefore, that when she asked me to help her make the patients' beds I should accept her invitation with the utmost pleasure.

As we were making one bed, Nurse Argyle turned the patient, an old man, towards her, so that I could smooth the draw sheet. As I did so, I felt my hand touch something sloppy. It did not take long for me to discover what it was. Sometimes, I wished that Nature had not compensated me for my blindness by increasing the efficiency of my other senses. On that occasion, my sense of smell appeared to be particularly acute.

'Oh, dear!' said Nurse Argyle. 'I think we'd better hurry to the bathroom. Shall I tell you what's happened?'

'I know what's happened,' I told her. 'The Greeks have a word for it. *Caca!*'

The patients were laughing and hooting as I hurried down the ward, holding my hand at arm's length, trying to keep it as far away from my nose as possible.

'What have you done, Kosta?'

'Dirty boy!'

In the bathroom she washed and dried my hand.

'That's it!' I told her crossly. 'No more making beds. I'm finished.'

I could tell that she was laughing and I was even more annoyed because she appeared to find it so funny. Personally, I was not in the least amused.

It did not take long, however, for my good humour to return. I could not be ill-tempered with Nurse Argyle around. In her presence, I could feel nothing but happiness.

As the weeks passed, I began to miss her more and more.

During the daytime, I longed for eight o'clock to arrive. On her days off, when she returned home, I longed for her to return. I missed her more than I imagined possible.

'Thank God you're back,' I told her when she returned from one weekend off duty. 'I've missed you.'

'Have you?' she said non-committally. 'Let me tell you about my weekend.'

My days, when she was off-duty, were spent in dreaming up schemes to inveigle her into spending her spare time with me.

'Nurse Argyle,' I said to her one day. 'Being a good Catholic, I naturally would like to attend mass. But I need someone to take me there. How about you?'

'Yes, I'll take you,' she said.

I was both surprised and overjoyed. When Sunday came round, however, it was not Nurse Argyle who arrived to take me to mass. It was Maureen, my girl-friend. I was disappointed and, when Nurse Argyle next came on duty, I tackled her about it.

'Why didn't you take me?' I asked.

'Because Maureen had already arranged to take you, before you asked me,' she said.

It was true. I had forgotten. I had been thinking only of Nurse Argyle.

At that moment, I realised that I could no longer continue to be Maureen's boyfriend. She had shown great kindness to me and I liked her immensely. My feelings for her, however, were feelings only of close friendship.

For Nurse Argyle, I felt something more.

Christmas in hospital was always a particularly happy time. Like most patients, I thoroughly enjoyed it. Mistletoe was hung over my bed and all the nurses made a point of kissing me.

'I bet you daren't kiss Matron when she comes on her rounds,' somebody shouted.

'I bet I dare,' I shouted back.

When she arrived, I called her over.

'How about a Christmas kiss, Matron?' I asked cheekily.

She laughed, bent down and, to a mixture of cheers and boos from the other patients, kissed me on the lips.

The good humour and cheerfulness that I had always tried to show in the face of adversity – except when the adversity occurred while making patients' beds – proved to be of considerable help in assisting another patient, Roland, to come to terms with misfortune.

Roland was a young boy, only sixteen, who was in hospital as a result of a cycling accident. He had crashed into a farmyard gate and, somehow, a spike had been driven into his eye, blinding him. The sight in his other eye was not impaired but, when I first met him, both eyes were bandaged and, as a result, he could not see.

It was tragic that it had happened to such a young lad and, not surprisingly, he was very upset. Often, after lights out, when everyone else had settled down to sleep, I lay in bed, listening to him weeping. At times like those, I tried my best to talk to him, to comfort him. He was frightened, frightened of the future. His life was finished, he said. Over.

I understood how he felt, I told him. I had felt exactly the same way. I had been through it all. He had lost only one eye. I had lost two. He must have courage. I tried to convince him that, by being cheerful, by giving himself to other people, not only would he make other people happy but he would forget his own troubles, too.

What I told him was the truth, I knew, not simply a tissue of lies, of half-truths even, in order to bolster his confidence. It was true because, that way, I had found happiness myself. Other patients had often said to me, 'You give me courage, Kosta, seeing you blind and yet so happy.'

I tried hard to show Roland, both by my own past experience and by the example of my actions and behaviour in the ward, that life could still have meaning, could still be well worth living.

Gradually, my constant message, repeated over and over again like water dripping on to a stone, had its desired therapeutic effect. Roland overcame his depressed, fearful, tearful state, began to take a new interest in life and, at last, found happiness.

I was discharged once more to Rita's care while making regular weekly attendances at Mr Boxill's out-patients' clinic. Each week, he put me on the operating table, gave me an injection in the eye and cleared away more scar tissue. I could hear the sound of the scissors, cutting, rasping, the blades snipping away the damaged and unwanted tissue. Unfortunately, almost as soon as the old scar tissue was cleared away, new scar tissue formed. It grew like weeds, they said. It was a thankless task.

On one occasion, as Mr Boxill was cutting furiously, I heard a noise, a commotion, and the sound of something falling. Mr Boxill and the nurses who were helping him stopped what they were doing. There was silence. Then there were voices and the sound of the door opening and then closing again.

I was unable to tell what was happening but, because there were no signs of panic around me, because everyone resumed what he or she had been doing at the time of the interruption, because the operation proceeded as if nothing had happened, I was not concerned.

What had occurred, I discovered later, was that Rosemary, an Irish nurse whom I knew well, had been horrified and awe-struck as she watched Mr Boxill cutting the flesh underneath my eye and the blood spurting out while I was fully conscious, and had fainted.

'It looked awful,' she told me. 'I thought it must be agony for you.'

'I'd had an injection,' I assured her. 'I didn't feel a thing.'

My inevitable return to hospital as an out-patient – Mr Boxill wanted to carry out some more skin-grafting operations – came in the summer of 1950.

When I regained consciousness, I realised that my tongue felt extremely sore, my mouth was decidedly swollen and I was in great pain.

'Keep still!' said a gentle voice at my bedside. 'Don't move your head.'

Even though I was in such agony, my heart leapt at the sound. It was the voice of my angel! The words that I wanted to say would not come. I wanted to tell her how kind she was, how gentle, how sweet, how much I missed her when she was not near me. The words that came out, however, if more sensibly practical, were decidedly less romantic.

'I'm thirsty, nurse!' I croaked. The stitches on my tongue were painful, the tongue itself felt like an over-inflated balloon, and I found that I could scarcely speak.

With one hand, she gently raised my bandaged head, almost imperceptibly. With the other hand, she slipped a drinking tube into the side of my mouth.

'Only a little,' she said. 'Just enough to moisten your mouth.'

Cool water trickled into my bruised mouth, my bloody mouth. It was difficult for me to swallow, even water, but her soft voice gave me encouragement. She removed the tube almost, it seemed, before I had begun to drink and my thirst was unslaked.

'Some more, please, nurse.'

'You're not allowed to drink too much. You're too sick.'

I lay back on my pillow, resigned to the fact that she would not permit me any more, too ill and exhausted to argue.

'What's wrong with my mouth?' I mumbled. 'My tongue is swollen.'

'The tip of your tongue has been removed to provide the mucous membrane that was needed for the graft on to your eyelids,' she explained.

Her slender, cool hands – such gentle hands, so full of tenderness – sponged my sweating body, dampened my fevered forehead, stroked my hair, encouraged me to take deep breaths and gently rolled me on to my side and massaged my aching back. What comfort she gave me! If only I could see her!

She sat at my bedside all through the long, painful night. I was half-asleep, half-awake, in agony, feeling very ill. Even a pain-killing injection brought little relief to my suffering. I knew, however, that she was there and, because of it, I was filled with happiness. My angel was with me, talking to me, whispering to me, her gentle voice like beautiful music in my ear, soothing me, comforting me. I knew I could not want for more.

Mr Boxill visited me each day but did not remove the bandages to examine me. My tongue began to heal but, four days after the operation, I noticed a nasty smell. My suspicions, my worst fears, began to be aroused. It was not the first time I had experienced a nasty smell coming from my face.

'What's that smell, sister?' I asked anxiously. 'From under my bandages?'

'It's nothing to worry about,' she said reassuringly. 'It's just with the bandages being left on for such a long time.'

For two weeks I had to lie flat on my back. Nurses washed me, bathed me, fed me. The bandages were not removed. The dressings were not changed. The eye was not disturbed. All precautions were taken to ensure that the results of Mr Boxill's delicate surgery were not put in jeopardy.

At the end of a fortnight, I was taken to the operating theatre to have the dressing removed. Mr Boxill was already there. I could hear him washing his hands. He was laughing and joking and was obviously happy.

Sister removed my bandages and Mr Boxill lifted the dressing. Immediately, his entire mood changed. The laughter died on his lips. The lilt left his voice. His happiness lay in the surgical waste-bin, along with the dressing from my eyes.

'Damn!' he exclaimed. 'The bloody job ruined again!'

Chapter Nineteen

The operation, like much of the previous plastic surgery I had undergone both in Egypt and in England, had failed. The skin graft, like many of the previous grafts that had been performed, using skin taken from my bottom lip, my forehead, the back of my neck and behind my ears, in an attempt to build new eyelids, had not taken. It had been probably the most important graft that had been attempted, the first one using mucous membrane from my tongue, the one for which Mr Boxill had seemed to hold the most hope. Now that had died, too.

I was crestfallen, demoralised, not so much at the failure of the operation as at Mr Boxill's reaction to it. At one moment, he had been happy, laughing, joking and, at the next, cursing, angry, obviously bitterly disappointed for his own sake as well as for mine. He cut away the dead graft, cleaned the wound and dressed the eye. Then he departed, without saying another word.

My feelings were like those of a child who has had his ice-cream snatched away, of a dog who finds that the bone he had so carefully buried is no longer there. Four years before, I had been promised that I would see. Major Gillan had told me that, once I reached England, a corneal graft could be performed and my sight would be restored. I had believed Major Gillan. Now, however, it seemed that the doctors were fated not to succeed. Even before any attempt at all had been made to restore my sight, to operate on the eyes themselves, most of the vital building-up operations, the essential preliminaries to the operations on the eyes themselves, had failed. In most cases, no sooner was plastic surgery performed than it died. No sooner was scar tissue removed than it re-formed. Most of the pain, most of the suffering, had been for nothing.

The very real fear that I had was that Mr Boxill, disappointed and frustrated by repeated failures, might lose interest in my case, might give it up, might say, 'Sorry, Kosta, there's nothing more I can do for you.' Worse, perhaps he would genuinely lose confidence in himself, lose his belief in his ability to help me, decide that there was really nothing he could do. He had been so cheerful, so hopeful. Now this.

Oh, Lord, I prayed, please give me strength to carry on.

Strengthen Mr Boxill's resolve to give me my sight. Don't let Ena lose interest in me now.

My spirits were low. I was depressed. I was allowed out of bed for the first time in a fortnight and sat morosely in the ward. The nurses seemed to be especially kind but I viewed the extra attention with suspicion. Perhaps it was pity, sympathy. Perhaps they knew that nothing could be done for me.

The other patients came to talk, to try to cheer me up. Somebody gave me a cigarette. It burned my sore tongue but it made me feel better.

Three days later, I knew that my prayers had been answered. I knew that I need not have worried on any of the three counts. I was determined to carry on my fight for my sight. Ena was as friendly as ever and was giving as much of her time as before. Mr Boxill had returned, his confidence restored, and had promised me that he would try something else. He had ordered a course of injections, one each day to be given in my thigh, to soften the scar tissue. Then he would try again.

The experience of being nursed back to health by Ena during the painful post-operative period that followed the removal of the mucous membrane from my tongue had brought us even closer together. She took me for walks in the hospital grounds and during one of them, I felt a sudden, overpowering desire to get away, away from the hospital, the staff, the other patients, away from everything, somewhere that Ena and I could be alone together, just the two of us. Suddenly, I knew that I could keep my feelings to myself no longer, that I had to tell her, that I was bursting to tell her, how I felt about her.

'Let's go out,' I said. 'Out of the hospital grounds.'

'Should we?' She sounded doubtful. 'You have to ask permission.'

'Come on,' I urged. 'Just for an hour. Nobody will know.'

We sneaked out of a back exit. Ena led me along Warren Road, towards Stoke Park. The road, which ran alongside the park, seemed busy. I could hear pedestrians passing on the pavement and the noise of the traffic. What I longed for was a quiet spot, a peaceful place where we could be alone, where I could talk to her without other people hearing. In the ward, there were always forty pairs of eyes watching us. It was impossible to talk to her seriously. In the hospital grounds, too, there were always people passing, people watching, people listening.

'Is there somewhere quieter we can go?' I asked.

'We could go into the park,' she said.

She led me through the gates, but even in the park, I could tell that there were people passing by.

'Are there many people around?' I asked anxiously.

'Quite a few.'

'Can you take me somewhere quieter?'

'What for?' she asked suspiciously.

'I want a little chat with you. There must be a seat. Let's sit down.'

'There's one over here,' she said. 'Under a tree.'

It was a warm, late-summer, early-autumn day. A hazy sun was shining. I could feel the first crisp, fallen leaves underfoot. We sat on the seat under the tree. I could hear the rustling of the trees in the gentle breeze and the singing of the birds in the branches.

'Is there anybody about?' I asked.

'There's a couple over there.'

Ena described the view to me, the path, the grass, the trees, the sky.

'Is there anybody about now?'

'Not now.'

I turned to her and cupped her face between my hands.

'I want to feel your face,' I told her quietly.

'Not my ugly old nose,' she said, with all the self-consciousness of a teenager, convinced of her unattractiveness as only an eighteen-year-old can be.

I knew, from the other patients, that she was tall and slim, with fair hair, blue eyes, classic features and a firm chin. I had lain on my bed for many hours picturing her face in my mind. Now I was to 'see' it for myself.

I held her face for a moment and then let my hands move over it. My fingers felt her eyes, her eyebrows, her forehead, her ears, her classical, high cheek-bones, the gentle curve of her chin. They smoothed lovingly over her hair. They traced the outline of her lips, her nose. They provided me with a more graphic picture, a more detailed description, than my eyes could ever have done. It was a lovely, oval face and, to me, her nose was beautiful.

'It's a beautiful nose,' I assured her.

'It isn't. It's too long.'

'It's part of you and I like it because it's part of you.'

'I feel self-conscious about it.'

'Don't be silly! If you don't like your nose, what about me with my scarred face?'

She paused, wondering whether she ought to say what she wanted to say, what she felt she had to say.

'I don't notice the scars at all,' she said quietly. 'Not as being ugly, anyway. They are beautiful to me.'

I took a deep breath, put my hands on her shoulders and turned her gently towards me.

'Darling,' I whispered. 'I love you. I love you very much.'

'I love you, too,' she said.

My heart leapt. It pounded against my ribs. My hands began to tremble and I clutched her shoulders more tightly in order to calm the movement. She loved me! She loved me! Blind and scarred, she loved me!

'I've been wanting to tell you that for a long time,' I told her.

'I know,' she said simply.

I took her face in my hands again. I kissed her eyebrows, her eyes, her cheeks, her nose, and then I kissed her full on the lips. It was not a lovers' kiss, a passionate kiss. It was clear that she was not experienced in the art of kissing, that she did not know how to kiss, but the kiss that passed between us was no less pleasurable for that. It was a gentle kiss, a tender kiss, a loving kiss, a kiss that sent my senses reeling and, when it had ended, we stayed there for a long time, our heads together, cheek to cheek, silent, lost for words, lost in thought.

'How did you know?' I asked at last.

'From the way you used to come into the kitchen when I was on duty. I knew you had planted your typewriter in there. And from the way you looked at me, even though you couldn't see me.'

'I couldn't have pulled through the operation without your strength, without you beside me. You know that, don't you?'

'Of course you would.'

'You came to me when I needed you. You came like an angel from heaven. Your kindness, your understanding, your sweetness, they all sustained me. You were so tender, so nice, so kind. I couldn't stop myself loving you.'

'Is that why you love me?'

'No, not only that.'

'Why then?'

'Because you're never moody. Because your voice is always smiling. Because you're always happy and gay. The other patients like you, too. You walk so quickly from one end of the ward to the other that you are like a passing wind.'

'What else?' she laughed.

'Because you are very sweet.'

'And?'

'Because you are innocent. I love your innocence.'

She remained uncertain, unconvinced, unable to believe that it was really true.

'But why me?'

'Because I can't help it. I love every part of you.'

'But you know so many beautiful nurses with gorgeous faces and lovely dark hair. Why choose plain old me?'

'Because I love your nose,' I smiled.

I held her in my arms, anxious to give her the reassurance that she obviously needed so badly, the confidence in herself that she obviously lacked so seriously, and to dispel the self-doubts that her sheltered upbringing, and its consequent limited contact with the opposite sex, had so painfully and needlessly inflicted upon her. I slipped my left hand behind her head and gently drew her towards me, so that her head was cradled on my shoulder.

'I love you,' I told her deliberately, 'because you are you. And, because I love you, I feel happier than I have ever felt in my whole life.'

My words were not intended solely to boost her confidence in herself. They were true. It was ecstasy to be alone with her. I knew a happiness that I had never known before. I had told her that I loved her. I had done it! What was even more exciting was that she loved me.

'When did you first know?' she asked. 'That you loved me?'

'That very first night you came on night duty, the night I asked you for a glass of water and held on to your cape strings. I used to listen for you, for the swish of your starched skirt and the squeak of your shoes. You always had squeaky shoes.'

'What if I'd changed them?' she laughed.

'I would still have known it was you.'

'How?'

'By your perfume.'

She was silent for a moment before asking her next question.

'What was it about me,' she asked, 'that you first fell in love with?'

'It was your voice,' I said. 'The moment I heard it, I knew it would come to this.'

We were silent for what seemed a long time. Ena, obviously

becoming nervous about our absence from the hospital, was the first to speak.

'It's getting late,' she said.

'We've plenty of time.'

'We must be going.'

'Just a few minutes longer, darling.' I kissed her again.

'There's someone coming. Someone will see us. We must go back now.'

'Not yet, darling. Just a few minutes more.' I was reluctant to go, to leave her, to return to the ward.

'I'm getting worried,' she said. 'We're out without permission. Let's not spoil everything by getting into trouble. We don't want to spoil it by being called to matron's office. It's been so beautiful.'

We walked arm-in-arm towards the park exit. I stopped and kissed her tenderly on the lips.

'You have a nice name, darling,' I told her. 'But I won't call you Ena. To me, you will be Inneta.'

'Why?' she laughed.

'Because it is more tender. Because you are tender and small and Inneta sounds tender and small.'

'Is it a Turkish name?'

'No, I just made it up. It has a tender sound. Nice and sweet, like you.'

'And what can I call you?' she smiled.

'You can call me Nino.'

'But everybody calls you Kosta.'

'That's because my name is Constantine. It's shortened by my friends. But to everyone close to me, to my own family, it is Nino.'

Suddenly, she was overcome by fear at the thought of what had passed between us, of the thought of the difficulties that lay ahead.

'Oh, Nino!' she cried. 'What are we going to do?'

'What do you mean?'

'We must keep this a secret,' she said. 'We mustn't show our feelings in the ward.'

'Why not?'

'Because if anyone finds out, the first thing they will do is part us!'

'They can't do that.'

'They can and they will. But how can I fail to show my feelings for you? I can't keep it hidden any more!'

'If they will part us, then you must try.'

'You mustn't call me Inneta in the ward. Nor Ena. It has to be Nurse Argyle.'

I tried to make her laugh.

'All right, Nurse Argyle.'

'Seriously,' she said. 'I mean it. And you mustn't try to kiss me when other people are around.'

'Not even on the hand?' I joked.

'Not even on the hand,' she said.

'Never mind,' I laughed. 'You can always kiss me goodnight when you tuck me up in bed.'

'No!' she shrieked, horrified. 'We must be discreet! We have to keep this quiet for both our sakes!'

'But I must see you!'

'Then we'll have to meet somewhere. Where can we meet?'

'In the bathroom,' I told her. 'Just before lights out. When I go to clean my teeth.'

'It's not very romantic.'

'It's better than nothing.'

'It seems so deceitful.'

'I know. But it's the only thing we can do until I get out of hospital.'

'The bathroom it is, then.'

'It won't be for ever, darling.'

'I hope not.'

'Be patient, my angel, until I get out of hospital. Then we will be able to meet and I will take you to the pictures and out to dinner.'

'That will be nice.'

I squeezed her hand.

'You are so delicate,' I told her. 'I want to look after you.'

'But I'm the nurse!' she laughed. 'I'm the one looking after you!'

'I know you're the nurse,' I said. 'I know you look after me. But, although you may wash me and dress me and feed me as if I were a baby, I know you need protecting. There's a femininity about you that appeals to me. You are crushable. I don't need protecting. Not now. I'm no longer a baby. I'm a man. From now on, I shall protect you and you will be my baby.'

We walked along in silence.

'What about Maureen?' she asked suddenly.

'She's just a friend. I don't love her. I love you.'

'Are you going to tell her? About us?'

'No, not yet.'

'Perhaps it's best.'

As we neared the hospital, she moved away from me, releasing the close link of our arms, easing her shoulder and her head away from mine. The pose she adopted was that of a nurse walking a blind patient.

'Let's not worry about the difficulties now,' I told her. 'Let us just think about meeting each other and getting to know each other.'

'All right.'

'Look,' I said. 'When you are in the ward, I shall say *Je t' aime,* right out in the middle of the ward in a loud voice so that you can hear but nobody else but you will know what I'm saying. Only you. Do you know what that means?'

'Yes.'

'What?'

'I want you to say it.'

'It means I love you.'

'Say it again,' she whispered.

'I love you,' I said. '*Je t'aime.*'

'Don't say *chéri*,' she warned. 'They might know what that means.'

'Here's another one in French,' I told her. '*Tu me manque.* It means I shall miss you. They will be our secret phrases.'

'I shall miss you, too.'

Nobody at the hospital had missed us, however.

'Hello, Kosta,' said the ward sister. 'You've been a long time out in the grounds.'

I squeezed Ena's hand, discreetly, as she had asked, a squeeze that said, without the need of words, that I would see her later.

I walked into the ward. I could not see but I knew that Ena was watching me until I was out of sight.

Chapter Twenty

I lay on my bed and thought about the events of the afternoon.
I was overwhelmed, deliriously happy, at the discovery that Ena
loved me. Even though she had previously given no indication
of her feelings for me, I had known, sensed, felt in my heart,
that she liked me very much. Had I discovered, in the park, that
my love for her was not returned, I would have been extremely
hurt and upset, although I had hardly dared to hope that it
would be. I had had to break the silence that had existed between
us on the subject, to tell her how I felt about her. I had told her
that I loved her without any thought of my blindness, without
any thought of the future, without any thought of the consequences of my confession, without any thought of marriage. We
had discussed none of those matters. All that I had wanted was
to tell her, 'I love you.' I had had to tell her and, having done
so, having heard and felt her response, I knew now, for certain,
that nothing would part us.

That evening, when Ena came on duty, I was seated at my
typewriter in the kitchen but the ward was busy and we had
little opportunity to talk.

'The more time I spend away from you the more I dislike my
job,' she told me as she tucked me into bed for the night. 'More
patients seem to have wanted bedpans tonight than ever before.
I've hardly seen you.'

I took her hand and, under the cover of the bedclothes, kissed
it.

'Don't!' she whispered in alarm. 'Someone will see!' I ignored
her warning and continued to kiss her hand.

Ena was terrified that the other patients, the other nurses,
would begin to notice, to wonder, to suspect. It was inevitable
that, eventually, they did. They began to notice me dropping
out of card games when Ena came on duty. They began to notice
me disappearing even more regularly into the kitchen with my
typewriter. They began to notice me slipping off to the bathroom and, a few minutes later, Ena following.

I had always been a keen card-player. Because of my blindness, we played games in which it was not necessary for those
participating to keep their hands secret and the other players

told me which cards I had been dealt and which cards I turned up from the pack. It was my inattentiveness when Ena came on duty, and my reluctance to continue, that first caused them to suspect, more than anything else, that ulterior motives lay behind my actions.

Before long, my lame excuses began to be met by knowing comments and sly chuckles.

'I'm dropping out – I've had enough of cards for today.'

'Funny how you get sick of cards now, Kosta. You never used to.'

'I have some letters I must write.'

'Yes, we know – on your typewriter in the kitchen! Why don't you type them out here, Kosta?'

Soon afterwards, the hints from the patients became even broader.

'Where's your girlfriend tonight, Kosta?' they used to ask when Ena failed to arrive because it was her day off.

'Here she is, Kosta!' they used to shout when she walked in the following evening.

Even Mr Bubb, the charge nurse, began to notice and, one evening, took Ena into the kitchen and asked her what was going on between us.

'I denied everything, of course,' Ena told me afterwards. 'But I was blushing a bright red, I'm afraid.'

The other patients were a mischievous crowd and, each evening when I went to brush my teeth, they watched as Ena waited the compulsory few minutes before following me – nonchalantly and unsuspected, she thought – and then followed her to the bathroom, listening outside the door for a joke, trying desperately hard to stifle their mirth. The novelty lasted for only a few evenings, however, after which they not only left us in peace during our surreptitious meetings in the bathroom but actually gave Ena the thumbs-up sign as she followed me from the ward. What was more, they apparently decided to put their talents to better use by acting as look-outs for us so that we would not be caught unawares by sister on her patrol. Invariably, as sister arrived in the ward, one of them would open the bathroom door and hiss a warning.

'Kosta! The old bag is on her rounds!'

Ena would disappear into the linen cupboard, pretending to be sorting the sheets and pillow-cases, and I would stroll innocently back to the ward.

One evening, however, the other patients decided to play a

trick on us. When, at the first hint of danger, Ena disappeared into the linen cupboard, Taffy Frost, a patient who used to act as one of our watch-dogs, and who was always playing pranks, locked her in. I could not understand why she did not reappear within a few minutes.

'Where is Nurse Argyle?' I asked.

'It's all right,' replied Taffy. 'She'll be coming soon.'

Inside the cupboard, Ena was tapping on the door to be let out. She did not dare to tap too loudly, however, for fear that the night sister would hear her. After a few minutes, she stopped tapping altogether. She waited until she heard sister walk past, until her footsteps had died away, and then resumed the tapping.

'Where is Nurse Argyle?' I repeated.

'She'll be here in a minute,' said Taffy. 'Don't worry.'

Unconvinced, I felt my way out on to the landing. I could not hear her. Then I realised that there was a faint tapping noise coming from the linen cupboard. I turned the key and opened the door. As I did so, Taffy pushed me inside. I fell into Ena's arms. The key turned in the lock.

'You can stay there for the night!' shouted Taffy, chuckling. The other patients were crowded round the door, laughing.

'No!' squeaked Ena in alarm. 'Let us out!'

'There's a mattress in there – what more do you want?' shouted Taffy. 'Stay the night, you two love birds!'

'No, no, no!' Ena squealed.

After a while, after they had all extracted the last ounce of hilarity from the situation, they opened the door and let us out.

In a way, I was rather sorry.

The patients were a cheerful crowd. Scarcely a day passed without someone – usually Taffy – or something providing an amusing diversion that lifted everyone's spirits in the midst of pain and suffering and death.

On one evening, I decided to give the ward the benefit of my considerable acting talents, to provide a Thespian performance of hitherto unequalled perfection, by dressing up as, and producing an impersonation of, the night sister. I borrowed Ena's cloak and wrapped it round me. I borrowed her cap to go on my head. Ena fixed it in place with hair grips and then, realising what I was up to, and not wishing to be associated with it, made a hasty escape to the sanctuary of the linen cupboard. Dressed in my uniform, I began my tour of the beds.

'Good evening! How are you?' I said, imitating sister's voice. I moved on from bed to bed. 'Do you want a sleeping pill?' I asked someone. 'Do you want an aperient?' I asked someone else. 'Do you want your bowels opened?' Even I had to admit that the impersonation was a good one.

The patients were shouting, laughing, booing and jeering as I walked round the ward. I was met by a hail of wolf-whistles and rude remarks.

'Cor! What a smasher!'

'Oh, Sister – you've got a lovely pair!'

'Come on, Sister – get into my bed!'

'Cor, Sister – what I'd like to do to you!'

I was so carried away by the brilliance of my performance that I failed to notice that the shouts and squeals of the patients had suddenly subsided. I blithely blundered on, thoroughly enjoying myself, basking in the gratifying response of my captive audience, delighted at the quality and the success of my obviously popular impersonation. It came to an end only when, to my horror, I was interrupted by an all-too-familiar voice.

'Good evening, Kosta!'

I stood there in my pyjamas, the cloak round my shoulders, the nurse's cap perched on the top of my head, the hair grips sticking out from under it.

'Good evening, Sister,' I said, sheepishly, wishing that it had been tonight that Taffy had locked me in the linen cupboard.

'What are you doing?' she asked. 'That voice sounds familiar somehow.'

There was a twinkle, a smile, in the way that she said it. I knew that she realised that it was she who was the butt of my joke and that she had accepted it with good humour. I decided to brazen it out.

'I was standing in for you because you are late, Sister,' I told her cheekily.

When she had gone, Ena told me that she had heard sister coming but had been unable to warn me because I was wearing her cap. Had Ena appeared without her cap on her head, she would have been in trouble with sister.

Our clandestine meetings in the ward, in the bathroom and in the linen cupboard continued. Ena took me for walks in the hospital grounds and, occasionally, outside the hospital on Pewley Downs. Then, a few weeks later, I was discharged from hospital once more for a rest while awaiting further operations.

In the park, on the afternoon I had told Ena I loved her, I had promised that, as soon as I was discharged, I would take her out for a meal and to the cinema. Before leaving hospital, we had arranged that, on the first Saturday afternoon, we would meet for our first real date, our first outing together away from the hospital, as free people, when, for the first time, I was no longer a patient and she was no longer my nurse.

It was a lovely autumn day. I had been preparing myself for the date all morning. As the minutes passed, my excitement mounted. When, in the afternoon, Ena called for me at Rita's home, I was waiting for her in my neatly-pressed best suit. My shoes were shining.

'Let us go and have high tea,' I said as we walked into Farnborough.

'Oh, no, darling,' Ena replied. 'Let's go to the pictures.'

'We'll have high tea and then go to the pictures,' I told her. 'We must. It's our first real date. I must treat you to high tea.'

She seemed strangely reluctant to do both, as if anxious to hurry off to the cinema without first having a meal. I concluded that, perhaps, she was being thoughtful in considering my pocket, that she was uncertain about the expense, uncertain whether I could really afford to pay both for a meal and for cinema seats but not daring to offer to pay her share, knowing what my reaction would be.

Her anxiety continued throughout the meal, however. I was thoroughly relaxed, enjoying the mixed grill of steak, lamb chops, tomatoes, mushrooms and chips, with bread and butter and a pot of tea, revelling in the chance of a leisurely meal with unhurried conversation away from the hospital, away from the ward sisters, in a comfortable atmosphere where there was no need for us to hide our feelings, no need for us to converse in snatched whispers. Ena, however, was clearly not relaxed. She laughed at my jokes but her laughter seemed forced. She ate her meal quickly and had finished long before I had. She seemed to be in a hurry and I could sense that she kept looking at her watch.

'What's the matter, darling?' I asked.

'It's all right,' she said. 'It's nothing. I'm just excited at going off to the pictures with you.'

'Are you looking forward to it?'

'Yes, darling, very much. Ought we to be going?'

'There's plenty of time. I want to go in those lovers' seats at the back – the ones without arm-rests between them!'

'Have you finished your meal?'

'Why are you in such a hurry?'

'It's just that I don't want to miss the film.'

At half-past five I decided that it was time to be going. I had lingered over the meal, over the conversation, for two-and-a-half hours. We walked across the road to the Rex Cinema and bought two tickets for the back stalls, in the lovers' seats, just as I wanted. It was a cowboy film called *Yellow Sky.* As my eyes were bandaged, Ena put her lips to my ear and whispered softly into it, describing what was happening on the screen in the parts where there was action but no dialogue to keep me informed. When there was background music accompanying the film, or the sounds of horses galloping, or of shots being fired, her whisperings were inaudible to the rest of the audience sitting around us. Occasionally, however, when the film was leading up to particularly dramatic moments, the sound-track was silent. At those times, Ena's whispered explanations began to irritate the other cinema-goers. Eventually, one of them could stand it no longer.

'Will you stop talking!' said a man's voice out of the darkness. 'Be quiet!'

He sounded angry. Ena stopped whispering at once. Undoubtedly, the man did not know that I was blind and that Ena had been explaining to me what was happening on the screen. She had been speaking extremely quietly, however, and the rebuke wounded both of us, spoiled the film completely, ruined our first date together. His tone, his complaint, shocked us, removed all our enjoyment. I put my arm round Ena and kissed her, trying to comfort her, but the rest of the film was watched in silence.

Towards the end of the performance, I sensed that Ena was becoming nervous and tense once more. When we left the cinema at half-past eight, I put my arm round her and she placed her head on my shoulder but, as we set off on the one mile walk to Rita's bungalow, her steps seemed to be hurried. Rita heard the crunch of our feet on the gravel path and was waiting for us at the front door.

'Nino,' she said. 'Ena's mother is very angry. Ena has to go home at once.' Her voice was shaking with anger.

'Why? What's wrong?'

She ignored my question and turned to Ena.

'Ena, didn't you know your mother wanted you back by seven o'clock?'

I turned to face Ena.

'Didn't you?' I asked.

'I'm sorry, darling,' she stammered, crestfallen. 'I was too ashamed to tell you I had to be back by seven like a small child.'

I was furious.

'Why didn't you tell me?' I demanded. 'Why didn't you tell me?'

Ena, near to tears, apologised to me and explained that, when she had told her parents that she was going to the cinema with me, they had demanded to know all about me. When she had told them that I was blind, her mother had become slightly hysterical and had insisted that she be home by seven o'clock. She had felt too ashamed to admit that she, a grown woman of nineteen, had been ordered by her mother to be home so early. That was the reason she had hurried through the meal.

I understood her explanation and realised how she must have felt but it did little to calm me.

'But why didn't you tell me?' I repeated. 'If you had told me, we could have gone to the cinema earlier and made a special effort to get you home on time or phoned your mother to let her know you would be late!'

We had been so happy in each other's arms as we had walked home from the cinema. Now, because of Ena's foolish pride in not telling me of her mother's insistence that she be home by seven o'clock, everything was ruined.

'Ena's mother phoned the night sister at the hospital to see if she was on night duty,' Rita grumbled. 'When she found out Ena wasn't, she rang my mother-in-law to see if she knew where you were. My mother-in-law in turn rang Mr Hook next door. Ena's mother has disturbed the night sister and my mother-in-law and my mother-in-law has disturbed Mr Hook. You know Mr Hook doesn't like to be disturbed.'

I was cross with Ena for not telling me the truth but I was cross with Rita, too, for making such a fuss. The way Rita was carrying on, anyone would have thought that Ena and I had committed the worst crime in the world.

Ena was almost in tears. Rita was babbling away in French and Greek. I lost my temper with Rita and we exchanged angry words.

'You're a guest in this house, Nino!' she shouted. 'You must behave yourself!'

By the time our anger had subsided and our quarrel had ended, I realised that I was no longer standing outside the bungalow on the gravel path. I was inside, standing in the hall. The front door was closed and Ena was no longer there.

In a sudden panic, I rushed to the front door, opened it, stepped on to the path outside and called Ena's name.

There was no reply.

Chapter Twenty-One

Three days later, a letter arrived for me in the post. Rita opened it and read it to me.

'Dear Nino,' it read. 'You are invited to join Ena and the family on a visit to the repertory theatre in Aldershot, to see *Tons of Money*, on Thursday evening. Please telephone to say whether or not you are able to accept. Evelyn Argyle.'

'It's Ena's mother!' I said excitedly. I was thrilled that Ena's family should invite me.

'Hmmm!' said Rita. 'Nice idea.' She sounded doubtful.

'What's the matter?' I asked.

'Nothing. It's just that . . . '

'What?'

'It seems a bit odd, that's all.'

'How odd?'

'Well, what's the good of inviting you to the theatre? They know you can't see.'

I thought about what she had said and had to admit that she had a point.

'It was nice of them, all the same.'

'Why invite you to the theatre? Why haven't they invited you to their home?'

'I don't know.'

'They seem a funny family, anyway, wanting a grown-up daughter home by seven o'clock.'

'Maybe they had good reason.'

'It might be better not to get mixed up with a family like that.'

'You think so?'

'It might be unwise. You don't want to get Ena into trouble with her father. He's a clergyman, you know.'

Rita did not actually tell me not to go but it was clear that she was wary of the invitation and was advising me not to go, not to become too involved with Ena and her family. Her obvious doubts began to produce doubts in my own mind and to turn me against the idea. I began to harbour suspicions about the reason for the invitation, to wonder whether it was as straightforward as it had at first seemed. I began to doubt my own feelings at the prospect of meeting Ena's parents, to wonder whether I was ready to meet them yet.

'Maybe you're right,' I told Rita at last. 'I won't go.'

'I think it's for the best.'

'What can I tell them?'

'I'll tell them you have another engagement that evening.'

Rita returned from using the telephone at Mr Hook's house.

'I spoke to Ena's mother,' she said. 'I explained that you were otherwise engaged that day.'

I felt sure that I had done the right thing.

A month later, I was standing in the kitchen talking to Rita when I moved away so that she could open the oven door. In doing so, I tripped and lost my balance. I could feel myself falling. I knew that Norman, Rita's little boy, was sitting on the floor playing with his toy cars and I knew, from the direction in which I was falling, that I was about to fall on to him. Trying not to think of the possible consequences of my thirteen stones in weight crashing on to Norman's tiny frame, I attempted, instead, to jump over him. Fortunately, I succeeded in my intention. Unfortunately, as I landed, I overbalanced and crashed heavily. My right arm smashed into an empty milk bottle which was waiting to be put outside for collection. The glass shattered. The jagged edges slashed the base of my right hand, almost at the wrist. Hot blood spurted out. I could feel it running over my arm and dripping on to the floor.

Rita screamed. Norman started to cry. I shouted for a towel. Rita threw one to me. I wrapped it round my hand tightly, but I could feel the blood soaking it almost immediately and starting to drip on to the floor once more. Rita ran out of the house in a panic. She returned seconds later with Mr Hook, the next door neighbour. He could see at once something that, even without sight, I already knew. I had severed a main artery. No matter how hard I pressed on to the wound with the towel, the blood still kept spurting out.

Mr Hook ran back indoors to telephone Frimley Hospital with a warning that an emergency case was on the way. He rushed back, guided me into his car and broke the speed limit to get there. The blood was still pumping out of the gash and seeping through the towel. My fingers were wet and sticky.

Fortunately, the hospital was only about one mile away. Nurses rushed out to meet the car. One was carrying a bowl. A tourniquet was tightened on my upper arm. I was hurried to the operating theatre. There was no time for an anaesthetic. I gritted my teeth and tried not to cry out with pain as the surgical needle sank into my tender flesh, in and out, inserting the stitches, closing the gap in the severed artery, sewing up the gaping wound, pulling together the bleeding flesh, mending the torn skin. I was put to bed and, because of the serious loss of blood, given blood transfusions. Had medical attention been delayed for another ten minutes, the doctor told me later, I would have bled to death.

After a week of being confined to bed, I was allowed to get up to go to the toilet. Because of my confinement, I was constipated and was forced to strain. Suddenly, I felt hot blood seeping from underneath the bandages on my hand. The straining had caused the wound to re-open. I was rushed to the operating theatre once more. New stitches were inserted, happily under a general anaesthetic this time.

I was learning the hard way about the perils of being unable to see.

In December 1950 I was recalled to St Luke's Hospital, Guildford, for yet another operation. Ena and I had not met for almost four months, not since the day of our quarrel. She was not on the ward. I assumed that she was working in one of the other wards. For all I knew, she could have been transferred not only to another ward but to another hospital.

On Christmas Eve, a choir of nurses, dressed in their cloaks and carrying lighted lanterns, was touring the hospital singing carols. They entered the ward and began to sing *Oh, come all ye faithful*. Their voices were like those of angels. I swallowed hard, overcome with emotion, thinking of my family in Istanbul, thinking of Christmas at home.

Suddenly, as the two ranks of nurses walked past my bed, still singing, I thought I heard something. I listened hard. For once, I was truly grateful for my acute sense of hearing. Yes, there it was again! My heart began to beat faster. Faster and faster! There was no mistaking it! Even above the glorious sounds of the carol, I could hear the familiar, the unmistakable, sounds of a pair of squeaky shoes!

The carol ended and the group of nurses dispersed throughout the ward to have a brief word with individual patients and to wish them a happy Christmas. I knew that she was standing beside my bed. My heart thumped against my ribs.

'Hello, nurse,' I said quietly, trying hard to keep the tremor from my voice.

'Hello,' she said.

I reached out my hands. She grasped them in a semi-hand-shake. She held my hands in both of hers. It was more than an ordinary handshake, more than a normal greeting of a nurse to a patient. I could feel a warmth coming through her hands and I knew that, even though we had not met for four months, she still felt the same. Our love had not died. Neither of us spoke. I was too overcome with emotion to speak and I sensed that she was, too.

Eventually, I broke the silence. I asked her where she was working, on which ward. On my ward, she said. She had just come on night duty after a few days' leave. She would be back as soon as the carol singing had ended.

When she returned to the ward and I heard the squeak of her shoes once more I called her over.

'Nurse, my hand needs to be dressed,' I told her.

'What have you done to it?'

I told her about the fall, the severed artery and my stay in Frimley Hospital.

'It's still quite painful,' I said, unashamedly seeking sympathy.

'I'll ask the charge nurse.'

'No, don't do that!'

'Why not?'

'Because I'm lying. The dressing has already been changed by the day staff. It doesn't really need to be changed again.'

'I see.'

'But just do it. Please.'

She was silent for a moment.

'Come with me to the treatment room,' she said. 'We'll see to it there.'

I put my hand on the back of her shoulder and followed her out of the ward. As she closed the door of the treatment room behind us, I grasped her shoulders, turned her gently towards me and kissed her on the lips.

We did not speak. There was no need for words. It was not necessary for either of us to say anything. The kiss spoke for both of us. It confirmed what the handshake had already told me, that nothing had changed between us, that she still loved me.

'I've been longing to see you,' I told her at last.

'Why didn't you come to the theatre?' she countered.

'I wanted to,' I said. 'But Rita put me off coming.'

'You were out with one of your other girlfriends, I suppose.'

'No, no, darling. It wasn't that. I wasn't out with anybody. I stayed in all evening.'

'My mother told me that Rita said you were going out with another girlfriend.'

'No, what Rita said was that I had another engagement. It was just an excuse. I hadn't really. Not with a girlfriend. Not with anybody. I wasn't going anywhere.'

'It was a lie, you mean.'

'It was an excuse.'

'I see.'

'But why didn't you contact me?' I asked. 'It's been nearly four months.'

'Because I thought you had another girlfriend,' she explained. 'I thought you were out with her on the night we went to the theatre.'

It was clear that there had been a mix-up. Somehow, Rita's telephoned message that I had another engagement had been misconstrued by Ena, or by her mother, as meaning that I was going out with another girl.

I was sitting on a chair. Ena started to remove the dressing from my hand. I pulled her gently on to my lap and kissed her lightly on the lips.

'I would never go out with anyone but you,' I told her. 'You ought to know that.'

'I know you've had loads of girlfriends.'

'I did have. But not now. Now I have only you.'

'You're such a charmer.'

'The only girl I want to charm now is you.'

'You see what I mean? You're such a charmer.'

We laughed. She placed a new dressing on my hand.

'But what happened on the night we went to the pictures?' I asked. 'Why didn't you tell me you had to be home early?'

'I thought it would sound so silly,' she laughed. 'A grown-up girl like me having to be home by seven.'

'I was cross because you hadn't told me.' I said. 'It caused a lot of trouble between Rita and me.'

'I'm sorry,' she said.

'Poor you! If only I'd known how you must have been choking on every mouthful of your meal! You must have been counting every minute! Just like Cinderella!'

'I was rather.'

'Why didn't you say goodbye?' I asked.

'I did,' she said. 'But you were so busy quarrelling with Rita that you didn't notice. You didn't reply. Then the two of you went inside and the door closed on me. I thought you'd gone. I was very upset and sad.'

'Darling, I'm sorry.'

'I went down the path in tears. It spoilt a lovely evening.'

I kissed her lightly on the forehead.

'It's all over now, anyway,' I told her. 'Let's forget it.'

There were footsteps outside the door. Mr Bubb, the charge nurse, opened the door and looked inside.

'Hurry up, Nurse Argyle,' he said. 'Matron's doing her Christmas Eve rounds.'

Ena led me back to my bed.

'I'll see you later,' I whispered.

As soon as matron had gone, I asked one of the patients to take me to the kitchen, where Ena was busily cutting bread.

Both Ena and I were delighted at the renewal of our close friendship. We started going out for walks together. As much as possible of her off-duty time was spent in my company. Her visits home became fewer.

One morning at about eleven o'clock, I was lying on my bed when one of the nurses told me that matron wanted to see me in her office. She did not know the reason.

I was puzzled. I put on my dressing-gown and slippers and the nurse led me to the office.

'Come in, Mr Fettel,' said matron's voice.

'Good morning, Miss Coyle.'

'Dr McMillan, the medical superintendent, is here, too,' she said.

'Good morning, doctor.'

'Sit down, will you?'

The doctor drew up a chair for me and I sat down. I waited for somebody to say something. Dr McMillan was the first to break the silence.

'Now, Mr Fettel,' he said, clearing his throat. 'The reason we have asked you here is that Nurse Argyle's father has been to the hospital to see us. He is insisting that we put a stop to your romance with his daughter.'

Between them, the medical superintendent and the matron explained that, although they did not have anything against me personally, it was against the rules and regulations for nurses and patients to fraternise. Personal relationships between nurses and patients were not permitted. It was not allowed for them to mix socially. The professional relationship must be maintained. For one thing, it was unfair to other patients for nurses to give too much of their attention to particular patients. In addition, Nurse Argyle was a student nurse who needed to concentrate on her studies without any outside distractions. Further, as my association with Nurse Argyle was specifically against the wishes of her parents, it must cease immediately. I was forbidden to associate with her any more.

'But we're not doing any harm,' I protested feebly. 'We're only friends.'

'According to Nurse Argyle's father, it's more than simply friendship,' said matron severely. 'We have nothing against you, Mr Fettel, but that is the way it is, I'm afraid. That is all. You may return to your ward now.'

I groped my way back to my bed and lay on it. I had had not the slightest suspicion of what lay in store for me when I had been summoned to matron's office. The ultimatum had come as a total surprise. I was shocked. I felt completely lost. It was the end of the world. My association with Ena must cease.

By that time, Ena had been moved to the women's ward on the ground floor, directly below my own first-floor ward. For some time, whenever she was off duty, she had been coming to see me as an ordinary visitor during normal visiting hours, always ensuring that she was dressed in civilian clothes and not in her nurse's uniform. Her period on night duty had ended and, during the daytime when she was on duty, we tried to meet secretly as often as possible. To that end, we had organised our own elaborate code signals. Whenever I wanted to speak to her, I wandered out of the ward on to the landing of the back staircase, pretending to go to the lavatory block which led off it. On the landing, I leaned over the railings and whistled our code tune, *Put Another Nickel In, In the Nickelodeon*, a song that was popular at the time. When Ena heard it, she would come out of her ward carrying a used bed pan, ostensibly to empty the contents in the sluice room, which was directly below the men's ward lavatory. In reality, her main object was to talk to me. I would lean over the banister rail, Ena would venture a little way up the staircase, three or four steps, and we would hold hurried, whispered conversations, arranging when next to meet, where to meet, whether she would be coming to see me during the next visiting time. Sometimes, as I stood expectantly on the landing, having already whistled my code tune, I heard the sound of footsteps coming out of the female ward and started to whistle my tune again. Sometimes it was not Ena but one of the other nurses. It did not matter, however. As they did not know the code, they took no notice of my whistling.

On the day that matron and the medical superintendent gave me their ultimatum, Ena had told me that she would be coming to see me that evening during the visiting half-hour. I was miserable and lonely, totally shattered, my world in ruins. I could scarcely wait for half-past seven to arrive so that I could tell her of the latest development, of my interview in matron's office, of their determination to keep us apart, of their decision that our association must end. Half-past seven arrived. Ena did not. By a quarter to eight I was becoming worried. At eight o'clock, when the bell sounded for the visitors to leave, Ena had still not arrived. By then I was in a panic. What had happened to her? Why had she not turned up? Had she, too, been told to end our association? Was she obeying the order she had been given? Had she decided never to see me again?

I lay silently on my bed, alone with my thoughts. The possibilities, the doubts, ran rampant in my mind.

'Goodnight, Kosta,' said Sister Parfitt as she went off duty.

'Goodnight, Sister.'

As soon as she had gone through the door, I made my way out on to the landing. It was a totally illogical action. I had no reason to believe that Ena would be in the ward. She was off duty. I had no reason to think that she might be down the stairs. It was simply that I had a vague, desperate hope that she might be somewhere around and that, if I went out on to the landing, I might find her.

I paced impatiently up and down. I whistled our code tune. The door below opened. Footsteps came out. They disappeared into the sluice room. There was no response to my whistling. The traffic out of the ward and into the sluice room seemed to be even busier than usual. Time after time, the ward door opened and the sound of footsteps came out. None of them, however, belonged to Ena.

Then, however, there was the sound of another door opening, not the ward door but the back door leading outside into the yard. Familiar footsteps made their way to the foot of the stone steps. An even more familiar voice called up to me.

'Nino!' It was Ena!

'Is that you, Inneta? Come up! Quickly!'

She could hear the agitation in my voice and she bounded up the steps.

'What is it?' She sounded anxious.

'Quickly, into the bathroom.'

In the bathroom, I held her close to me for a moment. It was a cold, bare room but, to us, it was a beautiful place where we could be alone for just a few minutes. Happiness for us was being together.

'What happened?' I asked. 'Why didn't you come to visit me?'

'I did,' she said. 'But Sister Parfitt turned me away.'

'I was worried when you didn't turn up.'

'She just wouldn't let me in. I don't know why.'

'I know why,' I told her grimly.

I recounted the unhappy events of my visit to matron's office and the dire warnings I had been given.

'So that's why Sister Parfitt wouldn't let me in,' she said. 'And that's why Matron wants to see me. I have to report to her office first thing in the morning. It means coming in on my day off.'

'Don't worry, darling.'

'I can't help but worry. She's going to tell me I can't see you any more. What really upsets me is not being able to see you during visiting hours. They were the only times we were able to meet openly without worrying about people seeing us. And now they're even going to take that away from us!'

'Don't worry, darling. We'll find a way.'

'Oh, Nino! I can't stand all this worry. What are we going to do?'

I took her in my arms.

'Listen, my darling. Nothing, nobody, can stop us seeing each other. Nothing can keep us apart. The more obstacles they put in our way, the more determined I shall be to see you.'

'They'll stop us somehow.'

'Have strength, my darling. The more they try to part us, the more determined they will make us to be together.'

My words seemed to revive Ena's flagging spirits, to give her fresh hope.

'You're right, darling,' she said. 'When I see Matron tomorrow, I shall ask her if I can still come to visit you. She can only say no.'

I made the sign of the cross on her forehead.

'God will give you the strength to speak up,' I told her. 'You'll see.'

The following morning, when I thought that her nerve-wracking interview with matron would be over, I groped my way on to the landing and began to whistle our code tune. After a while, Ena appeared.

I was right, she said. God had, indeed, given her the strength to speak up. She had stood up to matron over the question of being stopped from visiting me during normal visiting hours when she was off duty and in civilian clothes. In the end, matron had relented. Very well, yes, all right then, certainly, it would be permissible for her to visit me as an ordinary member of the public. There would have to be one condition, however. That was that, as her parents were opposed to the relationship, she would have to be discreet. Very discreet.

Chapter Twenty-Two

The course of daily injections in my thigh that Mr Boxill had ordered in a bid to soften the scar tissue had failed. After three days, pains developed in my chest. The injections had to be stopped.

Instead, he arranged for an appointment to be made for me at the world-famous Moorfields Eye Hospital in London. Rita accompanied me on the train journey. Mr Boxill was already there. He introduced me to the other eye specialists. They examined my eyes. One of them mentioned that the right eye appeared to be in better condition than the left but Mr Boxill explained that, for various reasons, the left eye provided the better chance of sight, except for the fact that new lids needed to be grafted on. The outcome of their deliberations was that it was decided that one of the specialists, a Mr Moffatt, would travel to St Luke's Hospital, where he and Mr Boxill would attempt a joint operation.

The surgery they carried out was a major skin graft, using the umbilical cord of a new-born baby in an attempt to build new eyelids for me. Grafts using skin and mucous membrane taken from various parts of my body had failed. A graft using an umbilical cord, they hoped, would be successful.

For a fortnight, I was made to lie flat on my back. Nurses fed me, washed me and provided me with bed-pans and bottles. At the end of the fortnight, Mr Boxill removed the dressing. After so many previous grafts had failed to take, I was prepared for the worst. Mr Boxill, unlike the occasion when he had removed the dressing following the operation for which mucous membrane had been taken from my tongue, did not show any signs of happiness or of elation and, because of that, there was no perceptible change of mood when he examined my eye. I knew that the graft had gone wrong, however, when he began cutting with his scissors. There was the old familiar sensation of little pieces of dead skin falling on to my cheeks.

I had been prepared for the worst and the worst had happened. The graft had died.

*

With or without the knowledge of her parents, Ena continued
to visit me in hospital and, when I was discharged once more,
continued to meet me regularly during her off-duty periods. She
travelled by train to collect me from Rita's home and we spent
afternoons walking in the countryside and evenings at the Rex
Cinema, Farnborough, where the kindly manager took pity on
us and began to let us in without payment for the seats. They
were happy days, spoiled only by the fact that, inevitably, they
had to come to an end, that Ena had to return by train to Guildford and to the hospital. Each day we were apart, Ena wrote to
me. Rita read me her letters.

During the summer of 1951, when I was back in hospital for
further operations, the continued opposition of Ena's parents to
our association took a more serious turn. Totally unexpectedly,
the Reverend Argyle knocked on the door of Rita's bungalow,
introduced himself and announced that he wished to discuss
with her my association with his daughter. According to Rita,
who recounted the event when she next visited me, he had begun
their discussion with a eulogy of Czechoslovakia and the
Czechoslovakian people. In his opinion, they were a wonderful
race. What culture they had! What a sense of humour! What
bravery they had shown during the war! Rita had pointed out to
him, somewhat tartly, that I was not a Czechoslovak but a
Yugoslav. Ah, yes! Quite so.

The Reverend Argyle had made it quite plain to Rita that,
while he had no objection to an ordinary friendship between his
daughter and me, he would not permit it to go further than that.
There must be nothing more. He had not uttered any threats.
His ultimatum had been delivered in a pleasant manner. He had
been agreeable but firm. Rita was not aware that Ena and I had
confessed our love for each other, that we were totally serious in
our commitment to each other. She was still under the impression that, as soon as my sight was restored, I was planning to
return to Turkey. As a result, she had told the Reverend Argyle
that he need have no worries about his daughter's relationship
with me as there were no plans for marriage. I was planning to
leave England as soon as possible. That, presumably, had
relieved some of his anxiety.

I had never met Ena's father and I was angry that he should
go to my cousin like that to state his objections. He had already
objected to the matron and the medical superintendent at the
hospital and now he had involved Rita, too. If he had wanted to
object to anyone, then he should have objected to me. I could

not understand what had made him talk to Rita. After all, she was only my cousin. She had no influence over me. It was simply that I lived in her home. I became convinced that there must be more sinister reasons for his visit than the one that he had stated. Perhaps he wanted to see what sort of a person my cousin was. Perhaps he wanted to see what sort of a home she lived in. Perhaps he wanted to know what her background was like – what my background was like – and whether it was good enough for his daughter. I did not know the man but I was cross that he had troubled Rita.

Ena, too, when I told her, was equally annoyed and puzzled. Neither of us could understand what had prompted her father to visit Rita. Ena was under age. We could not marry without her parents' consent until she was twenty-one and we knew that parental consent was out of the question. Why, then, did he appear to be so concerned by our continued relationship? Both Ena and I concluded that some plot was being hatched to part us.

The surprise that Ena and I felt at the unexpected visit of her father to Rita, however, was less than that experienced at an unexpected visit by her parents to me in hospital. I was taken completely unawares.

'You have some visitors, Kosta,' said one of the nurses.

'Good evening,' said a man's voice. 'I am the Reverend Leonard Argyle and this is my wife Evelyn.'

It was a strained first meeting. The atmosphere was tense. Ena's father tried to make conversation. His words were carefully chosen, extremely diplomatic. On the part of Ena's mother, however, I sensed a certain coolness. Even though she had brought me a big bunch of black grapes, she sounded cold towards me.

Ena received the news of the visit with a mixture of surprise, suspicion and pleasure.

'What did they say?' she asked anxiously, yet eagerly.

'Not very much,' I shrugged.

She was pleased that her parents had come to visit me, that, at last, they had met me. Yet, at the same time, she did not understand what lay behind it. She shared my suspicions. Like me, she feared the worst.

The worst – for me, if not for Ena – occurred not long afterwards.

'Darling!' Ena told me breathlessly. 'My parents have invited you home for the weekend! This weekend!'

Chapter Twenty-Three

According to Ena, her parents had been questioning her about the fact that she was spending more and more time at the hospital, even when she was off duty.

'Why aren't you coming home as often as you were?' her mother had asked.

'Because I like to be with Nino,' Ena had told her bravely.

'Very well. So why don't you bring him home with you?'

'Maybe I shall.'

'Right, how about this weekend?'

'I'll ask him.'

'He can stay overnight.'

I was apprehensive about the invitation and suspicious of the motives that lay behind it. Ena, however, was happy that, at last, her parents seemed to be accepting our relationship and softening in their attitude towards me. An invitation to their home was, at least, a step in the right direction.

'Please, darling!' Ena pleaded. 'Please come for my sake!'

By that time, I had been discharged from hospital once more and, on the following Friday, Ena collected me from Rita's home in Farnborough. I carried my pyjamas, slippers and shaving-gear in a small carrier-bag. Ena's father was no longer the Rector of Elvetham, in Hampshire. He had moved some time previously to a new living in Berkshire, where he had become the Rector of Bearwood, near Winnersh. On the train journey from Farnborough North to Winnersh Halt, the apprehension that I had felt when Ena had first told me of the invitation, and which had not left me since, increased in intensity until it had assumed proportions of sheer terror.

We walked the half-mile along the main Reading road from the station to the gates of the rectory. There was a long drive from the roadway to the house. I felt sick in the pit of my stomach. I felt like a lamb being led to the slaughter. Ena could feel my fear through the sweaty palm of my hand. She tried to calm me, to put me at my ease, to take my mind off what lay before me, by describing the scene as we walked up the laurel-and-rhododendron-fringed drive.

'Are we nearly there, darling?' I asked anxiously.

'Not far now,' she said.

'Darling,' I told her. 'I feel like turning round and running back to Farnborough.'

'Only a few steps more,' she said with forced brightness, ignoring my remark. 'We're nearly at the house.' Only small-talk passed between us. I could tell that Ena was as nervous as I was but she did not voice her fears.

Ena's mother opened the door in answer to her knock. She kissed Ena and then shook hands with me.

'How do you do, Nino?'

'How do you do, Mrs Argyle?'

I was led into their big kitchen and I could feel a flagstone floor under my feet. The Reverend Argyle was there. He sounded friendly but ill at ease. He cleared his throat nervously several times. Everyone seemed nervous, me most of all.

At Mrs Argyle's request, Ena took me to my bedroom and, after showing me where everything was, left me there and returned downstairs.

Ena's brother, Nigel, two years younger, and the second of her two sisters, Ruth, four years younger, were present at dinner. It was the first time that the family had had a blind man in their house and I could sense that they were waiting to see how I coped with the meal. Mrs Argyle put a plate in front of me. While I was wondering whether there was any food on it, or whether I was expected to help myself from serving dishes on the table, I heard Ena next to me busily, but discreetly, cutting up the food on her own plate. Without a word, she removed my plate and placed her own in front of me, the food already chopped up ready for eating. The Reverend Argyle said grace. I could feel their eyes watching me as I started to eat. Every fork-ful of food stuck in my throat. Ena tried to relax me, to make me laugh, by recounting more funny stories about her goats but I was too ill-at-ease to loosen up and to laugh. I was not able to bring myself to participate fully in the conversation. When I did speak, it was mainly in answer to questions put directly to me and, even then, my words were polite, reserved and guarded.

After dinner, the Reverend Argyle took me into the sitting-room. I thought that he wanted to speak to me on my own, about Ena, about my intentions towards her. Ena, however, was not mentioned. He began by speaking about the Yugoslavs. Wonderful people, he said. Great fighters. Perhaps he was sincere in what he said but, to me, his words sounded empty and false, without meaning. Next, he guided the conversation on to religion, first about the Dead Sea Scrolls, in which he was passionately interested, then about a scholarly book* that he had written on the Christian attitude to psychical phenomena and, finally, about my own beliefs. He had heard that I was a Roman Catholic, he said. A wonderful man, the Pope. A wonderful man. Again, I doubted the sincerity of his words. His praise for the Pope, like that for the Yugoslavs, seemed to me to be false, especially when, having praised him as a man, he immediately went on to criticise him theologically. He spoke to me for a long time about religion. He did not mention his daughter, nor my feelings for her, nor my intentions towards her, but I suspected that his many references to the Bible, his theological talk, his discussion of Catholicism, were intended to point out the religious differences between Ena and me, to emphasise the incompatibility of her Protestant beliefs and my Catholic beliefs, to drive a wedge between us. All the time he was talking, I was listening with one ear to Ena in the kitchen, where she was helping her mother with the washing-up, hoping that she would soon come to rescue me.

At bed-time, we had Horlicks to drink. Ena led me to the bathroom and then tucked me into bed.

I was awake early the following morning. I was anxious and could not sleep. I rose at half-past-five. I washed and dressed. Then I waited. I was not familiar with the layout of the house and, as a result, I had of necessity to stay where I was. I was a prisoner in my room, waiting, waiting for Ena, my rescuer, to arrive.

As it turned out, it was not Ena but her mother who arrived at eight o'clock with a cup of tea. Breakfast was a pleasant experience. The Reverend Argyle was still in bed. Nigel and Ruth had gone to their private school, which held classes on Saturday mornings. Only Mrs Argyle, Ena and I sat down to breakfast. The coldness that Mrs Argyle had shown towards me on her visit to the hospital seemed to have vanished. So, too, did the tension and awkwardness of the previous evening. She seemed to have warmed to me, seemed to go out of her way to make me feel comfortable and at ease.

'What are you going to do this morning, children?' she asked amiably.

'Perhaps we could do some shopping for you,' Ena suggested.

* *Nothing to Hide, An Exposition of the Great Prohibition*, by Leonard Argyle, BD, Hon. CF, published by the Churches' Fellowship for Psychical and Spiritual Studies.

'That would be a help. Could you get me two pounds of chops and some vegetables?'

I was much more relaxed as we walked down the drive on our way to the village shops.

'Darling, it's not so bad after all,' I told her. 'Your mother is quite nice.'

There was a queue of customers at the butcher's shop. When it was Ena's turn to be served, she detached herself from my arm. I stepped back so that I would not be in her way and, as I did so, I bumped into what I thought must be another customer.

'I beg your pardon!' I apologised, politely raising my grey trilby hat.

As we left the shop, I could hear Ena trying hard to stifle her laughter.

'What's the matter, darling?' I asked, puzzled.

'Darling!' she chortled. 'You've just apologised to a side of beef!'

Back at the rectory, Ena and I sat on a hollow oak tree that had been felled in the back garden. I could hear the quacking of ducks. Then I heard another sound.

'I can hear a baby crying,' I said.

'No, darling,' Ena told me. 'It's Ruth's Siamese cat. It cries just like a baby.'

The increasing confidence that I had felt on the Saturday, following my apprehension of the previous day, was not to last. Three incidents on the Sunday, three incidents caused by my own thoughtlessness and clumsiness, brought on a return of my former feelings of discomfort and anxiety.

On Sunday morning, the family attended a communion service at the Reverend Argyle's church. Ena led me up the aisle and, as she stopped to guide me into a pew, I faced the altar and made a genuflexion, as was my usual practice in my own church.

'Darling,' Ena whispered. 'You don't do that in the Church of England! Not in Daddy's church, anyway!'

I was embarrassed by my religious *faux pas* in not realising that, in most churches of the Church of England, it was not the custom to genuflect. I was more embarrassed, however, when, at Sunday lunch, I reached for a spoon and knocked over a glass of orange juice. There was a shocked silence. Then Ena's mother jumped up and ran to fetch a cloth.

'Don't worry, don't worry!' she said as she mopped up the table-cloth.

My face was red with embarrassment, however, and I could not help but worry.

My discomfiture continued at tea-time. Mrs Argyle had made a beautiful sponge cake filled with thick cream. She cut me a slice. Unknown to me, as I took my first bite, the cream squirted out of the middle and dropped on to the lapel of my best suit. Again, there was a shocked silence. Again, Ena's mother ran to fetch a cloth. Ena sponged the cream from my suit.

I had still not recovered my composure when it was time for Ena to return me to Rita's home.

'Do come again, Nino,' said Mrs Argyle. 'You are always welcome in this house.'

The Reverend Argyle cleared his throat.

'God bless you, Nino,' he said.

Privately, I thought it would be a long time before I dared to face Ena's parents again.

Chapter Twenty-Four

During yet another period in hospital for yet another operation, I discussed with Ena the question of our future together and the most suitable time to make an open declaration of our love for each other. We both wanted to make our relationship a recognised one in the eyes of the world by becoming officially engaged. It was simply a question of when to make the announcement and how to break the news to Ena's family.

'Let's do it now, straight away,' said Ena excitedly. 'I'm dying to let everyone know. I'm visiting my mother tomorrow. I'll tell her then. I'm longing to tell her!'

I was not the only patient Ena was visiting at that time. Mrs Argyle, too, was in hospital, in London, having undergone a gynaecological operation. I knew that, following surgery, she would not be in the best of spirits and might even be in considerable pain and in a depressed state of mind. I was dubious about what her reaction would be even when she had returned to perfect health. I knew that, in her present condition, it would be unwise, not to say foolish, to break the news.

'No, not while she's in hospital,' I told Ena. 'Wait until she comes home.'

Ena, however, was impulsive. On her next visit to me, she told me that she had broached the subject with her mother, had confessed that we were in love and had informed her that we wished to become engaged.

'How did she take it?' I asked anxiously.

There was a pause.

'She wasn't very pleased at all,' Ena said sheepishly. 'She cried. She's very sad about it.'

I could feel my stomach turning over with disappointment and then my face flushing with anger.

'Come outside with me,' I told Ena grimly. 'To the bathroom.'

Inside the white-tiled bathroom, where we had held so many surreptitious meetings, I turned to face her.

'Why did you have to tell her when she's in hospital?' I demanded. 'I told you not to.'

'I had to,' she said. 'I couldn't help myself. I was longing to tell her we are in love.'

'You had no right to tell her,' I raged. 'We are in this together, we decided to get engaged together and we should have gone together to tell your mother when she was at home and feeling better!'

'I couldn't wait any longer.'

'Why now, when she's in hospital? It's the worst possible moment. She's got all the time in the world to lie there thinking about it while she's in hospital.'

'But I didn't know she would take it like that! I wouldn't have told her if I'd known!'

'You should have known! What did you expect when she's just had an operation?'

Ena was surprised at my reaction to her news and shocked at my anger. She felt guilty about what she had done and her guilt caused her to lose her temper.

'Right, goodbye then!' she shouted at me. 'We're finished! It's all off!'

She stalked away, hurt and angry at my attitude. Although she had declared quite clearly that our romance was ended, I suspected that she was secretly hoping that I would call her back, apologise and make up the quarrel. I, however, was angry, too, angry that she should have chosen such an inappropriate time to tell her mother that we were in love, a time when she was in need of sympathy and understanding, a time when family problems that were likely to upset her should have been kept from her. It had been silly of Ena to upset not only her mother but probably the entire Argyle family as well. Not only was I angry, I was stubborn, too, and I did not call her back. I let her go.

A whole day passed and Ena did not return. By the time the visiting half-hour arrived on the evening after our quarrel, I was becoming anxious. By the time the bell rang, the visitors began to leave, and there was still no sign of Ena, I was becoming desperate. I had felt confident that, once her temper had cooled, Ena would come to me and the angry words that had passed between us would be forgiven on both sides. Now, however, my confidence had evaporated. I was no longer confident. I was afraid, terrified, that she had gone for ever.

At eleven o'clock that night, long after lights out, I could not bear the suspense a moment longer. I persuaded one of my friends to lead me downstairs to the public telephone boxes. I rang the nurses' home and asked to speak to Ena. She was a long time coming to take the call.

'Hello?'

'Hello, darling. Can you come straight away?'

'I have my hair in curlers.'

'Come straight away. Please, darling.'

'At once?'

'At once.'

She flew to my side. We fell into each other's arms.

'I'm sorry for being so nasty, darling,' I told her.

'I'm sorry for telling my mother,' she said.

We made up the quarrel and decided that, for the sake of harmony in Ena's family, we would not consider becoming engaged, nor mention the matter again, at least for the time being.

Despite the misgivings I had had following my first visit to Ena's family home, my self-confidence eventually returned and I became a frequent visitor to Bearwood Rectory.

During the winter, in between several more stays in hospital, Ena and I became regular theatre-goers, travelling to Reading to see plays and variety shows. Topping the bill on one occasion was the disc jockey Jimmy Young, one of the most popular singers in Britain at that time. We became regular ballroom dancers, too, at the weekly dances held at the Stoke Hotel, in Guildford. The quality of my dancing still left much to be desired but the other dancers good-naturedly endured the bruised shins and grazed ankles that resulted from their dance-floor encounters with me. On one occasion, however, when Ena and I began to perform a tango, the prospect of sharing the floor with me in such a tempestuous Latin-American routine appeared to be such a daunting one that none of them was prepared to take the risk. Presumably deciding that discretion was the better part of valour, everyone else hurriedly evacuated the dance area and retreated to the tables, leaving the entire floor to the two of us.

During the spring and summer, we went for picnics, walking for miles in the countryside before sitting down in cornfields to eat our packed lunches and drink piping-hot coffee from a vacuum flask. We attended horse-racing meetings at Windsor. We travelled on coach trips to places of interest and spent days at the seaside. On one trip, to Hayling Island, near Portsmouth, we lost a ten shilling note, our only money, on a fair-ground big-wheel and, as a result, had to sit in the coach during a stop on the return journey while everyone else trooped into a village inn for a drink. We did not mind, however. We had each other.

One of the several stays in hospital at that time coincided with my twenty-eighth birthday on 1 June. It seemed that almost all of the birthdays and Christmases that had occurred in the six years that had passed since Staka's attack had been spent in hospital. That particular birthday was memorable, however, for the fact that Ena had spent her wages – six pounds, a lot of money at that time – on an enormous iced birthday cake which she brought to me in the ward. I asked sister to cut it up and give a slice to each patient and each member of the staff. When she had done so, and when Ena and I had celebrated with the rest of the ward, the considerable remainder of the cake was placed on the table across my bed, where it stood in white-iced splendour earning the admiration of everyone who entered the ward.

Later that evening, I felt the need to move my bowels. A nurse brought me a bedpan and drew screens round my bed. Unknown to me, when she departed, she took away the cake from the table top.

When I had completed my toilet, the nurse returned to remove the bedpan and take away the screens. Before she could do so, however, she had to hurry away to attend to another patient whose need was, by then, greater than mine. She had time – again unknown to me – only to place the used bedpan on to the table.

A few minutes later, a sister from another ward popped her head through the curtains round my bed.

'I hear it's your birthday, Kosta,' she said brightly. 'I just came to wish you many happy returns of the day!'

'Thank you, Sister,' I said. I waved my hand expansively towards the table and added with generosity, 'Please help yourself to a slice!'

The happy days that Ena and I spent together were marred only by the continued opposition of the Argyle family towards our relationship. Although I had become a regular visitor to their home, I felt that they had accepted neither me nor the situation, that they were hoping that, given time, the relationship would come to an end. I sensed that, the longer my association with Ena continued without showing any signs of ending, however, the more concerned her family was becoming. I became more and more aware of a growing feeling of antipathy to me and of a determination to part us.

On one visit to the rectory, Ena and I were sitting talking in the kitchen when Nigel, her brother, walked in. It was a sunny day and I was feeling happy.

'Hello, Nigel,' I said cheerfully.

I could feel the coldness emanating from Nigel even before he spoke.

'You are not wanted in this house,' he replied icily.

His words shocked me and then angered me.

'Right, in that case I'm going,' I said. 'I shall leave.'

Ena was as upset as I was. She begged me to stay. Her mother, however, was in no mood to appease me.

'If he wants to go, let him go,' she said.

I went.

As far as I was aware, there was no reason for Nigel's rudeness and hostility towards me. I had done nothing to offend him. He was a young boy and, undoubtedly, he had uttered the words either with the thoughtlessness of youth or without realising how hurtful to me they would be and, because of that, it was not difficult to forgive him. In addition, I felt that the hostility he had displayed was not really his own. He was simply reflecting the feelings that were there in other members of the family.

Not long afterwards, Ena confessed to me that, on one of her visits home, her parents had taken her into the kitchen to discuss what they called 'something very important'. When she had been seated, they had told her that Uncle Henry was prepared to pay for her to spend a fortnight in Paris if she would go there, enjoy herself and 'forget this man'.

I felt a sudden sense of foreboding.

'They are trying to part us,' I said dully.

She squeezed my hand.

'I shall never leave you,' she said.

'What did you tell them?'

'I told them I wouldn't go and I wouldn't forget you. Absolutely not.'

Her answer had triggered off a stormy scene that had ended with both Ena and her mother in tears.

It was not difficult for me to understand the opposition of the Argyles to our relationship. They were very much a middle-class family, some way up the class structure of English society. Church of England clergymen were highly-respected and influential members of that society. Ena had been expensively educated and had acquired all the fringe benefits of a middle-class family upbringing and of a private education, like poise, personality, good deportment, correct elocution. She was ready-made either for dedicating her life to her profession and becoming a matron or marrying into the same sort of middle-class society in which she had been raised. There were many well-to-do, eligible young men in her family circle. Undoubtedly, her parents expected her to marry a young curate, a bank official, an architect or some other young, professional man with sound prospects.

Even I had to admit that, as a potential husband, I did not have a lot to commend me. I was blind, penniless, stateless and a foreigner.

Worse, perhaps, in the eyes of a staunch and traditional Church of England family, I was a Roman Catholic.

Chapter Twenty-Five

As so many of the skin grafts performed on my left eye had failed to take, Mr Boxill decided that, instead, he would attempt to carry out a corneal graft on my right eye, the lids of which were undamaged. Before the operation could take place, however, I had to attend the Royal Surrey County Hospital at Guildford, to which Mr Boxill's eye cases had been transferred from St Luke's, for heat treatment on my eye. Three times a week for many weeks, I attended the physiotherapy department, where a pad was placed over my right eye and, for fifteen minutes each time, an electric current was passed through it.

My quest for sight was even stronger than previously. Now I had Ena. She filled me with happiness. Every moment away from her was an eternity. There was nobody on earth but her with whom I wanted to spend my life. I wanted her to be my wife. I wanted to see so that I could earn my living and marry her. How could I now, blind and penniless, ask her to marry me?

At last, my eye was ready for the operation. I was admitted to the Royal Surrey County Hospital. The preliminary operations, the building-up operations, were ended, finished with. Now, at last, at long last, after six years of blindness, I was to have an operation on the eye itself, an operation that, if successful, would restore my sight.

I was shown to my bed in a small, three-bedded side room. A nurse introduced me to one of the other patients, a Mr Smith. I unpacked my suitcase and put my belongings into the bedside locker. When I had finished, I went to talk to Mr Smith.

'I've had an eye removed,' he told me.

'I'm sorry to hear that.'

'There was a blood clot. Mr Boxill advised that the eye should come out. Still, it will do somebody else a good turn.'

'How's that?'

'They're using my cornea to do a graft on someone else.'

Suddenly, I knew where the cornea was coming from. Nobody had told me and I had imagined that it would be obtained from a dead person's eye. Now, however, I knew that it was to be donated by a living person, by Mr Smith. His loss of sight would give me back mine. I did not tell him that I was in hospital for a corneal graft. He was sad, he said, to have lost his sight but happy that his cornea would give sight to somebody else.

I was wheeled, fully-conscious, to the operating theatre. After so many operations to repair the damage to my ravaged face and eyes, the first operation to attempt to restore my sight was to be performed under local anaesthetic. I could tell that there were bright, hot lights shining overhead. Mr Boxill tapped me on the forehead.

'This is the moment you have been waiting for, Kosta,' he said.

I was given an injection of morphine in the arm to sedate me. A saline bottle containing the local anaesthetic was attached to a vein in my ankle. Cocaine drops were put in my eye. My eyelashes were cut off. Soon my entire body tingled with pins and needles and then went completely numb. My mind, however, was alert. I was aware of everything that was happening.

'You will be conscious all the time, Kosta, but your body will be numb and you will not be in any pain,' Mr Boxill assured me. 'You won't feel a thing.'

The operation began. I could sense Mr Boxill bending over me and the masked and gowned figures of the other surgeons and nurses surrounding me.

'Retractors,' said Mr Boxill. They were passed to him. I felt what appeared to be two small spoons sliding underneath my eyelids and the lids being drawn apart. Then, suddenly, I felt as if my eye had popped right out.

Mr Boxill rapped out another order.

'Knife, please.'

The silence was broken only by the chink of metal as the knife was passed to him.

'Clamp!'

The atmosphere in the operating theatre was electric.

'Forceps!'

He was moving the eyeball but I could feel no pain.

'Scissors!'

He paused to give instructions to someone standing near him.

'Put another drop of cocaine in.'

I could feel him cutting my eye. Suddenly, I saw a big flash of yellowish light. It came and went in a split second.

'Pass me the eye,' Mr Boxill ordered.

An assistant passed him Mr Smith's eye. The cornea was

removed from it and then placed into my own eye. I could feel the stitches being inserted as it was sewn into place but, still, there was no pain.

Then, without warning, just as suddenly as the yellow light had appeared, something else flashed into view. It was misty and dark, almost like a negative photograph, and at first I could not tell what it was. Then, with an overwhelming feeling of surprise and delight, I realised that it was a surgical instrument and that an object beside it was Mr Boxill's finger! I could not contain my joy.

'Oh, I see!' I cried out. 'I see! I see your finger!'

'Keep still, Kosta!' said Mr Boxill. 'You'll ruin everything – the whole job!'

I did as I was ordered and lay still, scarcely daring to breathe. My vision was still misty but the image was still there. I could see the silver glint of the instrument and the finger holding it. Then it vanished again as the operation proceeded.

The instrument and the finger were the first objects I had seen for six years. I had seen them when the operation was still in progress, still unfinished. What, then, would I be able to see when the surgeon had completed his work? I was thrilled, delighted, excited and I had to make a conscious effort to remain immobile. I was certain that, at last, I would be able to see, that all my trials and tribulations, all the pain and suffering, were over, that soon I would be able to see Ena for the first time and that we would be able to marry.

'Thank you, Lord,' I prayed. 'The miracle has happened after so many years.'

Mr Boxill stitched the cornea with immense care. Then, after three hours, the operation was concluded. My eyes were bandaged.

'You had to keep still after the skin-grafting operations, Kosta, but this time you mustn't do anything for yourself – nothing at all,' said Mr Boxill. 'You will have two sandbags, one on each side of your face, and you must keep perfectly still and lie there in your bandages just like a mummy.'

I was taken back to the three-bedded ward. Six people lifted me gently from the trolley and put me to bed. The sandbags were packed round my head. Then they left me to my thoughts, to my dreams of the future, to my dreams of Ena.

For three weeks, I lay immobile, not daring to move a muscle. Nurses did everything for me. They washed me, fed me and wiped my bottom. I hated having to ask them to do it.

'Don't worry,' they said cheerfully. 'It's our job. That's nursing.'

Ena visited me every day after she had finished work at St Luke's. She sat beside me and read to me in her soft voice. By then, she had passed her final examinations and was a fully-qualified State Registered Nurse. The ward sister knew that she was from St Luke's and, at meal times, allowed Ena to feed me.

Ena was not the only daily visitor to my bedside. The nurses had confirmed to me that the cornea that had been grafted on to my eye was, indeed, that of Mr Smith and he, too, had heard the news. He had been discharged from hospital by then but, three days after my operation, he came to see me from his Guildford home. From the sound of his voice, I guessed that he was middle-aged, possibly in his fifties.

'How happy I am to know who my eye was used for – and to know that it was you,' he told me. 'At least, I know that in losing my eye I have been able to do some good for someone else and that, because of it, a young man will be able to see again.'

I was moved by his first visit, by his clear concern for me, by the happiness that was apparent behind the undoubted sadness at his own loss. I was not able adequately to express my gratitude.

'Thank you,' I said. 'I'm sorry that you have lost your eye. But it has certainly done me a good turn.'

'Never mind,' he said. 'My eye was no good to me. The blood clot could have killed me.'

The three weeks passed, three weeks in which I lay like a mummy, just as Mr Boxill had ordered, three weeks in which I twitched not even an eyebrow. Mr Boxill visited me regularly. Then came the great day, the day for which I had been waiting for six years, the day when the bandages would be removed from my eyes and I would see. My heart was beating madly and yet, at the same time, missing quite a few beats. Mr Boxill took off the bandages personally. I could not see clearly. I could not see a picture. I could not see Mr Boxill or the nurses. It was as if there was a thick mist over my eyes.

'Can you see daylight?' Mr Boxill asked.

'Yes.'

'Anything else?'

'No.'

'Don't worry. The cornea is misty. A few days of drops and

the cornea will start to clear.' He turned to sister. 'Leave the eye uncovered and he can start getting up.'

I was confined to a chair for the first two days I was allowed out of bed. Then I was permitted to move around the ward. I made my way over to what I knew must be a window, because of the strength of the light, and looked out. I could see nothing. My vision was still very foggy. Hope did not desert me, however. My spirits remained high. A few days of drops and the cornea would clear, Mr Boxill had said. It was only a matter of a few days. Then I would be able to see. Mr Boxill had said so and, therefore, it must happen.

A week after the bandages had been removed, however, Mr Boxill took me to the dark room and shone strong lights into the eye. He turned to his assistants.

'The cornea is opaque,' he announced. 'We will have to do a deeper graft.'

Chapter Twenty-Six

The corneal graft was a failure. I could not see. Still, however, my hopes were high. Mr Boxill had said that he would do a deeper graft and, before leaving the dark-room, he had instructed his assistants to find him another eye.

I was not discharged. I remained in hospital until, three weeks later, another eye became available and a repeat operation was performed. Unlike the first occasion, I was given a general anaesthetic and knew nothing of what occurred.

Once more, however, the fates were against me. Sister explained that it was essential that I did not become constipated lest, in straining, I put pressure on the graft and ruin the delicate surgery. With that object in view, three days after the operation I was given cascara to ensure that my bowels remained open. It was a most unpleasant medicine to take, however, and, unfortunately, it caused me to be violently ill. The vomiting, in turn, caused me to move my head and, as a result, my eye began to twitch. I could feel it jumping underneath the bandages.

When Mr Boxill arrived on his rounds, I told him about the twitching. He removed the bandages, examined the eye and dropped fluid into it. After a few minutes, he spoke.

'It has changed colour,' he said. 'There's a leak. We shall have to cauterise it.'

Once more, I was rushed to the operating theatre. Cocaine drops were put into my eye. The leak was sealed with an electric instrument. I was made to lie flat on my back, not moving a muscle, for another sixteen days.

When the bandages were removed, my vision was still not clear. I could not see a distinct image. I could, however, see shadows and I could see vague shapes moving in front of my right eye. It was not much but, for me, after six years of total darkness, it was something. It was progress. It was thrilling. After examining my eye in the dark-room, Mr Boxill, too, expressed delight.

I was discharged from hospital. Ena returned me to Rita's home. I went to the bathroom and washed my hands. Incredibly, I could see them moving, like the shadows of two great birds, in front of my face. Ena led me into Rita's garden and picked a flower. She held it close to me. I could not tell what kind of flower it was but I could see its colour. Ena and I went for a meal at a little restaurant we knew in Farnborough and, although I could not see the table itself, I could see the white of the table-cloth. We were both overjoyed at the partial, hazy vision that had been achieved. Technically, I was still blind but, to me, it was heaven. As we walked back to Rita's bungalow, she looked up at me. I could not see her features. I knew those well enough by touch. In the sunlight, however, with her face and hair bathed in its golden glow, I could discern the shape of her head, the frame of her face, which was more than I had ever seen before.

Mr Boxill continued to monitor my progress during my regular visits to the out-patients' department. As Ena and I were returning from one appointment, to which she had taken me on her day off, I was suddenly overcome by an urgent desire to make our relationship official. The second corneal graft had given new hope to both of us. Even though my vision was still so hazy, the fact that I could see shadows had convinced us that, soon, I would be able to see. We had discussed our plans for the future even more excitedly than previously.

As we walked along North Street in Guildford, I was in a happy mood. Suddenly, I stopped.

'I want to buy you an engagement ring,' I told her impulsively.

Although we were not officially engaged, although there was no ring, we both knew, in our hearts, in our minds, that we were engaged. We both knew that we would never be parted.

'Oh, no!' she said. 'They're so expensive!'

I could tell, however, from the way that she said it, that she was secretly thrilled at my decision and that, despite her protest, she was longing for me to buy her one.

'Let's find a jewellers,' I told her.

'There's one right here, darling,' she said.

We went inside. It was a small shop. We were shown a tray of engagement rings. In my pocket, still in the registered envelope, were five crisp one-pound notes that had just arrived from a benevolent fund of the Royal Yugoslav Guards. Since my arrival in England, I had received a five-pound payment from the fund every month. It had been the only income I had had in the four years I had been in the country. Whichever ring we chose, it would have to cost no more than the five pounds that I had in my pocket.

Ena selected several rings that came within our limited budget. She placed each one on the third finger of her left hand in turn before putting it into the palm of my hand for me to feel. With the aid of my finger-tips and Ena's description of them, I was able to visualise the appearance of each ring. Ena tried each one for size again. I felt each one again. Eventually, we were attracted to the one we had first tried on Ena's finger. I ran my fingers over it again to make certain that it was the one I wanted for her. It had three diamonds and, according to Ena, they were set in such a way that they appeared to be much bigger than they actually were. It cost four pounds. I paid the shopkeeper. I had one pound note to last me until the next benevolent fund payment arrived the following month.

As we left the shop, I closed the door behind us and then stopped in the doorway. I drew Ena gently towards me.

'I love you, darling,' I told her.

I kissed her finger and slipped the ring on to it.

Ena kissed me tenderly on the lips.

'Darling,' she said. 'I will marry you blind or sighted – because I love you.'

We were officially engaged. We had known each other for more than three years and had been going out together for most of that time. Our love for each other, despite my blindness, despite parental opposition, was stronger than ever. After knowing each other for so long, the actual private ceremony between us, the act of becoming officially engaged, had seemed to happen so naturally, so spontaneously. The ring was a symbol of our togetherness, our closeness, our love. I could hear people walking past the shop doorway and I could imagine their curious stares as we held each other close in busy North Street in the heart of Guildford, but I did not care.

Both Ena and I were apprehensive at the thought of how her parents might react. Before facing them, we needed time to gather our courage. We went first to Rita's home and broke the news to her. She said little. We did not stay long. The same afternoon, we caught a train to Winnersh Halt and walked to the rectory.

'Very nice, darling,' said Mrs Argyle, when Ena showed her the ring.

'Let's have a glass of sherry,' said her father.

By that time, Ena was over age. She was twenty-one. She

could make her own decisions and act upon them. Her parents knew that there was nothing they could do to stop her becoming engaged to me.

They were not unpleasant nor antagonistic. There were no tears, no recriminations, no distressing scenes, but neither were there any congratulations, any warmth. They were quiet and reserved and I knew that their hearts were breaking.

I was not the only one who loved Ena. Her parents, her sisters and brother, her entire family, loved her, too, and I knew that it was their love and devotion for her that had caused them to oppose our relationship. They were heartbroken because they had tried, and failed, to stop her committing what they were certain would be an act of the utmost folly, of sentencing herself to a life of penury and hardship, of sacrificing herself for the sake of a penniless blind man.

Over the previous months, we had both experienced many hurtful remarks from unthinking people. Ena's feelings for me were feelings of pity, not love, they had maintained. As for me, I was totally selfish. Had I really loved Ena, I would willingly have let her go, would have vowed never to see her again, would have given her the chance to find happiness with someone else, rather than condemn her to a life of misery with me, a blind man. All I wanted was a housekeeper, someone to look after me. I was thinking only of myself, of my own convenience, of my own future, of my own happiness, not of Ena's.

We had both been dreadfully hurt. I had marvelled that people could be so cruel, could imagine that I had not considered whether I was doing the right thing, whether I was, indeed, being selfish, whether I should, indeed, give up my Inneta for her sake. It had been a testing time for both of us and a tribute to our love that it had survived despite the opposition, despite the cruel remarks. I had known, still knew, that any unhappiness that might be caused to Ena by staying with me, by marrying me, would not compare with the unhappiness she would feel at losing me. Nothing, nothing, would shake our faith in each other. We needed each other, we loved each other and our love was above any criticism.

A week after we had bought the engagement ring, we visited the rectory again. Ena's godmother was staying there and came downstairs to meet us. She kissed Ena and then turned towards me. The Reverend Argyle introduced us.

'This is Nino,' he said. 'A friend of the family.'

I heard Ena catch her breath. Then she exploded into a

violent rage, not only the most violent rage I had ever seen her in, but the only one.

'Let's be honest, father!' she shouted, her voice quaking with fury. 'He's my fiancé and I'm engaged to be married to him whether you like it or not!'

I was shocked. I had never seen her so angry. I took her hand and tried to quieten her.

'Sshh!' I whispered in her ear.

Her father refused to be ruffled.

'I don't know why you are getting so excited about such a little matter,' he said calmly.

His words seemed to infuriate Ena even more.

'It's not a little matter!' she stormed. 'I'm engaged to him!'

I put my arm round her shoulders and tried to calm her.

'Don't worry, darling,' I said. 'Everything is all right.'

I took her outside. We went for a walk. Ena put her head on my shoulder and wept.

'Oh, Nino!' she sobbed. 'All the world is against us!'

Not long afterwards, on a visit to the out-patients' department, I told Mr Boxill that the light that was still filtering through my right eye appeared to have turned to a red colour. He explained that it was nothing to worry about, that it was caused by blood vessels and that he would cauterise them there and then.

I was placed on the operating table. Drops were put into my eye. I felt something touching my eyeball and then heard a sizzling sound as the electrically-heated instrument did its searing work. My eye became watery and misty but Mr Boxill assured me that it would clear and that I would no longer be seeing light and shadows in red.

Four days before Christmas, 1952, however, came another setback. I had been invited to spend Christmas with Ena and her family at the rectory. She collected me from Rita's home. We travelled by train from Farnborough to Wokingham and, from there, by bus to Winnersh. As we were walking to the rectory at Bearwood, my right eye began to water. It was as if tears were trickling from it.

'What's the matter, darling?' Ena asked anxiously. 'Have you caught a cold?'

'I don't know,' I told her. 'I don't think so.'

'You must have a piece of coal grit in your eye from the train,' she said. 'We'll wash it out when we get home.'

Despite the washing out, however, the watering became worse.

Soon, water was pouring from my eye. In desperation, Ena telephoned Mr Boxill. He instructed her to take me to the hospital. In his consulting room, he examined my eye.

'I'm afraid you will have to be admitted,' he said gravely. 'You are losing fluid from your eye.'

Chapter Twenty-Seven

The following six months were the worst I had to endure in the seven years since I had been blinded. For the whole of that time, from December 1952, until June 1953, I was not only confined to hospital but confined to bed, too, being made to lie flat on my back and to move as little as possible. Once a week, every week for six months, I was taken to the operating theatre, where repeated attempts were made to stitch up the leak that had started so suddenly just before Christmas. The repairs, however, would not hold. No sooner were the stitches inserted than they fell apart, like cotton in threadbare material. The precious fluid from the interior chamber of the eye continued to leak away. My eye was slowly collapsing.

During those six months, my only excitement, my only relief from boredom, was listening on my head-phones to the BBC radio commentary on the 1953 Football Association Cup Final between Blackpool and Bolton Wanderers, a match that became known as 'The Stanley Matthews Final'. After going behind by three goals to one, Blackpool, inspired by Matthews, the great English international outside-right, fought back and levelled the score. Then, in the last few minutes of the game, Matthews made yet another amazing dribble up the wing and crossed the ball low and accurately through a crowd of Bolton players for his outside-left, Perry, to slam the ball into the net. After looking certain losers, Blackpool had fought like tigers and had won by four goals to three! Stanley Matthews had, at last, managed to win an FA Cup winner's medal – the one major honour that had eluded him.

As the final whistle blew, one of the nurses stuck a thermometer in my mouth in a routine check on my temperature.

'Goodness! What's the matter with you, Kosta?' she said. 'It's over a hundred!'

'Don't worry – it's just my first excitement for months, that's all!' I told her happily.

The rest of the time, however, consisted of months of excruciating boredom, of lying flat on my back, of repeated operations, of repeated failures. I became decidedly wearied, frustrated, despondent and impatient, and it was in that mood of despair and disappointment that I had my first and only disagreement with Mr Boxill.

'When will I be able to get up?' I asked him irritably one day when he came to see me. 'I'm getting fed up lying here in bed.'

To my shock, his reply was short, sharp, terse and to the point. Worse, his voice revealed an equal amount of tetchiness as my own had done, if not more. I had to continue to lie immobile in bed if I did not want to lose my eye, he told me pointedly, and, if I did not like it, I could find someone else to treat me.

His words, his manner, cut me more deeply than any of the surgical knives he had used upon me so many times. I was shocked, demoralised. I had been his patient for almost five years. Not once during those five years had I complained. I had placed myself entirely in his hands. I had done everything that he had asked of me and I had asked nothing in return. Now, when I had complained for the first time in five years, the man in whom I had had so much faith and trust had rounded on me and was telling me, quite bluntly, that, if I were not satisfied, I could go elsewhere.

I knew that Mr Boxill had worked so hard on both my eyes. I had been a challenge to him. His greatest wish had been to give me back my sight. He had put so much time and effort into helping me and he had met with little success. Now, Mr Boxill, too, was displaying symptoms of irritability, frustration and despair at the repeated failures, at the repeated dashing of hopes. He, too, was showing impatience at the lack of progress. Was he also despairing that success would ever come, that I would ever see again?

The incident completely shattered my faith in the future, removed all the hopes that I had of regaining my sight. I was totally lost. I had nothing left but Ena's love for me.

A few weeks after the Cup Final, a pain developed in my right eye, a pain that almost drove me demented, a pain that made sleep impossible. At one o'clock in the morning, the night staff called Mr Boxill from his bed. He diagnosed an infection of the eye due to a cold and sore throat from which I had been suffering. Mr Boxill came to see me every day but, despite treatment, the condition of my eye, and the pain, became worse and worse. Finally, when he removed the bandages one day, I could see nothing at all – no shadows, no light, no movement, nothing but blackness. Once, I would have accepted anything that Mr Boxill had told me but, after so many frustrations, so many failures, I had lost all hope. Despite his assurances that the light would return, I was not convinced.

The day arrived when, for the first time in six months, I was allowed out of bed. My immediate thought was that I must go to church. I was in need of the spiritual uplift that I knew a visit to church would provide. I knew that I had to find strength from somewhere. It was not only spiritual strength that I was lacking. After so many months of inactivity, I was woefully deficient in physical strength, too. Despite my bodily weakness, however, I was able, with Ena's help, to walk to church. It necessitated considerable effort on my part and, inevitably, I paid the price of my foolishness in attempting to walk so far when I had not walked a single step in six months. By the time I returned to the hospital, my right ankle had swollen to the size of a balloon.

In the dark room, Mr Boxill examined my eye. His verdict was no more than I had expected. My right eye was finished. There was nothing more that could be done with it.

'But don't worry,' he said cheerfully, as optimistic as ever. 'We will start on your left eye again.'

By then, however, my spirit was broken, my confidence had evaporated, my hopes had died along with the numerous skin grafts and corneal grafts. I had been receiving continual treatment from Mr Boxill and his team for nearly five years, from 1948 until 1953, I had undergone numerous painful and harrowing surgical operations, and I was no nearer to being able to see. Worse, my right eye, the eye with which I had been able to see light and shadows, and with which I could now see only darkness, was completely finished, completely useless. I was not convinced by Mr Boxill's optimism, by his enthusiasm for starting again on my left eye, nor by his mention of the possibility of consulting specialists in London. Nor was I convinced that, in his heart, Mr Boxill was as confident of achieving ultimate success as his voice and his words suggested. I was sorry for Mr Boxill, sorry that there was no tangible result to all his efforts, sorry that, together, we had not succeeded, but I could not go on.

Back in the ward, I fought back the bitter tears of disappointment. I wanted to be alone. I groped my way to the bathroom. The tears flowed.

Suddenly, Ena was by my side, holding me, consoling me, comforting me. She held my face to her shoulder. My tears wet the collar of her coat.

She had arrived in the ward to visit me and, finding an empty bed, had guessed that I was in the bathroom. She knew that something was seriously wrong even before I told her. She seemed to read my thoughts, to sense that I could take no more.

'You've suffered enough,' she told me quietly. 'We won't bother with your eyes any more. You and I will get married instead.'

Chapter Twenty-Eight

I was ecstatic. Ena was prepared to take me as her husband even though I was blind, even though the miracle for which we had been praying had not occurred. I was to be with the woman I loved and who loved me, for ever. I longed to begin a new life as a married man.

The Reverend Argyle had obtained a new living at Great Witley, in Worcestershire, and Ena accompanied her mother on a shopping trip to Reading in preparation for the move. Over tea and cakes in a department store restaurant, she broke the news of our plans.

'Look, Mummy,' she said, as Mrs Argyle was pouring the tea. 'Nino has had enough of all these operations. As you and Daddy are moving away, we would love to get married and settle down.'

She waited for the reaction, for the hurt and, possibly, for the tears. There were none. Instead, Mrs Argyle accepted the news cheerfully.

'Darling! That's what I've been hoping you would say. Daddy and I have been most worried at the prospect of leaving you down here, a single girl, with no home to go to. We know Nino will look after you.'

Ena was surprised. So, too, when she told me later of her mother's reaction, was I. We had both been prepared for the worst and were delighted that she had taken it so well.

We were even more delighted and happy at the fact that Ena's parents offered to share their new home with us after we were married, wanted us to move with them to Worcestershire and begin our married life together in the comfort of their new rectory. It was extremely kind of them but Ena declined their generous offer. Gently, she explained that, when we were married, we wanted to be independent.

Only Ena knew how much it meant to me that her parents had, finally, come to accept me. Only she knew how happy I was that they had dropped their opposition, had given their blessing to our marriage and were ready to welcome me into the family as a son-in-law. From the beginning, their one concern had been for Ena's happiness. Finally, they had come to realise that Ena was a grown woman, that she was old enough to know her own mind, that she had carefully considered all the implications of marrying a blind man, that she was fully aware of all the difficulties that lay ahead and that she was still convinced that her future happiness lay with me. Finally, they had come to realise that Ena was not marrying me out of pity but out of love. We loved each other and that was enough.

In the weeks leading up to the wedding, the Argyles were particularly kind to me, as if anxious to atone for the hurt that, in their anxiety to avoid unhappiness for Ena, they had done me. To my delight, Ena's father even insisted that we marry in a Roman Catholic church and agreed to participate in a Catholic marriage ceremony by giving her away.

'I want you to marry in a Catholic church because I know it will mean so much more to you than marrying anywhere else,' he told me. 'And to show that I am not prejudiced against you as a Catholic, I will give my daughter away.'

I knew that, as an Anglican clergyman, he was making a considerable concession. It was a kindly gesture and I was grateful for it.

The day of the wedding arrived, the day for which both of us had been waiting for so long, through so many difficulties, so many setbacks. Ena was twenty-two years old. I was twenty-nine. We had known each other for four years and had been in love for almost the whole of that time.

My hair was newly-cut. My black shoes were shining. I hoped that I did not look too idiotic in my morning suit, hired for the day from Moss Bros. Although I had finally succumbed to Ena's persuasions and had agreed to wear tails, I had stubbornly refused to make a total fool of myself by completing the clown's outfit and turning up in a top hat. Ena had eventually conceded defeat.

John was my best man. It was five years since we had first met, as total strangers, on the quayside at Southampton docks, on my arrival from Egypt. It was John and Rita who had given me a home in England, who had cared for me for five years, who had provided for me even though, with no income other than the five pounds a month I received from the Royal Yugoslav Guards' benevolent fund, I had been able to contribute little to my keep. I had become one of the family and I was grateful for their care and friendship.

'Let's all have a glass of sherry!' said John, before we set off from the bungalow for the Church of Our Lady, Help of Christians, at Farnborough.

There were tears in his eyes as the three of us sipped our drinks, Rita told me later.

At the church, John guided me up the aisle towards the altar. We sat in the front pew on the right side of the aisle. Like many brides, Ena was late. Fifteen minutes after the ceremony was due to start, she still had not arrived. By that time, I had begun to fidget but I was not worried. I was confident that she would come. I was sure of her love.

Suddenly, the organist halted the incidental music that he had been playing. There was a pause. Then the church reverberated to the sound of the tune that I had been waiting for. *Here Comes the Bride.*

'Here she comes!' John whispered, glancing excitedly over his shoulder.

Ena walked up the aisle on her father's arm. There was a lump in my throat as we came together before the altar. I knew that she looked radiant in her simple ivory satin dress with the beautiful antique Limerick lace veil in which her mother had been married. I could smell the scent of the posy of ivory-coloured roses that she carried. I could visualise the scene but, nevertheless, I wished that I could have seen her.

The service began. I felt as though I were in a dream, as though I were floating. I was vaguely aware of Ena's father and John standing behind us and, between them, young Norman, John and Rita's son, dressed in a page-boy's uniform of black velvet trousers and white lace shirt. I was vaguely aware of the priest's voice and of the prayers that were being recited. I could think only of Ena standing beside me and of the fact that, at last, our dreams were about to come true. The sudden mention of my name brought me back to reality, to full attentiveness.

'Constantine Jean Natalis. Wilt thou take Ena Elizabeth, here present, for thy lawful wife, according to the rite of our Holy Mother the Church?'

It was an emotional moment. I swallowed hard.

'I will.'

'Ena Elizabeth. Wilt thou take Constantine Jean Natalis, here present, for thy lawful husband, according to the rite of our Holy Mother the Church?'

I waited breathlessly for her reply. She answered quietly but clearly.

'I will.'

The Reverend Argyle stepped forward to give away Ena. I repeated the solemn vow after the priest.

Ena began to take her own vow. I could tell that she was not only nervous but emotional, too.

'I, Ena Elizabeth, take thee, Constantine Jean Natalis, to my wedded husband . . . ' Her voice was trembling. ' . . . to have and to hold from this day forward . . . ' There was a long pause. ' . . . for better, for worse, for richer, for poorer, in sickness . . . ' Her voice broke and I could tell that she was choking back the tears. ' . . . in sickness and in health, till death do us part, and thereto I plight thee my troth.'

Tears pricked my own eyes. I heard a sob from somewhere in the congregation. The priest continued with the ceremony.

'I join you in holy matrimony in the name of the Father and of the Son and of the Holy Ghost. Amen.'

He beckoned John forward and took the ring from him.

'Bless, O Lord, this ring, which we bless in Thy name, that she who shall wear it, keeping true faith unto her husband, may abide in Thy peace and will, and ever live in mutual charity. Through Christ our Lord. Amen.'

The priest passed the ring to me. I turned to face Ena.

'Repeat after me,' said the priest.

'With this ring I thee wed,' I repeated. 'With my body I thee worship; and with all my worldly goods I thee endow.'

I took Ena's left hand in mine and, with my right, placed the gold ring on to her third finger. I kissed her gently on the lips. Her cheeks were wet with tears. I knew, however, that they were tears of joy. Even though we were both emotionally drained with the solemnity of the occasion, we were bursting with happiness, overwhelmed that, at last, we would be together for always. At last, we were husband and wife!

We retired to an ante-room for the signing of the marriage register. The sounds of Bach's *Ave Maria* drifted from the organ. We walked down the aisle, arm in arm, man and wife, to the crashing, joyful, celebratory sounds of Mendelssohn's *Wedding March*. Even above the organ music, I could hear stifled sobs coming from both sides of the aisle as women guests clutched screwed-up handkerchiefs, clasped them to their mouths, blew their noses and wiped away the tears from their eyes.

Ena and I were driven to the reception at the Prior's Kitchen Hotel at Frimley. In the back of the car, we held hands, kissed and laughed like a couple of children whose birthdays had all come at once. We were overwhelmed with happiness.

The guests at the reception were mainly relatives and close

friends. They included hospital nursing staff and three usherettes from the Rex Cinema at Farnborough, where the manager had, for so long, provided us with free seats. John read telegrams from relatives and friends who were unable to be present, including a large number from my family in Istanbul.

Later, as we prepared to leave the reception for a four-day honeymoon in London, one of the hospital sisters took our hands.

'You've earned it after all these years,' she told us. 'You've been so patient waiting all this time. If only he could have seen you, Ena!'

Ena's mother embraced me.

'Take care of her, Nino, darling,' she said. 'She is very precious.'

Our relatives and friends gathered outside the hotel to wave goodbye as we drove off to our honeymoon. I relaxed in the back seat of the car and held Ena's hand.

One woman had destroyed me. Another woman had saved me.

Chapter Twenty-Nine

Ena and I began our married life in two furnished rooms in a house at Mytchett, near Frimley, in Surrey. It was a pleasant house owned by an equally pleasant spinster who worked as secretary to the manager of the local water board. Its name, Sunray, seemed a happy omen. The rent of our two rooms was thirty shillings a week, which more than swallowed up the five pounds a month I received from my old regiment's benevolent fund. I had no other income and, painful though it was, I was forced to live on the wages Ena received from her new job at Aldershot General Hospital, to which she had moved from St Luke's at Guildford.

I had my loved one with me. We were together at last. Although we had won one battle, however, I knew that a new battle was just beginning and that the first stage of the battle, the first advance, the first step towards winning it, was to strive for self-sufficiency, for physical and financial independence, to give myself the pride that would result from earning my own living and being the family breadwinner.

For the first time in seven years, I accepted my blindness. I prepared myself to face the future as a blind man. I made contact with a welfare organisation for the blind and arranged for a course of training. I visited the Labour Exchange and found out about courses designed specifically to equip blind people for particular jobs. I discussed the prospects of obtaining employment at the end of them. I had hoped to train for a position in which the many languages at which I was proficient could be used but, unfortunately, it seemed that the principal vocational training courses available for the blind, and the opportunities most readily open to them, were in industrial occupations.

Until that time, I had known nothing of the blind. Like many people, I had vaguely thought of the blind man as being a beggar. Now, however, I realised that, far from being condemned to a life of uselessness, as I had at first thought, I could become a useful member of society. There were opportunities to make myself independent, to learn a trade, to earn my living, just like any other husband. With Ena beside me, the future held no fears. No matter what the future had in store, I was determined that I would not accept the blind man's conventional mantle, his popular image, his begging role. No matter how menial the task, I was determined to work to maintain my wife.

The first months of our marriage, while I was waiting for a place on a training course, were joyous ones. We had little money but, although our lives were uneventful, we were happy simply to be together. For the first time in the four years that we had known each other, we were totally free from worries and pressures of any kind. For the first time, we were able to relax together, both mentally and physically, in our own home. Our pleasures were simple. Our greatest joys were walking in the countryside and listening to our little battery wireless. Once, when the battery ran down, we tramped in the snow to Aldershot to buy a replacement and, as a special treat, sat down to steak and chips in a cosy café.

In 1954, the year after our marriage, I was asked to attend a rehabilitation centre for the blind at Torquay in preparation for starting a full-time course there lasting for twelve weeks. I travelled alone by train from Reading to Torquay, a journey of about four hours. It was the first time that I had been by myself on a British train and the apprehension that I felt at finding myself alone, at not being able to see, at the strangeness, was increased by the unexpected discovery of what I later learned was the perfectly normal and typical reserve displayed by the British on train journeys. I tried hard to make conversation with my fellow passengers, to indulge in small talk, to ask the time of day, to pass observations on the state of the weather – the latter a typically-English habit that I had acquired during my six years in the country. I was met, however, by conversation that could scarcely be described as illuminating, consisting as it did of one-word negatives or affirmatives in answer to my questions and comments and a series of non-committal and discouraging grunts. I could tell from the rustling of pages that their heads were buried in newspapers and, after a while, I abandoned my futile attempts at communication.

Soon after my first visit to Torquay, I returned to begin the course itself. I was unhappy to be leaving Ena. Twelve weeks seemed a long time to be away from her. I was apprehensive, too, at going to a new and unfamiliar life. At the same time, however, I was pleased that I was taking the first step towards achieving my independence.

The course was not a vocational one. It was not designed to teach the blind to become proficient in particular industrial occupations. It was designed simply to teach the newly-blind, or the long-time blind who had received no formal training, how to cope with their blindness, how to become free and easy and confident without sight.

Our days began at eight o'clock with breakfast in a large dining-room, the trainees seated four to each table. Nobody helped us to cut up our sausages, take the rind from our bacon, remove the tops from our boiled eggs or butter our toast. We had to learn to do everything for ourselves. The mornings were spent learning the braille alphabet, followed by an hour of touch-typing, which, as Lois had already taught me, I found easy. Before lunch, the instructors, some of whom were also blind, took us on a half-hour walk into the town centre, down a steep hill, showing us how to walk with a white stick, how to cope in traffic. The afternoons were spent modelling in clay, playing bowls and at dancing classes. Every day I was learning something new. Every day I was becoming more and more independent.

One of the other trainees was a young man of twenty-three who was in love with a Scots girl. Because of his blindness, however, he was not ready for an emotional involvement, not self-confident enough to commit himself to his girl. He knew that I was married and he was interested in how my own problems had worked out.

'Don't be a fool!' I told him. 'Marry the girl!'

'I won't be able to support a wife,' he said.

'Of course you will!'

For a long time, he was able to produce a counter-argument to every argument of mine. In reality, they were excuses rather than arguments. He was trying to convince himself that he, a blind man, could never be a husband, could never make a wife happy.

Eventually, however, the confidence that I displayed as a result of my own experience persuaded him that, perhaps a blind man could make a good husband, could make a good marriage. His own confidence increased. He asked the girl to marry him and she accepted.

My own happiness was increased by the knowledge that my own marriage was about to be blessed by the arrival of our first child. Ena visited me at Torquay and we spent the weekend in a small hotel not far from the rehabilitation centre. When I held her close, it was clear that our baby was almost due and it was an enthralling moment for both of us when Ena placed my hand on her abdomen and I felt the baby kicking.

At three o'clock one Sunday morning, I awoke with a start, convinced that I had heard Ena calling my name and shouting for me to help her. It was impossible, of course. I was in Torquay and Ena was miles away in Mytchett. The following morning, I recounted my experience to the two blind trainees with whom I shared a room.

'I expect it will be good news,' one of them said.

At eleven o'clock that morning, I received the news that Ena had given birth to a daughter. I was a father! I could scarcely wait for the weekend to arrive so that I could visit them.

On the following Saturday, a nurse guided me into the maternity ward at Frimley Hospital, where I had once almost bled to death with a severed artery. There was a smell of baby powder, perfume and milk.

'Nino!' It was Ena's voice. 'Nino, darling!'

At last I was by her side, holding her close, my mackintosh damp with rain. We were together again. I kissed her tenderly and presented her with a spray of flowers.

Ena was excited both at seeing me and at the birth of our first child.

'Where is she?' I asked eagerly.

'She's asleep. In a cot at the foot of the bed.'

A nurse picked up the baby and passed her to Ena. I felt a tiny bundle being lowered into my arms. She seemed so fragile that I feared she would break.

I peered down at my baby with sightless eyes, at my daughter, who was to be named Linda Angela Teresa. It was a moving experience. I was mesmerised. I gazed at her as if I could see every strand of hair, every tiny finger-nail. I held her in the crook of one arm and, with the fingers of my free hand, traced the outlines of her nose, her cheeks, her forehead, her chin, trying to capture a clear image of her features. The little bundle stirred, disturbed by my discovery of her beauty. She was none too fond of such a strange object trailing over her face. She woke up, turned her head away, stretched, yawned and went back to sleep. I had not even taken off my raincoat.

Ena touched my hand. She was obviously moved.

'Oh, Nino!' she whispered. 'The joy on your face! It was a picture! Nobody would ever think you were blind, seeing you peering down at the baby like that!'

How fortunate I was to have such a wonderful wife and, now, a beautiful daughter!

Our landlady had accompanied me to the hospital and I returned with her to the house in Mytchett before visiting Ena again in the evening. The following day, I had to return to Torquay. I was sad to be leaving Ena and the baby but my sadness was made bearable by the knowledge that, in only a few more weeks, I would be home with them to stay.

At the end of the twelve-week course, I could cut up my meals, read braille, make toast and coffee, do the washing up and walk by myself in the street with the aid of a white stick. I was on my way to becoming independent.

Back at our two rooms, Ena set about making me even more independent. Fearful that she might fall ill or have an accident and be unable to look after our daughter, she started to train me in baby care so that I would be capable of looking after Linda by myself. Soon, I was proficient at bathing Linda, feeding her, changing her nappies. I began to learn to cook and to carry out the household chores. When I was not helping in the home or with the baby, I made wooden stools with sea-grass seats (an art in which I had become proficient both in hospital and on the training course).

Considerable though my progress was, however, the increasing number of skills I was acquiring were not achieved without some setbacks. On one occasion, after Ena and I had had a tiff and while she was sulking in the bedroom, I decided to assert myself and cook a meal, thus showing that not only was I capable of looking after myself but that Ena did not have a monopoly of skill in the culinary arts and that, when I was hungry, I was adequately equipped to feed myself. The particular gastronomic delight that I decided to create was a plain omelette. Unfortunately, my culinary accomplishments did not extend to a knowledge of the length of time a three-egg omelette should be permitted to cook. Previously, when I had made omelettes, Ena had been on hand to tell me when they had been ready. Consequently, the time I allowed for cooking my masterpiece was rather less than that required. What I tipped on to my plate was not so much an omelette but more like three raw eggs. By that time, however, Ena had returned to the room and nothing would have persuaded me to admit that there was the slightest flaw in my creation. Sheer pride forced me to sit at the table and eat it, a not inconsiderable accomplishment, considering that the eggs were not only so runny but unpalatable, too.

It was apparent to Ena that my omelette was revoltingly unappetising and decidedly underdone. She sat there, gleefully watching my every mouthful, increasingly marvelling at the evident relish with which I devoured it.

On another occasion, I was digging a vegetable patch for our landlady, whom I often helped with the gardening, when I heard a sudden shout of alarm. It was the landlady, in a considerable state of agitation. I had thought that I was doing a grand job but, unfortunately, in my enthusiasm, I had dug right out of the garden and had excavated half of a neighbour's garden as well. Fortunately, the neighbour had a sense of humour.

Our long-suffering landlady was the victim of yet another of my attempts at being helpful. While Ena was out shopping one day, I decided to assist her by polishing the doors and furniture of the two rooms in which we lived. By the time she returned, I knew that they must be shining.

'Come and see what I've done,' I told her proudly.

I could tell almost immediately that something was wrong.

'Oh, dear!' I heard Ena say to herself, obviously worried, probably wringing her hands.

I had picked up the wrong tin of polish. The beautiful, cream-painted doors, the white woodwork and furniture, had turned a horrible dark brown. Frantically, Ena tried to rub off the dark streaks but to no avail. They could not be removed. There was nothing we could do but wait anxiously for the return of our landlady and face her wrath. To our relief, however, she took it well. Like the neighbour whose garden I had dug up, she showed that she had a remarkable sense of humour.

Although the arrival of Linda had provided Ena and me with a family, had cemented our marriage and had brought us enormous joy, it had also brought us considerable financial difficulties. Previously, when Ena had been working, we had just been able to manage on her wage and my benevolent fund payment. She had continued in her nursing career until the last possible moment but, with Linda's birth imminent, she had finally been forced to give up her job. Without her wages, our sole income was the six pounds a week National Assistance payment that we were forced to accept and my five pounds a month from the benevolent fund. For thirteen weeks following Linda's birth, Ena received thirty shillings a week in maternity benefit but, as my National Assistance payment was reduced by a similar amount, we were no better off. Times were hard but our love and happiness compensated for the lack of material possessions.

In one particular week, however, we seemed to have manipulated our money rather less well than usual. Ena's housekeeping allowance had been spent. We had no money to pay the rent. The situation was desperate. Then, suddenly, I had a bright idea.

'Let's make a bit of money selling stools from door-to-door,' I suggested.

The stools that I had been making with materials bought at special cheap prices from the welfare association for the blind had been intended primarily as occupational therapy but the woman welfare worker who had introduced me to it had suggested that we could make a little money from my hobby by selling the stools to relatives. As the months had gone by, however, the generosity of Ena's relatives had become exhausted. Six stools had been sold to Ena's mother alone for re-sale at the church fete. There were no other sales outlets left among our relatives and friends. Selling them round the houses seemed to be the obvious answer to our immediate financial problems.

Time was short. The rent was almost due and we had to find the money from somewhere. Ena telephoned the welfare association and ordered the materials for six stools. As soon as they arrived, we set to work. As speed was essential, Ena helped me. For the whole of one evening, I sandpapered the wooden legs and struts. Ena assembled the frames by sticking the wooden pieces together with glue. Then she varnished them in different colours. Finally, while Ena slept, I wove the sea-grass seats. I worked right through the night. By seven o'clock in the morning, the last one was finished.

Straight after breakfast, we put Linda into her pram and carefully arranged the six stools round her, two at her feet, two tied on to the hood and the other two dangling from the handle.

'I feel like a gipsy selling her wares!' Ena giggled self-consciously as we trudged along the road towards a wealthy private estate in Mytchett.

We laughed.

'Never mind!' I told her. 'Think of the money!'

'Let's try Coleford Bridge Road,' said Ena. 'There are some very wealthy people living there.'

She left me standing on the pavement, holding the pram, and set off determinedly up the drive of a big detached house.

'Good morning, madam!' Ena said in her best vicarage tea-party voice. 'Would you care to buy a stool?'

'No, thank you,' said a woman's voice.

Ena returned, disappointed but not dispirited. She tried again . . . and again . . . and again. At some houses, she was met with polite refusals. At others, not a word was spoken. Doors were slammed in her face. Poor Ena, the middle-class, privately-educated, genteel daughter of an unworldly, religious family, had never had occasion, never had the need, to try to sell anything. She lacked the confidence, the expertise, the persuasive chat, the thick skin, of the successful door-to-door salesman and her inexperienced efforts failed to produce a single sale. Near to tears, she was on the point of giving up.

Our critical financial situation, however, drove her on to make one final attempt. At the next house, in sheer desperation, she decided to try a new sales pitch, to appeal blatantly and shamelessly to the sympathies of the prospective customer.

The door was opened by a middle-aged, expensively-dressed woman. Ena held out two stools in different colours.

'My husband is blind,' she said simply. 'He has made these stools with his own hands. Would you care to buy one?'

'Come in,' the woman said.

It had started to rain. I heard the door close. I stood there, at the end of the drive, wondering what was happening inside. Ena seemed to be in the house for a long time. Then I heard her footsteps on the drive.

'What happened?' I asked.

'I sold the first stool!' she said, trying to keep the excitement and pride from her voice.

She pressed something into my hand. With my other hand, I felt a one-pound note, a ten-shilling note and two half-crowns.

'Thirty-five shillings!' I cried.

She fell into my arms. I hugged her. We were both half-laughing, half-crying.

'Come on!' she said, fired with enthusiasm by her first and unexpected success. 'Let's try some more!'

We pushed Linda's pram along the rain-drenched roads, knocking at every door we came to. At some houses, Ena was successful. At others, not even her new hearts-and-flowers approach could melt her way into their purses.

I could feel a rough track under my feet. The pram started slipping in the mud.

'Where are you taking me?'

'Down a cart-track. There's a farm at the end of it. I thought we'd try somewhere different.'

The farmer's wife bought a stool on the spot. Within four hours, we had sold the lot.

We stood in the road and counted the money. Linda was asleep in her pram. Our hair was plastered over our faces, our clothes were soaking, we looked bedraggled but the rain had stopped and we were happy.

'Ten pounds ten shillings!' Ena announced excitedly.

I quickly calculated in my head.

'That will pay the rent for seven weeks!'

We hugged each other, laughing deliriously. It was more money than we had had in the whole of our married life, in all the years we had known each other.

'We're rich, darling!' Ena shouted. 'We're rich!'

The following morning, there was a knock on the door. It was the farmer's wife. She had been delighted with her stool, she said. Unfortunately, it appeared that it had been made for looking at, not for sitting upon. When she had done the latter, the frame had come apart and the stool had collapsed underneath her.

In our haste to earn some money quickly in order to pay the rent, we had varnished the stools without allowing sufficient time for the glue to dry properly. I had known that, according to the instructions I had been given, it was recommended that two days be allowed between applying the glue and the varnish but our urgent need for money had over-ridden other considerations. The rent had been due and two days had been too long to wait. Although I had had slight doubts when Ena had carried out the varnishing, I had been confident that the glue would hold, even though the time allowed for it to set had been less than ideal. Had I suspected that the stools might collapse, I would not have allowed them to be sold.

In all, three out of the six stools were returned to us, all in a considerable state of disarray. Fortunately, we were able to mollify the farmer's wife and the other two purchasers and, even more fortunately, when I promised to re-make the stools, none of them demanded their money back.

Encouraged by our stupendous success in selling six stools for ten pounds ten shillings, Ena developed grandiose ideas about not only selling them from door-to-door but also to shops for re-sale. So carried away was she that, for a moment, she had visions of me turning out sea-grass stools by the hundred while

she knocked on doors and made our fortune. Her flight of
fancy, however, was soon to come down to earth with a bump.

Three days later, the welfare worker from the blind association called to collect the money we owed for the materials from
which we had made the stools. The cost was thirty-six shillings
– six shillings for each stool. Even after deducting the cost of the
materials, the profit from our labour was still eight pounds
fourteen shillings.

Ena counted out the money from her purse into the welfare
lady's hand.

'Could I have six more, please?' she said enthusiastically.

'Of course,' said the welfare lady amiably. 'You must have a
lot of relatives.'

'Oh, no!' Ena innocently replied, her voice swelling with
pride. 'We tie them on the pram and sell them round the
houses. They go like hot cakes.'

I pinched Ena's arm, hard, but it was too late. The damage
was done. The welfare lady's pleasant manner changed immediately.

'I'm afraid you won't be allowed to sell any more stools in
that manner,' she said frostily. 'To sell them like that, you have
to have a hawker's licence.'

Ena – poor, innocent, unworldly Ena – had unwittingly ruined
our chance of riches almost before it had begun.

Chapter Thirty

Although I was fluent in seven languages, and although the area in which we lived could by no stretch of the imagination be described as an industrial one, it was decided that my vocation in life would be found in industry. My destiny awaited me on a factory floor. I was sent on an eight-week course at an industrial training centre at Letchworth, in Hertfordshire, to train as a capstan operator.

The centre existed not only for blind trainees but for sighted ones, too. I knew nothing of life in industry and I was not enamoured of the industrial atmosphere of the place, of the stench of oil and metal, of the deafening grinding and screech-ing of machinery. Was that what factory life was like? Was that the life that lay before me?

The trainees learned their various crafts in little cubicles. My working day, from eight o'clock until noon and again from two o'clock until five o'clock, consisted of assembling and dismantling machinery, reading a braille micrometer and, finally, operating a capstan itself. At first, I was decidedly nervous, not to say terrified. Pieces of machinery were revolving in front of me and, in order to perform the tasks required of me, it was necessary for me to touch controls close to the revolving parts. I was afraid, petrified, that I would lose at least a finger if not a hand. Gradually, however, my confidence increased until the time arrived when I was able to operate the capstan as skilfully as a sighted man.

Almost every weekend, I visited Ena and our baby. Our love sustained me during the eight long, lonely weeks of the course and, in that respect, I was considerably more fortunate than one of the other blind trainees whom I had come to know. He was a young man in his twenties whose wife, he discovered, was having an affair with another man. The shock of his discovery, the realisation of his wife's faithlessness, broke him completely. One day, as he worked near me in one of the other cubicles, he tried to commit suicide by taking an overdose of sleeping tablets. He was found slumped and unconscious over his work-bench. I heard shouts and the sound of running footsteps. A doctor was called and he was rushed by ambulance to hospital where, mercifully, his life was saved.

The incident upset me and I was thankful when the course ended and I returned to Ena and Linda. I was a fully-trained, totally-competent, highly-skilled and impeccably-qualified capstan operator. I was not entirely surprised, however, to find that there was no job available for me. Although the absence of any large industries in the area was a decided drawback, my blindness was an even bigger handicap. Ministry of Labour officials tried hard to find employment for me but were unsuccessful in persuading any employer to take me on to the pay-roll. The few small engineering firms that existed in the area were unwilling to employ a disabled person of any kind (and the term *disabled* covered a wide field of disability) let alone one whose disablement was blindness.

Our only income was a grant of six pounds twelve shillings a week from the Ministry of Labour, to which I became entitled on completion of my industrial training course and which was paid instead of unemployment benefit, plus a small National Assistance payment and my monthly benevolent fund money. Each week, after the rent, gas and electricity had been paid, we had only four pounds twelve shillings to provide for the three of us. We had a roof over our heads and food to eat but, apart from each other, little else.

Sometimes, not even the food we ate provided the enjoyment to which we felt entitled. Somehow, even the cheapest cuts of meat and low-cost, in-season vegetables seemed to lose their flavour with the realisation that, because we had no money, they had been bought on tick and had still to be paid for. Occasionally, when debts to the butcher, the grocer and the greengrocer remained unpaid and we knew that, even with the current week's income, we would be unable to settle them, Ena's culinary offerings, through no fault of her own, assumed particularly unappetising and indigestible qualities.

Once, when Ena's debt to the grocer had reached five pounds and she had suffered the humiliation of being asked to settle it, our permanent financial problems reached crisis point.

'There's only one thing for it,' said Ena. 'We'll have to go to the pawn shop.'

She said it as if she had been doing business with pawnbrokers all her life.

Ena had been given a beautiful piece of Victorian pearl jewellery by a close friend of her mother, Aunt Violet. It broke Ena's heart to part with it but we had no other choice. Together, we took it to a pawn shop in Reading. Ena placed it on the counter.

'I want two pounds,' she said decisively.

The pawnbroker scrutinised us closely. He scrutinised the jewellery even more sceptically, obviously suspecting that it was stolen.

'Thirty bob,' he said, in a way that meant take it or leave it.

Ena's nerve cracked. Faced with the pawnbroker's professional inscrutability (was he bluffing or did he really mean thirty bob?), her own decisive two-pounds-and-no-haggling stance began to weaken. Instead of maintaining her insistence, she changed her tactics. She began to wheedle.

'Oh, no, please!' she said. 'It's an antique. Look at it again. Those pearls . . . they're beautiful. A man with your experience obviously knows what they're worth!'

The flattery began to soften him. He examined the jewellery again.

'How much did you say?'

'Two pounds. Please. We must have two pounds.'

'Okay. Two pounds.'

Perhaps it was the flattery. Perhaps it was the desperation in Ena's voice. Perhaps it was my blindness. Perhaps it was simply that pawnbrokers, too, have hearts.

In the months that followed, repeated financial crises were relieved by many more visits to the pawn shops. It seemed that some of our best friends were pawnbrokers. Delicate pearl brooches and necklaces, a beautiful garnet pendant and other cherished pieces from Ena's jewellery case suffered the same fate as had Aunt Violet's pearls. Of necessity, our mercenary instincts became so highly developed that every birthday or Christmas gift we received was eagerly scrutinised and mentally assessed for its pawnable value.

Desperate though our financial position was, however, only gifts donated to Ena and me were considered for conversion to cash. Presents bought by relatives and friends for Linda – including beautiful hand-embroidered clothes and pram rugs sent by my twin sister in Istanbul – were strictly not for pawning. Linda had grown into a beautiful baby, so everyone said. Each time Ena and I took her for walks in her pram, people stopped to admire her.

In 1955, the year after I had completed the industrial training course, the Ministry of Labour officer who dealt with the disabled called on his regular weekly visit. Over the months, his visits had become a routine. He had called simply to inform me that, still, there was no job available for me. On this occasion, however, his news was different – and excitingly different. A small engineering firm in Tongham, not too far away, had agreed to give me a chance. He would accompany me to an interview and, provided that I could satisfy my prospective employer that I was capable of operating a capstan, there was a job waiting.

The four-mile journey to Tongham seemed to be over all too soon. I had not had time to collect my thoughts, to recollect the training that I had received almost a year before. Had I forgotten everything I had learned? Would I remember how to operate, by touch alone, the intricate workings of the capstan?

The firm was run by two brothers, Jim and Eric Neaves. I was introduced to them and, after answering some questions about myself and the training I had received, I found myself in front of a capstan in the factory. Nervously, I started it up. To my relief, I managed to demonstrate my ability without a single error. My prospective employers seemed to be pleased.

'Right, Mr Fettel,' Eric Neaves said. 'Can you start tomorrow?'

Could I? You bet I could! Yippee! I was starting work!

'Yes,' I said. 'Thank you very much.'

My weekly wage would be six pounds ten shillings, they said. If I found that the work was becoming easier and that I could increase my speed, however, I could earn a bonus. If I found I could work really quickly, it might be possible to increase my earnings to as much as nine pounds a week.

Ena was overjoyed. She rushed out to the shops and bought a workman's lunch-box.

The following morning, we were up early. Ena prepared my sandwiches, put them into my lunch-box and took me to the bus stop, which was outside our front door.

The factory was noisy and smelled of oil and industrial dirt but I did not mind. I cared only that I was working, that I had obtained a job at last, that I was doing my first day's work for nine years, that I was earning my living, that my labours would provide for my wife and daughter and for the unborn child that was growing daily inside Ena. My new workmates were friendly and the factory was an exciting place in which to be.

All that week, I returned home each evening at six o'clock, tired and wearied not only by the physical effort after so many years of inactivity but also by the mental concentration needed to operate the capstan efficiently and without error or accident. It was an exhaustion, however, that was accompanied by incredible happiness, contentment and sense of achievement.

On the following Friday, a wage packet was placed into my hands. I counted the notes. There were eight and a few coins. Eight pounds!

At the end of the day, one of my workmates guided me to the nearby shops. I bought a bunch of chrysanthemums and a big box of Ena's favourite Black Magic chocolates.

She greeted me at the door. An appetising smell of cooking drifted through from the kitchen. I kissed her and presented her with the flowers, the chocolates and my first wage packet.

'I am the proudest man in the world,' I told her simply. 'I have earned these for you with the sweat of my own hands.'

Chapter Thirty-One

Ena's pregnancy resulted in an enforced move from our two rooms. Our kindly landlady was sorry but there was simply insufficient space for two babies as well as two adults. We understood.

The notice to quit that she so reluctantly gave us, however, proved to be an unexpectedly happy occurrence. For some time, we had had our names down on the local authority's waiting list for a council house. Because of our threatened homelessness, our application rose rapidly to the top of the list. We became a priority case. It was unthinkable that a pregnant wife with a young child and a blind husband should be turned out on to the streets.

Our delight at being allocated a two-bedroom council house was increased by the discovery that it was in Tongham, only a hundred yards from the factory where I worked. Even though we were to move into the first real home of our own, it was with some regret that we said goodbye to our landlady and to the two rooms in which we had shared so much happiness.

We had only the bare essentials with which to furnish our new home. We had a carpet. Ena's mother gave us a double bed. An anonymous donor provided an old couch and a chair. The main bedroom had a built-in wardrobe so, at least, we had somewhere to hang our clothes. We scoured second-hand shops searching for bargains. We bought some barely-worn linoleum, which a friend kindly laid for us in one of the bedrooms. The garden was a big one and extremely well-stocked. The previous tenant had planted vegetables, for which one day we would be truly thankful.

We were on our own at last, in our own home, just the three of us. The house came alive with the infectious laughter of baby Linda.

Another source of pleasure was the fact that, because of the nearness of the factory, I was able, with the aid of my white stick, to guide myself to work and return home for lunch.

One morning, just after Christmas 1955, Ena rose at five o'clock. Without a word, she began to bake fruit cakes and wash mountains of clothes. Not surprisingly, I found her behaviour a little strange. Ena, however, knew what she was doing.

At seven o'clock, the ambulance arrived and took Ena to hospital. Her baby was already two weeks overdue. I could not conceal my agitation. I was desperately anxious for her. Ena, however, seemed unusually calm.

Ena's parents arrived the same day and stayed for a week to take care of baby Linda and me. Ena gave birth to a boy. I had a son! We named him Paul.

Every evening for ten days, a young apprentice, only fifteen, who worked alongside me, took me to hospital to visit Ena and our newly-born son. I was grateful for his kindness and his thoughtfulness in giving up his evenings to help me and I was extremely saddened, fourteen years later, to learn that he had collapsed and died while on a training run.

The arrival of a son meant that we now had two children of different sexes. Because of that, the council informed us that we would soon have need of an additional bedroom and that, in the near future, we would qualify for a three-bedroom house.

Building work was still taking place on the estate in which we lived and, one day, Ena took me to inspect some of the half-built houses. She held my hand and led me round one house that she liked only fifty yards from our home. As we walked through the shells of the rooms, stepping over planks and piles of bricks, she described it to me. Then she guided me into the back garden.

'It's just a mass of mud and builder's rubble at the moment,' she said. 'But it's a lovely secluded garden with lots of trees to keep it private. And at the bottom there's the railway line. It's disused now, as you know, so there won't be any trains to make a noise. Oh, Nino! Can't you just imagine the peace and beauty in this garden in the summer time?'

She had clearly set her heart on it and, from her description, I rather liked the sound of it myself. We telephoned the council's housing department and asked if the house we were due to be allocated could be that one. They could promise nothing, they said, but they would try.

Three months later, we were handed the keys of our chosen house. Once more, we had only the bare essentials with which to furnish it and, to our slight consternation, there were no built-in wardrobes. Ena, however, cleverly found an old wardrobe in a second-hand shop and bought it for four pounds. The large, airy living-room had a hatch through which prepared meals could be passed from the kitchen but, with two young children, it was easier and less messy to eat in the roomy kitchen.

For six pounds, we hired a workman and a cultivator to turn the soil of the garden and level the ground. We scattered grass seed and, when the sun had brought the tiny seeds to life, Ena took me into the garden to feel the tender, green shoots peeping through.

Later, when the lawn became lush and green, we became aware of random bare patches but we did not mind. The birds had had their fill and the damage could soon be repaired.

Two years after I had started work, my boss, Eric Neaves, called me to his office.

'Kosta,' he said sadly. 'I'm afraid I won't be able to keep you on after another fortnight. You'll have to find a new job.'

A decline in orders, which Mr Neaves hoped would be only temporary, meant that there was insufficient work available to keep the entire work-force in employment. Redundancies were necessary. Whether it was because I was blind or because a last-in-first-out policy operated I did not know, but I was the first to go.

Sick with worry, I telephoned the Labour Exchange. Jobs were not readily available, especially for the blind, but a possible opening for me was found with a firm at Farnham, only four miles away. An interview was arranged but, before it took place, a sudden and unexpected increase of orders meant that it was possible for Mr Neaves to keep me on. I was happy to stay in a job that was only one hundred yards from home and the interview with the Farnham firm was cancelled.

The incident, however, had given us a fright. Even though the redundancy notice had been withdrawn, my position at work was not so secure that we could contemplate the future free from worry. I knew that a slackening of business could recur and that, if it did, I would be the first to be sacked once more. Quite independently, Ena decided that, as a precaution against my future possible unemployment, she would return to nursing on a part-time basis. During the day, I went off to work as usual while Ena cared for Linda and Paul. On five evenings each week, after I had helped her to bath and feed the children, Ena left them in my care while she caught a bus to the local hospital, where she worked from seven o'clock until ten o'clock for three pounds a week.

Ena's foresight in obtaining a part-time nursing post could not have been improved upon had she been clairvoyant. My future prospects did, indeed, turn out to be as uncertain as we had suspected and, after being laid off several times and then recalled when new orders came in, I was finally made redundant with no hope of an early recall.

The Farnham firm at which I had previously been offered an interview no longer had a vacancy. Nor did any other factory in the area. Mr Neaves, in an effort to relieve my financial difficulties, found me part-time work that I could do at home, threading plastic candle-holders to cards, six different-coloured holders to each card. As the rate of pay was only ninepence for each dozen cards completed, however, it was fortunate that Ena had had the foresight to obtain a part-time job, modest though her wages were.

Soon afterwards, however, Ena's wages were no more. She was pregnant again. Not surprisingly, the physical and mental effort of looking after the house, a blind husband and two young children, as well as working at the hospital in the evenings, proved too much. With the birth four months away, she resigned her job.

After having had her first two babies in hospital, Ena was determined to give birth to her third at home. She wanted to find out, she said, what a home confinement was like.

The district nurse who attended her was young and kind. She placed her foetal stethoscope on Ena's abdomen and let little Linda listen through the ear-pieces. Linda's lovely eyes widened in wonderment as she heard the heart-beat of the unborn baby.

Early one morning, Ena began to display the same early-warning signals as she had done before the birth of Paul. There was a sudden flurry of activity. Piles of dirty linen were washed clean and hung out to dry. Cake mixtures were whipped up in bowls and left in the oven to bake.

The pains started long before lunch. Kindly neighbours gathered in Ena's room to offer help. It was evening, however, before Ena asked me to call the district nurse on the telephone that, by then, we had had installed.

The nurse arrived and ushered our friends from the room. Linda and Paul were asleep in the next bedroom. Only I remained with Ena and the midwife.

I was euphoric that Ena wanted me to be present at the birth of our third child yet, at the same time, I was nervous, anxious and a little afraid. I sat at the head of the bed holding Ena's hand. She took several deep breaths and then pushed, hard. It seemed for ever before she breathed again.

For the next half-hour, the longest half-hour I had ever

known, Ena pushed, panted, gasped for breath, groaned with pain and pushed again. In between contractions, she squeezed my hand and urged me not to worry. Why, until then, had I not realised what hard work it was? Why had no one told me that giving birth was quite like this?

Suddenly, Ena gave a little cry. She fell back into my arms. Seconds later, I heard a slap and then another cry – the gurgling, infuriated cry of our second son, Adrian.

The midwife allowed me to hold him for a few moments before placing him into Ena's arms. She was tired after all her efforts but happy to have another fine son.

I was relieved that Ena had come safely through her ordeal. It had been an ordeal for me, too, and I could feel the perspiration on my forehead.

There and then, I decided that our family was complete. We had a lovely daughter and two splendid sons. Ena had done enough.

The following morning, I called Linda and Paul into our bedroom.

'Look!' Ena told them. 'We have a present for you.'

She placed Adrian into Linda's arms. Little Paul looked on, amazed.

In the months that followed, so that Linda and Paul would not be jealous, Ena encouraged them to help her bath and feed the new baby. Sometimes, during the daytime, we went for walks in the green countryside that was on our doorstep, Ena pushing Paul and Adrian in the pram, I holding the handle with one hand for guidance and Linda's tiny hand with my other. Often, when little Linda grew tired of toddling beside us, I lifted her on to my shoulders and carried her home. On Sundays, we walked across the fields to attend mass. By that time, Ena had become a Catholic, a conversion that had brought us even closer.

I was happy. I had Ena. I had my little ones. As I traced my children's faces with my finger, however, as I romped with them on the living-room floor and in the garden, I knew that my happiness was not complete. I longed actually to *see* their faces, their expressions at play, their naughty exploits.

My right eye was finished. My left eye had no lids. I could, however, still see daylight with it.

'Darling,' I said suddenly to Ena one day. 'If only I could see them . . .'

Chapter Thirty-Two

For almost eighteen months, my dream of seeing my wife and children for the first time remained . . . a dream.

The last lingering hopes of ever seeing them with my right eye had long since been extinguished. Mr Boxill, though, had always insisted that my left eye was the better one and that, behind the scar tissue, there was definitely a recognisable eye. Innumerable skin grafts had died. Innumerable operations to clear away the scar tissue had scarcely improved the prospects. If only someone, somewhere, could successfully build me new eyelids and remove the unwanted debris then, perhaps, another attempt could be made to restore my sight.

The question was . . . who?

The answer was . . . Sir Archibald McIndoe.*

Sir Archibald, a New Zealander, was the most famous plastic surgeon in Britain and, probably, in the world. His fame had been achieved during World War II when he and his team at the plastic surgery unit of the Queen Victoria Hospital at East Grinstead, in Sussex, had performed miracles in rebuilding the horribly-burned and mutilated faces and bodies of pilots and other aircrew whose aircraft had caught fire and, sometimes, crashed and burst into flames. At the time of the war, plastic surgery had been a comparatively new medical technique. McIndoe had been a pioneer in the field. His surgery had, to a large extent, been experimental – a fact that both he and his grotesquely-burned patients had cheerfully recognised by the formation of the famous 'Guinea Pig Club', membership of which was restricted to the many hundreds of skingrafted airmen of many nationalities who had been re-built and re-born by his tremendous skills. Since then, the Queen Victoria plastic surgery unit had become world-renowned.

* Sir Archibald Hector McIndoe, CBE; MB, ChB. (Medal, Clinical Medicine and Surgery) New Zealand 1923; MSC (Pathology) Mayo Foundation, University of Minnesota 1927; MS 1929; FRCS Eng. 1932; FACS 1934; MD (Hon. Causa) Uppsala; Commander Order of the White Lion (Czechoslovakia); Officer Order Polonia Restituta (Poland); Plastic Surgeon St Bartholomew's Hospital, London; Consultant Plastic Surgeon RAF; Surgeon in charge of Maxillo-Facial Unit, East Grinstead; Consultant Plastic Surgeon Chelsea Hospital for Women; Member (ex-President) Association of Plastic Surgeons; Fellow Medical Society, London. Died 12 April 1960.

'Let's see if we can see him and get his opinion,' said Ena excitedly. 'We might just as well go to the top!'

My general practitioner arranged an appointment and handed me a letter to give to Sir Archibald. Ena's parents had moved to a new parish by the sea at Rustington, in Sussex, and Mrs Argyle drove us from their home to East Grinstead.

My first impression of the great man was decidedly favourable. He sounded solid, dependable and kindly. His New Zealand accent was noticeably pronounced.

He examined my eyes and asked why, after so many years, I wanted new eyelids. How many years was it? Thirteen? Yes, nearly thirteen.

I explained that, contrary to what he had assumed, it was not for cosmetic reasons. It was because I had been told that, underneath the scar tissue and burned flesh, there was an eye, an eye on which I could have an operation to restore my sight if only it could be freed from what was left of my eyelids, if only the surrounding damage could be repaired.

'Oh!' he said, surprised. 'We can arrange for you to see Mr Rycroft.* We have an eye unit here.'

A bed would be reserved, he said. I would be informed of my admission date.

Unknown to me, after we had left, Sir Archibald dictated a letter to my own doctor. Dated 2 February 1959, it said: 'This is a very considerable problem. Before any attack is made on his left eye in the way of corneal grafting he would of course have to have a reconstruction of his lids. I would say at once that after a very extensive experience of corneal grafting in burns of the eyes, no single case that I have ever seen or known about with a burn as bad as this has ever recovered sight. However, I think that an attempt should be made to reconstruct his eyelids, and at the same time something can be done to improve his scarring. I will arrange his admission here when a bed becomes available.'

Not long afterwards, knowing nothing of Sir Archibald's dismal and pessimistic prognosis, I entered the unit's America

* Benjamin William Rycroft, later Sir Benjamin, Kt. (1960), OBE.; MD St Andrew's University 1928; MB, ChB 1924; FRCS Eng. 1931; MRCS Eng., LRCP Lond. 1924; DOMS 1929; Moorfields Research Scholar 1934; Occulist to HRH the Princess Royal; Consultant Ophthalmic Surgeon, Corneo-Plastic Unit, Queen Victoria Hospital, East Grinstead, Plastic Unit, Kent County Ophthalmic and Aural Hospital, Sussex Eye Hospital and BEA; Consultant Ophthalmologist, Zoological Society, London. Died 29 March, 1967, aged 64.

Wing full of hope for the outcome. Sir Archibald operated. He separated my left eyeball from the surrounding tissue and, with skin removed from my right upper arm, fashioned shapely new eyelids and grafted them into place.

I awoke to find my eyes bandaged. Gauze covered a sore patch on my arm. The dressings remained untouched for two weeks. Then they were removed. The graft had taken.

'Darling!' Ena exclaimed. 'What a lovely job they've done! You've got some terrific lids!'

'They even have a bit of movement in them,' I told her.

My appearance, so everyone assured me, was considerably enhanced.

Three days later, I was transferred to the eye ward. Mr Werb,* the eye specialist who was assistant to Mr Rycroft, the consultant ophthalmic surgeon, inserted a glass shield to ensure that the eyeball did not adhere to my newly-grafted eyelids.

Later, Mr Rycroft himself examined me. He sent me home with instructions to return in one month's time.

Shortly before my next appointment, however, a pain developed in my eye.

'What is it, doctor?' I asked our GP, whom Ena had called.

'I'm not sure,' he said. 'You will have to be admitted to East Grinstead.'

It was clearly serious. It was a Sunday. Only emergencies were admitted at weekends.

I was operated upon the same day. They sent me home without the shield. The shield, I knew, should have stayed in place for several months. Now, it had been removed.

I had my new lids. Mr Rycroft had tried to prepare my eye for yet another corneal graft. Yet again, however, something had gone awry.

A year passed. The urge to see my wife and children returned. Back at the Queen Victoria Hospital, a swab was taken from my eye. An infection, I learned, had precipitated the previous premature removal of the glass shield and, this time, there was to be no repeat. They were determined. The taking of the swab was a precaution to ensure that my eye was not infected. It was a wise precaution. It was. The swab was swarming with bacteria. Three

* Abraham Werb, MB, ChB Cape Town 1945; FRCS Eng. 1970; DOMS Dublin 1956; DO Eng. 1956; 1st Assistant, Corneo-Plastic Unit, Queen Victoria Hospital, East Grinstead; Fellow Royal Society of Medicine; Member Ophthalmic Society UK.

days of eye drops eliminated the danger. Another glass shield
was inserted.

I discarded the white eye-pad that I had worn for years and
returned home to Tongham, confident that my new eyelids had
so improved my appearance that only dark glasses were now
required as camouflage.

Ena had been instructed in the routine requirements for keeping infection at bay. With meticulous regularity, she deftly
flipped the shield from my eye, sterilised it in a solution and then
nimbly inserted it again behind the lids.

Not long afterwards, I was recalled. To my sorrow, Sir
Archibald McIndoe had died. The new consultant plastic
surgeon in charge of my case, Mr Beare,* decided that my
bottom lid needed to be further built up. Another operation was
performed. That skin-graft, too, proved successful. I was making
progress.

The progress, however, was slow. Inexhaustible patience was
required not only by me but by the doctors. During the eighteen
months that the shield remained in my eye, frequent stays in
hospital were interspersed with innumerable visits to the out-
patients' department and, when I was required in neither,
occasional spells back at my old job, which had become unexpectedly available once more.

It was the first specialist eye ward in which I had been a
patient. In charge of it was a dedicated and brilliant nursing
sister who was the first lieutenant of the specialist eye team, not
only running the ward but also taking her own out-patients'
clinics and assisting at operations. The ward itself abounded
with aids to assist the blind and partially-sighted. I spent my
time listening to long-playing records and 'talking-books' and, in
the sitting-room that separated the men's and women's wards,
smoking, talking and reading braille books. Unfortunately, my
knowledge of braille was still decidedly elementary and I found
that patience was required for me to read it. I had not practised
braille reading since completing the course on which I had
learned the art, at Torquay, six years before. Paradoxically,
although I had accepted my blindness, I had always refused to
have a braille book in the house, a quirk that Freud would
doubtless have found significant. It would not have taken him

* Robin Lyell Blin Beare, MB, BS (Honours; Distinction Surgery) London
1952; FRCS Eng. 1955; Consultant Plastic Surgeon, St Mary's Hospital,
London, and Queen Victoria Hospital, East Grinstead; Member of British
Association of Plastic Surgeons; Fellow of Royal Society of Medicine.

many hours of probing to discover that, in my subconscious if not in my conscious, braille books were symbolic of finality. They signified more than an acceptance of blindness. They signified an acceptance of blindness *for ever,* a resignation to a lifetime in the dark, not just in the present but in the future, for all time.

During one seven-week stay in hospital for yet another operation, I made the acquaintance of a patient from the women's ward, a Welsh woman, the wife of a soldier, who was living in army quarters at Aldershot, only a few miles from my own home. She was waiting for a corneal graft to be performed and was afraid of being in the dark when she awoke to find her eyes bandaged.

'I don't know what I shall do,' she said anxiously. 'I won't be able to do anything for myself.'

'Don't worry,' I told her. 'When you've had your operation I'll try to help you.'

On the first day she was allowed out of bed, she asked a nurse to take her to the sitting-room that separated the two wards.

'Where's Kosta?' she asked.

The nurse brought her to sit beside me. Together, we spent hours each day, practising the dozens of different everyday acts that sighted people take for granted. I taught her to walk without bumping into tables and chairs, how to sit down without missing the chair, how to locate the food on her plate, how to ensure that she did not misplace the cap of her tooth-paste tube. She enjoyed a cigarette and never imagined that she would ever be able to light her own. I taught her how to do so by holding the cigarette and the match together, so that the match head projected just beyond the end of the cigarette. Then, when the match was struck, still with the cigarette alongside, the flame was in exactly the right position to ignite the tobacco at the first draw. When she wanted letters written, I typed them out to her dictation.

She was grateful for my help but the pleasure was mine. Just like in Egypt all those years before, when I had been able to help Mary, the girl in the ATS ward, and to teach French to Dorothy, I was happy and proud to be of use to someone, even though I was blind.

Towards the end of 1960, even though I was back at my old job in between spells in hospital, the Ministry of Labour official dealing with the blind thoughtfully found me a new position that promised more regular employment. It was at Martonair, a bigger engineering company employing about two hundred people at Farnham, four miles from my home. The pay was to be thirteen pounds a week. There was no bonus for increased productivity but there was a good pension scheme and job security. Like the Neaves brothers, they were prepared to keep my job open during the many periods when I would be away in hospital.

Ena and I discussed the offer and decided to accept. Even though my old job was so near to home, the insecurity had begun to worry me. With three children to feed as well as Ena and myself, frequent spells of unemployment were not conducive to peace of mind.

The noise of so many more machines seemed deafening at first, but it was a friendly place. Everyone went out of his way to help me. On the second day, I was called to the office of Mr Moore, the works manager. It was the first time they had seen a blind man working a capstan, he said. They had been watching me and were incredulous at the way in which I was able to find the controls.

There was another reason why I decided to opt for the security that was offered at Martonair. Ena and I planned to visit my family in Istanbul, my parents and two sisters, whom I had not seen since leaving for the army, nineteen years before. My father was both ageing and ailing and I longed to see them all again.

Ena had begun a new job, too, as night sister in charge of a geriatric unit near Guildford, earning eleven pounds for a four-night week. Our regular earnings produced a distinct improvement in our financial position. By the time that Ena had been working as a night sister for a year, our savings had increased to an amount that would almost pay for our train and boat fares. My family in Istanbul were excited at the prospect of seeing both me after so many years and the girl who had become my wife and whom they had never seen.

Sadly, however, further frequent spells in hospital meant more lost wages. Months of living on sickness benefit wreaked havoc with our budget. The cost of day-to-day living was increasing all the time. Unexpected bills had to be paid. Our savings dwindled. Inevitably, in July 1961, I had to write to Istanbul. The trip was off.

Three months later, in October, I was in the bathroom when I heard a knock at the door. The children were playing in the garden. Ena was busy in the kitchen. She answered the door. I heard voices in the hall and realised that Ena was talking to my cousin, Rita. I was surprised.

Rita rarely visited us and, when she did, usually let us know when she was coming. She had obviously been unable to ring because, by then, we had given up the telephone in order to save money for the trip to Turkey.

Rita spoke to Ena in a low voice. Even though I was in the bathroom, the hyper-sensitive hearing that I had developed since being blinded turned what was scarcely more than a whisper into a sentence of total clarity.

'Ena,' she said. 'Nino's father has died.'

Stunned by her words, I groped my way to the bedroom and flung myself on to the bed. The tears flowed from the grievously injured eyes and wet the pillow. My dearest father was dead and, but for the shortage of money, I would have been by his side.

Ena came into the room. It had not just happened, she said. My father had been seriously ill for two weeks and had died two months before. Rita had just returned from a holiday in Istanbul and had learned the news while she was there. Knowing that I was in hospital having operations, my family had decided to keep the news from me, to remain silent, to save upsetting me.

Two months! Two months and they had told me nothing! My initial grief gave way to anger. If only they had let me know that my father was ill, if only they had told me, I would have postponed the operations on my eyes! Somehow, I would have got to Istanbul. Somehow, I would have been at his side. It was twenty years since I had seen my father. Now I would never see him again.

I was distraught with grief. Ena looked at my tear-streaked face, heard the uncontrollable sobs, and sensed that I needed to be alone. She closed the door quietly behind her. My cousin left without seeing me. I did not want to speak to anyone. Nobody, not even Ena, could console me then.

I wept again for my father. The pillow dried and became wet yet again with tears. Ena put the children to bed. Somehow, they sensed that there was trouble in the house and were unusually good and quiet.

Later that evening, Ena came in with a cup of coffee. She sat on the edge of the bed. How long I had lain there I did not know.

'Darling,' she said. 'I've been thinking. I'm going to get a better nursing post with more money. You and I *will* make that journey to Istanbul. You *must* meet your mother again.'

We sat on the bed and talked. Listening to Ena's plans to visit my family in Istanbul gradually eased my grief and pain at my father's death.

Ena was right. The journey *must* be made.

Chapter Thirty-Three

Straight away, Ena set out to achieve her self-imposed objective. She obtained a new post, as ward sister at the Cambridge Military Hospital at Aldershot, which carried a higher salary. As I was working, too, our savings began to mount.

The penalty for Ena's increased salary, however, was the fact that she was obliged to work split duties and occasional weekends, leaving home at a quarter past seven in the mornings and, sometimes, not returning until nine o'clock in the evenings.

Ena's determination to earn sufficient money for us to visit my family in Istanbul was matched only by her determination that, because of her irregular working hours, the children should not lack their usual care. She was determined that Linda, Paul and Adrian should not become latch-key children, arriving home from school, letting themselves into an empty house with their own door-keys and waiting, lonely and hungry and miserable, until their parents returned from work. Clearly, with both Ena and me being out at work each day, the children needed someone to look after them. The solution was an *au pair* girl. Michelle, an extremely pleasant French teenager, was welcomed into our home. Her duties were to accompany the children to and from school and, in case they arrived home unexpectedly from school because of some minor mishap or emergency, to be in the house whenever Ena and I were at work.

Although, because of frequent stays in hospital, my own earnings were intermittent, by the summer of 1963 we had managed, between us, to save the grand total of one hundred and forty pounds. It had taken us almost two years to amass what seemed to us like a fortune. It was almost two years since we had learned of my father's death and Ena had vowed to take me to visit my family, but the amount that we had saved was sufficient to pay the boat and train fares not only of ourselves but of the children, too. As, by then, they were all well past the toddler stage – even Adrian, the youngest, was almost six and had been at school for nearly a year – we decided to take them with us.

At last, the great day, the day of our departure, arrived. It was the Monday of the first week in August. Michelle returned to

France for a month's holiday. Everything was packed. I could tell that Ena was nervous. She had never been abroad before, never been out of Britain, yet here she was, about to embark on the journey of a lifetime, a journey that was to last for three-and-a-half days, a journey right across Europe to the very door-step of Asia Minor, towing a blind husband and three children, all under nine years, behind her.

It was fortunate that I had grown up in a cosmopolitan society in which foreign tongues were learned quickly by the young and that, as a result, I had seven languages at my disposal.

In the evening, loaded with suitcases, picnic hampers, thermos flasks, shopping bags, and a shoulder bag containing our family passport and the visas required to travel through Yugoslavia and Bulgaria, we set off. I had had no difficulty in obtaining a pass-port. My nationality was no longer a problem. I had become a naturalised British citizen. I was no longer a stateless person.

To our surprise, waiting for us at Aldershot railway station were the Reverend and Mrs Argyle. They had unexpectedly turned up to bid us goodbye and wish us *bon voyage*, a kindly gesture that was greatly appreciated, and I was moved when, as a memento of a memorable occasion, they presented me with the gift of a cigarette lighter.

The train from Aldershot arrived at Victoria Station in London at nine o'clock. The boat train to Dover did not leave for another hour. Knowing that we would not be able to afford to eat on the trains, we had brought with us well-stocked picnic hampers, prepared to exist for the next three-and-a-half days on cold meats, biscuits and chocolate. Because of that, Ena sug-gested (with the gloomy air of a condemned man about to meet his doom) that we should all eat a hearty dinner, our last hot meal until arriving in Istanbul in almost four days' time.

The railway snack bars at Victoria Station could offer nothing more exciting than cold pies and sandwiches.

'Never mind,' said Ena. 'There's a restaurant over here.'

She guided us through the restaurant door. My feet sank into the thick pile of a plush carpet.

'Are you sure this is a restaurant, darling?' I asked anxiously.

'Of course,' Ena replied. 'It says so outside.'

Waiters appeared out of thin air, like wraiths. They sur-rounded us and ushered us to a table. Chairs were pulled out and slid underneath us as we sat down. It was accomplished with the professional dexterity of the highly-skilled and experienced waiter.

'Madam,' said a silky voice. 'Sir,' said the same flunky. Huge menu cards were placed into our hands.

'Oh, darling!' Ena wailed when the waiters had discreetly withdrawn to await our further bidding. 'I've made a terrible mistake. Everyone here is in evening dress!'

My heart sank. I was acutely aware that we were all wearing old travelling clothes and that the ancient, battered shoulder bag containing the passport and visas was hanging round Ena's neck.

Ena studied the menu.

'Oh, Nino!' she squeaked. 'The price of the food!'

'What does it say?'

'I can't read it all. It's in French!'

My heart sank even further. My worst fears were confirmed. The plush carpets, the obsequious waiters, the high prices, the menus in French, all indicated that we had inadvertently entered a select and exclusive establishment.

'Where are we?' I whispered.

'I don't know.'

'The menu!' I hissed. 'What does it say on the menu?'

Ena looked.

'Grosvenor Hotel Restaurant,' she said.

The Grosvenor Hotel! *The* Grosvenor Hotel, one of the best-known, most select, most luxurious and most expensive hotels in London! We had found our way into it through an entrance leading directly from Victoria Station and were now sitting uncomfortably in the hotel dining-room.

The discovery of our unfortunate error had come too late. Neither of us could face the humiliation of getting up and shuffling shamefacedly out, trailing the children behind us.

Ena read the menu to me in French. I translated. The cheapest dish on the menu was *sole meunière* served with *pommes frites*. It was priced at one pound five shillings. There were no half-portions – and no half-prices – for children.

'Twenty-five bob!' I exclaimed. 'And that's plain fish and chips without any trimmings!'

'Tell them we want fish and chips five times,' joked Ena who, having spent many hungry evenings while living on the meagre fare offered at nurses' homes, had become rather partial to the homely, unpretentious repast. She had also become quite knowledgeable on the colloquial expressions employed by the English working classes when ordering the dish.

I could tell by her flippant remark that she was trying to make light of her appalling blunder in bringing us to such a place but I was in no humour to be easily amused. Ena had managed to obtain a loan of two hundred pounds from our bank to cover the expenses we were bound to incur during our visit and I could foresee that we were about to be relieved of a large portion of it before we managed to escape from the Grosvenor Hotel.

Wine waiters hovered expectantly. Ena shooed them away with the sort of imperious wave of the hand that she fondly imagined was expected of her.

'No, thank you,' she said nonchalantly. 'Just water, please.'

Ena was gazing around the dining-room and was becoming more anxious with each passing minute.

'Nino!' she whispered. 'You've never seen anything like it. The women are all in fabulous, long evening gowns. And they all have the most marvellous jewellery dripping from their ears and dangling round their necks. It looks so heavy I'm surprised they can keep their heads up out of the soup!'

Suddenly, Paul, our elder son, spotted a familiar face across the other side of the dining-room.

'Mummy, mummy!' he shouted excitedly. 'Look, look! There's the man from *No Hiding Place!*'

Diners in dinner jackets and exquisite gowns turned and glared towards our table.

'Yes, darling,' Ena said calmly, trying hard to cover her embarrassment. 'Be quiet now, there's a good boy.'

'But Mummy ... !'

'Yes, darling! Just be quiet!'

When the attention of the other diners had returned to their *escalopes de veau chasseur* and their *crêpes suzette,* Ena risked a furtive glance in the direction in which Paul had pointed.

Sure enough, he was right. Sitting at a table across the room was Raymond Francis, a well-known British actor who played the leading role in *No Hiding Place,* a television police series that was extremely popular at the time.

The children left most of their meal. The bill totalled five pounds, plus a service charge of ten per cent. I was fuming. Our spending money was down by five pounds ten shillings already and we had not yet left London. We now had only one hundred and ninety-four pounds ten shillings left of our bank loan and that had to last us for eighteen days in Istanbul, plus the seven days spent travelling both ways. We could have bought fish and chips five times from a fish and chip shop for less than one pound.

The train from Victoria sped through the Kent countryside. It was a pleasant summer evening. Gradually, my good humour returned and Ena and I laughed about her expensive *faux pas*.

'What must they have thought when we all walked in?' Ena giggled.

'I bet they weren't as shocked as I was when you read out the prices,' I told her.

At Dover, there was a long queue of passengers waiting to get through the customs check.

'Stay there with the children, darling, and I'll go and see what's happening,' Ena said. She was gone before I could stop her. I waited anxiously. Five minutes passed. My anxiety was growing. Suddenly, she was back at my side.

'Where have you been? I was getting worried.'

'Come on. We're going through.'

We were ushered through customs and on to the ship.

'How did you manage that?' I asked.

'I told a policeman I had a blind husband and three very tired children and he let us to the front of the queue,' she explained.

We were shown to our cabin. We settled down for the night. The children and I slept throughout the whole of the Channel crossing. Ena slept hardly at all.

At Ostend, after continental breakfast on board ship, we boarded a train for Munich. The seats were hard, straight-backed and decidedly uncomfortable. At first, the children were excited but well-behaved. Riding on a train was a novelty to them. Later in the day, however, they became tired and irritable. In the afternoon, when the sun was at its highest and the carriage was at its hottest, the heat and sweat from our bodies caused our clothes to stick to the hard seats. Each time the train stopped, Ena jumped out to fill our water bottles, leaving me in the carriage, my stomach knotted with nerves, worried sick in case the train left without her, and I found myself alone, blind and with three children to look after.

Munich arrived at last. It was nine o'clock in the evening. We had been travelling all day. The platform loudspeakers crackled into life. An announcement was made in German, a language with which I was not familiar. Presumably, it was about train destinations, times of departure and platform numbers but the announcer was speaking so quickly and his voice echoed so confusingly around the lofty station that I could not even hear the word Istanbul. We had no idea where to find the Istanbul Express.

Ena rummaged into one of the bags and pulled out a ball of string. She tied the children together, fastening the string round their waists and knotting it at the backs of their coats, linking them together. Then she tied the three of them to me.

'That's better,' she said. 'They won't be able to wander off now and get lost while I'm away.'

'Where are you going?'

'To find our train.'

She led us, one behind the other like a line of shackled prisoners, to a noisy station café. She seated us at a table and then left us alone.

The Istanbul Express was due to leave at eleven o'clock that night, two hours after our arrival. It was already half-past-nine. I waited nervously for her to return. If only I could help her!

'I've found it!' I started at the sound of her voice. I sighed with relief. She had been away for at least fifteen minutes.

'Where is it?'

'Not far. Come on. I'll show you.'

'You seemed to be gone for ever.'

'I had a bit of trouble.'

'What happened?'

'I found the train eventually but I couldn't make the steward understand that I had a blind husband and three children waiting.'

'What did you do?'

'I'm afraid I had to resort to feminine tears before he understood. It's all right now though. He's waiting to help us aboard.'

Our *wagon-lit* compartment was quite roomy. The three bunks, which could be turned into seats during the day, were waiting for us. The sheets were crisp and clean. There was a wardrobe and a small sink with one tap, the water from which, Ena warned the children, was not for drinking. Ena helped me to climb up the steps to the top bunk. Paul and Adrian lay head-to-toe in the middle one. Ena and Linda crawled into the bottom one. Within minutes, we were all asleep.

The Istanbul Express roared on through the night. At dawn, Ena looked out of the window.

'Darling!' she said. 'The whole landscape has changed!'

'What does it look like?'

'There are lots of little chalets on the mountainside.'

'It must be Austria,' I told her.

'They're just like little dolls' houses with trees all round that one sees in the shops at Christmas!' She sounded enthralled.

Ena washed the children and I dried them. For breakfast, we ate rolls that were left from the previous day. When the steward came round with his trolley, we bought cups of coffee.

By lunch-time, the Yugoslav border was only a few miles away. Every turn of the wheels, every clickety-clack of the rails, was bringing me closer to my family.

We stumbled and bumped our way down the corridor to the dining car. We ate a mouth-watering meal. Ena and I treated ourselves to iced beer. The children drank Coca Cola.

At Belgrade, Ena left the train to re-fill the drinking bottles from a communal tap on the platform. Linda waved to her out of the window.

'Mummy's having to wait, Daddy,' Linda informed me. 'There's a big queue of people.'

A few minutes passed.

'Is she nearly there, darling?'

'Not yet. There's still a queue.'

I was becoming more anxious with each passing second.

'Have another look, please, Linda.'

'Mummy's getting her water now,' she said.

The guard's whistle blew. There was a hiss of steam. The train began to move slowly along the platform.

My God! Where was Ena?

'Can you see your mother, darling?'

I was becoming desperate.

'I can't see her, Daddy! I can't see her!'

'What's happened to Mummy, Daddy?' Paul shouted in alarm.

'Where is she?' Adrian asked, in a panic.

Linda began to cry. Paul and Adrian joined in. I felt like accompanying them.

Suddenly, the compartment door opened. Ena walked in.

'Now, now, it's all right, darlings!' she said. 'It's all right. Don't cry! I jumped in the last carriage and walked along the corridor.'

My feelings were a mixture of profound relief, gratitude and anger at the risk she had taken.

'Ena!' I heard myself saying as I mopped my brow. 'Don't you ever leave this train again! We'll ration the drinking water!'

The weather was unbearably hot. The children were tetchy and bored. The novelty of travelling on a train had long since worn off. Ena produced some children's toys and games that she had been keeping as a surprise for just such an occasion. They helped the children to pass the day more happily.

That evening, we put the children to bed and waited until they were asleep. Then we crept out of the stifling compartment into the cool of the corridor, where we sat on little wooden seats that pulled down from the carriage side. The train thundered on. The cool, evening air felt fresh against our travel-grimed faces. In about thirty hours, we would arrive in Istanbul.

During the night, Bulgaria and a corner of Greece sped past. The Turkish border was near. The train stopped. An hour passed. The sun beat down. Two hours passed and still the train did not move. The sun rose still higher. Its heat scorched down on to the roofs of the carriages, sending the temperatures soaring, turning the entire train into something resembling an oven. Sweat poured from our bodies. The children began to cry.

All that day, the train clattered on through the Turkish countryside. Although it still proudly sported the name Istanbul Express, it seemed that the title, for the Turkish section of the journey, at least, was something of a misnomer. The speed at which we progressed could scarcely be described as proceeding at an express pace. Indeed, after the earlier performance of the Istanbul Express, it seemed that we were proceeding at the pace of a senile snail.

'Look, Daddy!' Linda suddenly shouted. 'A mosque!'

At that age, the children always said, 'Look, Daddy!' I wished that I could.

The afternoon passed slowly. We dozed in the heat. It was late afternoon when I roused myself.

'Nino, I think we're nearly there,' Ena said. 'We're passing through a station.'

'What is its name?'

'Yeşil Köy.'

'Yeşil Köy!' I exclaimed. 'That's where I used to live as a boy! Remember me telling you?'

The train hissed to a stop. The corridor was full of pushing people.

'Let's stay in here until this mad animal stampede is over,' Ena said.

We had sent photographs of Ena and the children to my two sisters but she was anxious in case they failed to recognise us.

The last of the corridor crowds alighted. We followed. I stepped on to the concrete platform of Sirkëci railway station,

Istanbul. It was the first time in twenty-two years that I had set foot in Turkey.

Suddenly, arms were flung around my neck. There were two people, judging by the number of arms.

'Nino, Nino, Nino!'

I felt kisses on my face, again and again. I could feel the tears of joy that were streaming from their eyes and wetting their cheeks. I felt confused but happy. My weeping sisters left me for a moment to embrace Ena and the children and then started kissing me again.

My mother was not there. She was waiting for me in the family apartment. When the excitement and the emotion had subsided, we climbed into a taxi for the journey home. Home!

The taxi lurched over Galata Bridge. Ena, nervous in traffic, as always, held on tightly to me and to the children.

There was no lift. The stairs to my mother's fourth-floor apartment seemed never to end. Eventually, to my surprise, they did.

Suddenly, my mother's arms clasped me to her. She touched my face. Her hand slipped behind my head and pressed my face to hers. She held me close. She wept.

Years before, her only son had left to start a new life in the army, a new life in a foreign land. Now, twenty-two years and sixty-seven operations later, I had returned, blinded and older, but my feelings for my mother unchanged. Our devotion to each other had bridged the years, survived the separation. Our love remained untarnished, undiminished.

The apartment, only two hundred yards from the British Consulate, was not only my mother's home but also that of my elder sister, Lucia, her husband, Emile, and their four children, Nadia, aged eighteen, who was studying to become a schoolteacher, Michel, seventeen, Pierrot, sixteen, and Paulette, fifteen. Emile was away on one of the many business trips that kept him from home for long periods.

Nina, my twin sister, had an apartment two hundred yards along the road, where she lived with her husband, Joseph, her sixteen-year-old son, Arnaldo, and her thirteen-year-old daughter, Anita.

I was uncle to three nephews and three nieces and, for the first time, I met them all.

In the days that followed, Lucia and Nina took Ena and the children on trips to the seaside. I stayed in the apartment talking to my mother. We had twenty-two years on which to catch up.

Three times each week, the entire family gathered round the big, oval dining-table in my mother's apartment to have dinner together. They were convivial evenings. For two hours or more, we ate, drank, talked, joked and laughed. Ena could speak a little French but not sufficient to follow all the conversation and I acted as interpreter for her.

Towards the end of our second week, we accompanied my mother and two sisters to the Black Sea resort of Kilyos. We sat on the beach in the warm sunshine. The children began to dig in the sand. A large sand-castle began to take shape. Suddenly, there was a loud blast on a whistle. A beach guard was making frantic gestures to us to stop the children digging up his beach. It seemed that building sand-castles was not permitted because, as the Black Sea was not tidal, the water did not wash away the evidence of childish pleasures and restore the sand to its original smoothness. Instead, any digging activities on the beach remained as permanent, unsightly excavations.

On another day, Nadia, my eldest niece, took Ena to Sainte Sophie and the Blue Mosque and then on to Topkapi Palace and Yerebatan Sarai, the fabulous, underground palace with its famous water cisterns, huge, stone-built storage places filled with collected rainwater and built by Justinian between the years 527-565 AD to ensure adequate water supplies during sieges by his enemies. Ena marvelled that the thick, stone columns that supported the roof also had to bear the weight of modern roads, traffic and apartment blocks up above and decided it was a remarkable tribute to the skills of the builders of almost 1,500 years before.

Inevitably, all too soon, our holiday had to end. In the eighteen days that we had been in Istanbul, Ena and my mother had come to love each other. They embraced and said goodbye. My mother turned to me. She clutched me to her. I tried not to break down. Silent tears ran down her cheeks but she signalled to Ena not to let me know.

My sisters accompanied us in the taxi to Sirkëci Station. I was depressed and numbed by the parting from my mother. On the platform, I hugged my sisters. Their tears upset me. I did not know when we would meet again. It was ten o'clock in the morning. Right on time, the guard blew his whistle. The train moved off. We waved goodbye. The long trek home had begun.

Shortly before leaving Turkish soil, the train came to a halt. Ena looked out of the window.

'Quickly, children, look!' she said excitedly. 'Nino, it's incredible. There's an old man dressed just like they did in biblical days. He's carrying an earthen pitcher on his shoulder and he's selling something from it to the people on the train.'

The old man arrived outside our carriage. He said something to Ena in Turkish.

'He says it's beautiful, cool, fresh water straight from a natural spring,' I told her.

Through the night and the following day, at each stop the train made in the Communist countries of Bulgaria and Yugoslavia, guards with pistols boarded the carriages and locked the toilet doors, presumably with the intention of preventing would-be defectors hiding in the toilets and escaping to the West. Only when the train had moved off once more were the toilet doors unlocked.

When, eventually, we arrived at Munich, extremely late, our connection to Ostend had already departed. All was not lost, however. A kind German professor, who had been travelling in the same carriage, informed us that another train, for Brussels, was due to leave in ten minutes' time. At Brussels, there would be a train to Ostend.

Ena tied the children together with string once more so that they would not become lost. Then she set off to find a porter to help us with our luggage and take us to the Brussels train. The porters, however, ignored her pleas for help. With only five minutes left before the Brussels train was due to leave, Ena became desperate.

'There's an empty postal trolley over here,' she told me. 'We'll use that.'

She hauled our luggage over to the trolley and piled the suitcases into it. If only I could have helped her! The children were tied together in a line by string that was attached to my waist. I held on to Ena's shoulder with one hand. She set off, pushing the trolley, with the children and me in single file behind her.

A split-second later, however, I heard the clanking of chains. The trolley came to a sudden halt. The children fell against my back. I stumbled on to Ena. The dead stop and the unexpected push from behind by me caught her off balance. She clattered into the trolley. But for its high sides, she would undoubtedly have taken a headlong dive into it and would probably have ended up spreadeagled on the luggage.

'Blast!' Ena shouted. 'There's a chain and padlock round the wheels!'

Doubtless, it was a cunning ploy by fiendish German postal

officials to stop crazy Englishwomen running off with it.

Howls of laughter were coming from a train standing at a nearby platform. I could hear French voices. A crowd of French students were hanging out of the windows, tears streaming down their faces, helpless with mirth at the sight of the flustered Englishwoman, her bumbling husband and their three off-spring tied together with string, all bumping into each other and stumbling forward like a line of dominoes being pushed over.

Ena was frantically trying to heave the luggage out of the deep trolley. I could hear her panting and swearing with her efforts. The words she used were decidedly unbecoming for a clergyman's daughter.

Her head was buried in the trolley. At the sound of the laughter, she raised her head and glared at the students.

'You call yourselves gentlemen!' she screamed at them in her best broken French. 'Come down at once and help us with our luggage! We must catch the Brussels train and it's going in a minute!'

It was a passable imitation of a French fishwife. The genteel ladies of the Mothers' Union and the gentlefolk of the Reverend Argyle's congregation would never have recognised the rector's daughter.

Her wrath struck them dumb. The laughter died on their lips. Sheepishly, they climbed down from their carriage and collected our luggage from the trolley. Ena led me and the children in the direction of the Brussels train. The French students trailed behind like a file of native porters.

The train was packed. We walked its full length. All second-class seats were occupied. It was standing room only. Ena, however, was not to be beaten. She marched to an empty first-class compartment and ushered us inside. The French youths put our luggage on the rack. Ena thanked them in French and waved as they made their way back to their own train. We sank into the plush first-class seats. Although they did wonders for my physical comfort, however, they did nothing for my mental ease.

'What have you done, darling?' I asked anxiously. 'We'll have to pay the excess fare for the first-class seats. All we have are twenty pounds in travellers' cheques and a few German marks. Nothing else.'

The train moved off. Ena dismissed my worries. When the ticket inspector came on his rounds, I saw the reason why. She was like a tigress.

'Do you speak English?' she asked.

He did. 'The Istanbul Express was three hours late,' she continued. 'Our connection had already left. I will not tolerate standing in a corridor with my blind husband and three tired and hungry children.'

It was not a plea to be allowed to stay. It was a statement of fact.

'I understand, madam,' he said. 'You may stay in this compartment at no further charge.'

We spent our last few German marks on a meal for the children in the dining car. Comfortable and relaxed, we dozed the rest of the way to Brussels.

At Brussels, however, there was a further setback. To our dismay, the connection to Ostend had left. It was late in the evening. There was no train to Ostend until seven o'clock the following morning. We sat on our suitcases, our heads in our hands.

A Frenchwoman who had been sitting next to us on the train from Munich came to our aid. She spoke to station staff and confirmed our fears. It was true. There was no train until the morning. Ena asked her where we could change our travellers' cheques, so that we could buy some food.

'There is nowhere now,' she said. 'The *bureau de change* is closed until the morning.'

'I see. *Merci, madame.*'

The Frenchwoman rummaged in her handbag.

'Here, take this,' she said, thrusting something into Ena's hand. It was a one hundred franc note.

'But *madame*!'

'The waiting-rooms here are comfortable and the money will buy breakfast for you in the morning.'

Ena asked for her name and address so that we could write and thank her and pay back the one hundred francs. She refused.

'A gift,' she said. 'From me to you.'

Brussels Station, clean and beautiful, was our refuge for the night. The waiting-room had long, soft seats. We lay down and were soon asleep.

Soon after we awoke on the following morning, the station master came to see us. The French lady had paid him to show us where to get breakfast and also to see us safely on to the first Ostend train, he said.

'Nino,' said Ena, as we tucked into breakfast bought with the

Frenchwoman's one hundred franc note. 'There are some very kind people in the world.'

'That one,' I told her, 'was a saint.'

It was a slow journey to Ostend. The commuter train took two hours. On the boat, we changed our remaining travellers' cheques and had a meal. The Channel was rough. Ena and Linda were seasick.

By late evening, we were safely home in Tongham. Ena's sister, who had been caring for our pet terrier, returned her to us. We unpacked our suitcases. All the china souvenirs we had brought as presents from Istanbul were in pieces, doubtless smashed in the Munich postal trolley.

That night, as Ena slept a well-deserved sleep, I lay by her side and marvelled at her strength, determination and fortitude.

How many other women, I asked myself, would have the courage to make that tremendous trek across Europe, to the frontier of Asia, with a blind husband and three young children?

Not many, I answered.

Chapter Thirty-Four

Ena returned to work. Michelle, our *au pair* girl, returned from France but soon had to go home for good and was replaced by Jacqueline, a friend of hers from the same town, Dijon. I returned to the factory and to the hospital. The kindness, compassion, understanding and tolerance shown to me by everyone at Martonair was extraordinary. No matter how frequently I had to desert my post and leave my capstan idle in order to undergo operations or to attend out-patients' clinics, the situation was accepted without grumble or complaint. My job was always kept waiting for me, no matter how many weeks I was away. There was never any question of replacing me with a worker whose attendance would be more regular.

At the hospital, my progress was maintained under the skilled attention of Sir Benjamin Rycroft, who was no longer plain mister since being awarded a well-deserved knighthood in 1960. Whenever he toured the wards on his rounds, chairs were placed in position by the patients' beds for them to sit upon to await his arrival. It was almost like being back in the army. Any minute, I expected the old, familiar sergeant's cry of 'Stand by your beds!' to ring out except, in this case, we had to sit by our beds. Although he was regarded as something approaching a god by both staff and patients, however, he was a kindly and humane man.

One day, Sir Benjamin examined me and expressed surprise and delight at what he had seen.

'That looks more like an eye,' he said, patting me on the shoulder. After so many years of hospital treatment, it was heartening to hear such an optimistic comment.

Sometimes, my treatment seemed endless and, at those times, I often grew angry at the ingratitude and impatience of my fellow patients. I had been in and out of hospitals for years, undergoing operations, receiving treatment at out-patients' clinics and still had months, perhaps years, of treatment to endure before an attempt could be made to restore my sight. Virtually every other patient knew that he would be in hospital for a few days, a few weeks, a few months even, and would then leave the ward with perfect sight. Yet, still, they grumbled. They did not realise how fortunate they were. Patients came. Patients went. I remained.

By the autumn of 1965, a series of ten operations, all designed to build up my left eye in readiness for an operation that might give me my sight, had been completed. I had been a patient at the Queen Victoria for six years.

One morning, as the doctors were carrying out their rounds, I heard a new voice. It was a young man's voice. It sounded sparkling and fresh, full of enthusiasm, and when its owner arrived at my bedside I could smell the tangy perfume of an extremely pleasant after-shave. He introduced himself as Peter Rycroft.*

Because of increasing ill-health, Sir Benjamin Rycroft was finding the growing work-load more than he could conscientiously cope with. His son, Peter, had arrived at the Queen Victoria as clinical assistant in order to aid him. After service in the Royal Army Medical Corps, Peter Rycroft had specialised in ophthalmology. It had soon become apparent that he had inherited much of his father's considerable talent. He had proved himself to be a brilliant young ophthalmic surgeon with a great future ahead of him. He seemed destined to become as famous a name in the medical world as had Sir Benjamin.

I liked Peter Rycroft immediately. He was enthusiastic, dynamic and full of optimism and I felt confident and at ease with him from the start.

In the early months of 1966, he sat at my bedside one day, obviously intent upon a long and serious conversation with me. A friend of his, he said, a famous Italian eye surgeon named Professor Benedetto Strampelli, had developed a new and revolutionary surgical operation for restoring sight. Known as osteo-odontokérato-prosthesis, it was still in its infancy but had already proved to be successful in clinical cases for which nothing else remained to be done surgically. It appeared to be particularly suitable in the treatment of cases in which the cornea was badly altered and in which all or nearly all the corneal tissues had become substituted with a vascularised fibrous tissue, as happened after bad burns, especially chemical burns. In addition, it seemed particularly suitable in cases where previous grafts had failed.

* Peter Vere Rycroft, MA Cambridge 1957; MB, 1956; B. Chir. 1955; MD; DO; Fellow of Royal College of Surgeons; late Ophthalmic House Surgeon, St Bartholomew's Hospital, London; Clinical Assistant, Queen Victoria Hospital, East Grinstead.

My own case history suggested that I was an ideal candidate for the new operation.

Patiently, Peter Rycroft explained to me what the surgical technique involved. Two operations were necessary. The first, which was really a preparatory operation, consisted of covering the eyeball with mucous. The second, which was the main operation, consisted of implanting a specially-constructed sight-giving unit into the eye. The special unit would be built from a section cut from the root of one of my teeth with the living gum still attached. A hole would be drilled into the piece of tooth root and a plastic lens would be cemented into the hole. Finally, the gum tissue would be sewn to the eye. Placed in the exact spot where the eye's pupil previously was, and directly in line with the retina at the back of the eye, the unit should enable me to see again. As previous corneal grafts had failed, my best chance of sight was to have an artificial cornea implanted into my eye. The plastic lens would be the artificial cornea. It was not possible to insert the hard, artificial material of the lens into the eye on its own. It could not be grafted to the surrounding tissue. That was why it was necessary to have the tooth root, which would form a base for the artificial cornea. The gum tissue would take to the surrounding tissue of the eye.

It was obviously a very simple explanation of an extremely complicated surgical operation. To me, it sounded miraculous.

'You mean I would be seeing through my tooth?' I asked in amazement.

'That's exactly what you would be doing,' he said.

'It sounds incredible.'

'Professor Strampelli is a brilliant surgeon. It was sheer genius to think of using a tooth root like that.'

'To think of that, he *must* be a genius.'

Peter Rycroft paused.

'It's still in its experimental stages, of course,' he said. 'Only time will tell whether it lives up to its early promise. But results so far are encouraging. I'd like to try it on you. What do you think? Would you like to take the chance?'

I had no hesitation in agreeing to it.

'Yes,' I told him. 'I'll take the chance.'

'Perhaps you would like to think about it.'

'I don't need to think about it,' I said.

The preliminary operation was carried out in July 1966, by Peter Rycroft and Mr Beare. Instead of covering the eyeball with mucous, as originally planned, they used skin taken from

my arm. The object of the operation was to strengthen the eyeball by placing the skin over it so that it would be sturdy
enough to hold the tooth root and lens they were planning to
implant into it.

For two weeks, the eye was left strictly alone. The dressing
was not changed. Then, I was taken to the operating theatre.

'That's a lovely job we've done,' Peter Rycroft said to Mr
Beare. He was obviously pleased.

'Has your father seen him yet?' Mr Beare asked.

'No, I'll take him tomorrow.'

The following day, Peter Rycroft, full of enthusiasm, proudly
showed his handiwork to his father.

'Why did you not use mucous membrane on his eye?' Sir
Benjamin asked. 'Why have you used skin?'

'Because his eyelids were not good enough for mucous
membrane,' Peter Rycroft explained.

The great man sounded suitably impressed.

I was given a letter to take to my dentist. I would have to
have a few extractions, Peter Rycroft said.

After numerous X-rays had been taken, all my top teeth
were extracted with the exception of my two eye teeth.

'Wonderful, Mr Fettel!' said Peter Rycroft after he had
examined me. 'Your eye is ready for the operation. We'll have
you in for it in four or five weeks' time.'

A bed was booked for October. I was sent home with another
glass shield in my eye. Ena was instructed to sterilise it as she
had done on so many previous occasions.

Two weeks later, despite her considerable experience in
removing and replacing my shield, Ena was faced with what
proved to be an insurmountable problem. No matter how hard
she tried, she was unable to coax the newly-washed shield back
into my eye. For more than half-an-hour, she prised my artificial
lids apart, sliding the shield first under one and then the other,
pulling, pressing, pushing, easing, trying desperately to persuade
it to slip behind the second lid. Perspiring, nervous and terrified
lest she damaged either the eye itself or my man-made lids, she
finally admitted defeat.

The following day, I returned to the Queen Victoria. Peter
Rycroft decided that I must be admitted. I telephoned Ena to
break the news. She sounded worried. She was sad, too. East
Grinstead was some distance from Tongham. Visiting me was a
much more difficult proposition than when I was in hospital at
Guildford and, now, she had the children to care for.

The reason that Ena had been unable to replace the shield into my eye was that, unknown to both of us, my manufactured lids had begun to settle down and, in the process, had become fractionally smaller. Although the shrinkage was imperceptible, it was sufficient to ensure that it became mathematically and physically impossible to reconcile the two dimensions.

Peter Rycroft admitted me in order to keep me under observation. He prescribed eye-drop medication which eased the soreness and, with adjustments to the shield, I was soon able to return home.

One week before my October admission date for the operation that I hoped would restore my sight, Ena became seriously ill with agonising pains in the region of her liver. She was rushed to the Cambridge Military Hospital, where she worked. Doctors diagnosed gall-stones. An operation was necessary.

Immediately, all thoughts of my own operation vanished. It was impossible. There was no way in which both Ena and I could undergo surgery at the same time. Jacqueline, our *au pair*, could not possibly be expected to take on the responsibility of looking after the children alone for what would undoubtedly be several weeks. Besides, I could not go into hospital myself and be unable to visit Ena, to comfort her, to give her strength. I could not abandon her in her hour of need. I phoned Peter Rycroft and postponed my operation.

Ena had her gall-bladder removed. She spent one month in hospital and two months at home recuperating.

Due to Ena's hospital confinement and lengthy period of recuperation, plus a shortage of available beds at the Queen Victoria, it was February 1967, before I was re-admitted. The final, sight-giving operation should, ideally, have been performed three months after the preliminary one in which my eyeball had been covered with skin. Because of my belated admission, the skin had thickened and, because of that, a new unit had to be made, causing a delay of a further week.

At last, the day of the operation arrived. In the anaesthetic room, Peter Rycroft examined me.

'Mr Fettel,' he said. 'Anyone else would shake your hand and say goodbye. But I shall try my best to give you your sight.'

I waited for the anaesthetic and pondered his words. He was saying that nobody else could do anything to help me, nobody else would attempt to perform the operation he was about to carry out. Was he also advising me not to hold out too much hope, not to be too disappointed if it failed?

He turned to the theatre sister.

'This is the centre of the eye where we will put the unit,' he said. 'Would you mark it with some dye?'

My eye was marked with a coloured liquid. After so many years and so many operations, the moment for which I had waited had arrived. The skin grafts were finished. This time, the operation was to make me see. It was for real. I was excited as the anaesthetist's needle sank into my arm and, tingling, I drifted into sleep.

I regained consciousness in the recovery ward. The rest of the day passed in a haze. During the following night, I must have been restless. I awoke to find that, in my sleep, I had pushed all the bandages from my head. Fortunately, the pad protecting my eye was still in place. The night sister replaced the bandages but I was frightened that I had done some damage. That day, I was allowed to lie on my bed in a semi-recumbent position.

After three days in bed, my bandages were removed. I could see nothing. Light, though, was filtering through. Peter Rycroft examined me. He did not ask me if I could see.

'Everything appears to be quite satisfactory,' he told me. 'You can have some dark glasses and you can get up and move around.'

After the doctors had gone, I picked up my cigarettes and matches from the top of my locker and groped my way to the lavatory. I sat on the seat, alone with my thoughts, wondering whether, despite Peter Rycroft's assurance that all was well, the operation had failed. After all, I could not see.

I put a cigarette into my mouth and struck a match. Suddenly, I stopped. I stared in astonishment. In the darkness, even through my dark glasses, I could see something glowing . . . something yellow and flickering . . . a yellow light.

It was the light of the match.

I sat spellbound, staring at the flickering flame creeping up the match-stick. I watched, entranced, until the flame burnt my fingers. I dropped the spent match, hurriedly, and lit another one. The flame was still there. I could still see it. With mounting excitement, I lit a third match . . . and a fourth.

It could not be true. It was my imagination. I could not believe that it was true. Yet, despite my doubts, I knew that it *was* true. It was thrilling! It was terrific! It was the eighth wonder of the world! I could see for the first time in twenty years!

Suddenly, I realised that the sight of the match, the first object that I had seen in all those years, had caused me to abandon all logic, all reason. In the past, there had been so many raised hopes that had been subsequently dashed, so much exciting promise that had not fulfilled its expectations, so much apparent success that had turned to failure, so much delirious joy that had been transformed into despondency. Why should I assume that this time might be different? I made a conscious effort to dampen my excitement, to calm my euphoria. Not believing that such good fortune could possibly last, I returned to the ward and told no one.

To my surprise, when the lights were switched on in the ward that evening, I could see the glow from the electric bulbs. I looked down the ward. I was able to count the number of lights over the beds. The news could not be contained any longer. I called a nurse and told her what I could see.

'You just wait, Mr Fettel,' she said. 'Later on, you'll be able to see properly.'

At the weekend, Ena came to visit me. She bent to put some clean pyjamas into my bedside locker.

'What a nice blue hat you have on, darling,' I told her quietly.

There was a sudden intake of breath.

'Can you really see it?' she asked, equally quietly. Like me, she was trying to treat the matter calmly, not daring to hope that my sight would last.

In truth, I could not see Ena's hat, not sufficiently sharply to see its every detail, at least. What I could see was something blue. I could see other colours, too, and I could make out Ena's shape but my vision was hazy and the objects that I could see were indistinct. As the blue object was sitting on top of Ena's head, however, I was reasonably confident in my assertion that I could see her hat.

The medical term for the form of partial sight that had been restored was 'tunnel vision', so called because, for the patient, it was similar to looking down a tunnel or tube. I was seeing through the plastic lens which was centred on a small hole that punctured the skin covering my eyeball. The range of vision was restricted by the diameter of the hole and of the lens. The eyeball itself was immobile. I could see only objects straight ahead. I could not swivel my eye to focus on objects to the left or to the right, nor could I move my eyeball up or down. It was necessary for me to move my head until the desired objects came into my restricted line of vision.

Nevertheless, after twenty years of blindness, such restrictions were decidedly of little consequence. To be able to see colours, shapes and people moving was incredibly exhilarating. A whole, wonderful new life had opened up for me. Every day my vision was clearing. Every day I went to the lavatory, where it was dark, to strike matches, just to make sure it was really true. Every day, for half-an-hour or more, I sat there, striking match after match, watching them burn right down to my fingers. Dozens of boxes of matches went up in smoke.

Unfortunately, the hundreds of blackened match-sticks that littered the lavatory floor did not go unnoticed by the ward sister. Not for the first time since I had been blinded, I was branded a fire risk.

Two weeks after the operation, the caution with which I had regarded my apparent success appeared to be well justified. I awoke to find that I had severe pains over my left eyebrow. I was taken to the examination room. I had had a haemorrhage behind the unit in the interior chamber of the eye, they said.

My spirits sank. Was success yet again to be snatched from my grasp? Was the precious sight that had been recovered to be taken from me?

The doctors were worried. A pad was placed over my eye and an electric current was passed through it. The treatment continued for five days. The pain cleared. The doctors were guarded. Hopefully, all was well.

Unknown to me, in a letter dated 23 March 1967, Peter Rycroft wrote from the Queen Victoria Hospital's corneoplastic unit to my general practitioner.

'Your patient, Mr C. Fettel, underwent an odontokératoprosthesis on the left eye. Apart from a haemorrhage behind the prosthesis he has subsequently reported improved vision but it is a little early to assess prognosis. At present the tooth graft has been accepted and we shall keep him under close review. Certainly his vision has been improved as a result of this procedure, but whether any useful vision will result is too early to say.'

Six days later Peter Rycroft's father died. Sir Benjamin Rycroft had been the consultant in charge of my case for eight years. Even though, for the last two years, his son had been concerned mainly with my day-to-day welfare and had carried out the operation on my eye, I had remained Sir Benjamin's patient right up to the time of his death. The loss was not only mine, not only the hospital's, but everyone's. He was a wonderful, humane man who had given sight to patients not only from Britain but from all over the world.

The day arrived when I was to be sent home. Peter Rycroft removed my dark glasses and replaced them with a pair of magnifying glasses with thick, untinted lenses.

'I want you to look through these,' he said. 'They should help you to see even better.'

They did not. I could not see anything.

Norman, my cousin Rita's son, came to collect me from the hospital. He was no longer the small boy I had once known and played with and looked after while Rita and John went out for the evening. He was grown up, turned twenty-one, drove a car and brought a girlfriend with him. I climbed unaided into his car.

Despite the fact that I was unable to see when the new pair of glasses had been placed over my eyes, Peter Rycroft knew what he was doing. As Norman drove me home, I sat in the back seat staring out of the window. Gradually, objects began to come into view. Every so often, I could see coloured lights, greens, reds and yellows.

'They're traffic lights,' Norman explained when I asked.

Sometimes, when I had been driven from home by hospital car to the Queen Victoria, I had inquired about the frequent stops.

'It's because we're at traffic lights,' the drivers had always replied.

The term 'traffic lights' meant nothing to me. I had never seen traffic lights. I did not know what they were. Now, at last, I knew. I could *see* them, even though it was indistinctly.

I turned round to look out of the rear window. The more I tried to see, the more I was able to see. I was fascinated by the passing cars and by the brilliant green of the countryside.

The two-hour journey passed quickly. Soon I was home in Tongham. I could see close objects better than those in the distance and, as I stepped from the car, the house was a blur. I had no clear indication of what it looked like but, as I walked up the path and drew closer, I could see the front door and I could tell that it was green.

The door opened. I was in Ena's arms. The three children danced round us excitedly. I cupped Ena's face with my hands and looked . . . and looked. I was trying to see her but everything was misty. I could see her fair hair and her big, blue eyes looking straight into my new one but, although I could tell there was a face in front of me, I could not see it in detail. Nevertheless, it was a wonderful moment, the moment when, for the first time, I saw my wife's face. It was sheer joy! It was heaven!

'Daddy! Daddy! Look at me!' It was Linda's voice. She was obviously thrilled.

'No! I want Daddy to look at me first!' Paul sounded equally excited.

'See me first, Daddy!' shouted Adrian. 'See me!'

The children, pushing and scrambling for me to see them, tugging at my coat, finally prised me away from Ena.

One by one, I took the children's faces into my hands. They were so effervescent that it was impossible for them to keep still. They did not remain stationary long enough for me to fix them directly in line with my lens and, as they jumped about, they kept moving out of the range of my restricted vision. Eventually, Ena managed to calm them. She persuaded them to stand still for almost a whole minute (a not inconsiderable achievement considering their zestful state) and, for the first time, I saw my children's faces. From what I could see, they were every bit as beautiful as I had imagined.

'Can you see me, Daddy?' Linda asked breathlessly.

'Not perfectly, but I can see you,' I told her. 'It will improve.'

'When will it improve, Daddy?' Paul asked.

'We will have to be patient, my darling.'

Ena served coffee in the living-room. Every few seconds, I jumped up from my chair to take her face in my hands and peer at it. My coffee went cold. The children were brimming over with joy. For the first time in their lives, they brought their school books to show me.

'Look what I drew at school, Daddy!' said Paul proudly.

'Look at my sum book, Daddy!' said Adrian.

I willed myself to see them, the drawings and the sums, but I could not see them properly. My vision was still misty . . . but it would improve.

There were tears in Norman's eyes when he left for home, said Ena.

Peter Rycroft had given Ena instructions on how to clean my eye each day and gently polish the precious lens that enabled me to see. She was nervous at first but she soon acquired the necessary confidence and expertise.

The following day, I walked unaided to the village shops. It was marvellous to be able to walk without a guide. Instead of feeling my money to distinguish between the different notes, the different coins, I was able to look at it to pay for the groceries and meat that Ena had asked me to buy.

The days passed without any noticeable change in my vision. Then, at Easter, there occurred a sudden and dramatic improvement.

Ena was in bed, having an afternoon rest. I was idly staring out of the window. Suddenly, I saw something. It became clearly distinguishable as a leg . . . a child's leg. More legs flashed into view . . . then colours . . . blues, reds and yellows. I could see children running past the window.

'Ena! Ena!' I shouted. 'I can see colours!'

She leapt out of bed and raced downstairs.

'What is it, darling? What can you see?'

'Colours! And the children playing!'

'Have another look! What else can you see?'

'The green grass! The pavement!'

Ena hugged me.

'Oh, darling! I'm so pleased for you!'

I went outside so that I would have a better view.

'I'm going to buy a ball!' I suddenly decided. 'We'll have a game of football!'

It was a brown ball, a small one, but big enough for me to see it. My sons and I went into the garden and played at shooting-in. I was the goalkeeper. Paul and Adrian tried to score. Even with my limited vision, I was able to save quite a few shots.

After a while, Adrian ran out of the garden and returned with some of his friends.

'Come and see,' I heard him saying. 'My Daddy is playing football with us!'

Each day, as soon as the newspapers were delivered, I rushed to the door to take them from the letter-box. Eagerly, I read the biggest of the headlines. I returned home one day to find a dozen reporters and photographers swarming outside the house. The newspapers had heard that I had regained partial sight after twenty years and stories appeared in print throughout the world.

Silently, I blessed Peter Rycroft and his team of doctors and nurses for making it all possible, for fulfilling my dream . . . except that it wasn't a dream. It was true! I was awake . . . and I could see!

I had left hospital with an appointment to return for a check-up in one month's time. The journey from Tongham to East Grinstead was a revelation. It was like seeing a whole new world for the first time. To me, England *was* a new world . . . a new, exciting world that I had never seen before. Not only could I see the traffic lights (and much more plainly this time) but also the green of the trees and of the fields, the multitude of traffic signs, the variously-coloured cars on the roads, the women pedestrians carrying handbags.

My vision was not perfect. I could not recognise everything. Nevertheless, I could see the colours and they were beautiful.

It was April. It was spring. It was a lovely, sunny day. It was happiness. It was bliss.

Peter Rycroft was operating. I was shown into the consulting room to see Mr Werb.

'How many fingers am I holding up?' he asked.

'Two.'

'How many now?'

'Four.'

The quiet of the consulting room was shattered by an excited babble of voices. I was right both times. They were delighted. Until that moment, the same specialists had been quiet and reserved, decidedly uncommunicative, about the prospects of success. They had shown no excitement, expressed no great hopes. Now, however, they were positively ecstatic.

They called in the hospital dental surgeon who had cut from my upper jaw the eye tooth from which the section had been taken for grafting into my eye.

'How wonderful!' he exclaimed, patting me on the back. 'When you had that haemorrhage, we thought it was the end!'

Another appointment was made for me to return in a month's time.

The month passed in a haze of pleasure. It was thrilling being able to see Ena every day.

'You're smoking a cigarette!' I said in surprise one evening after dinner.

She looked up, startled, and gazed round guiltily as if searching for somewhere to put it.

'I shall have to be careful how many I smoke now that you can see me,' she said with a thin smile.

'Come and play football with us, Daddy!' the boys urged.

I did not need to be asked twice. No matter how tired I was, no matter how I longed to sit down, I was never too tired to play with my children, not now that I could see them, not now that I could see the football. Tina, the family mongrel, joined in, growling at the ball, pushing it with her paws, trying to pick it up in her mouth. It was the first time that I had seen Tina, too.

In the evenings, I relaxed in front of the television. Even though my vision was still misty, I could see the programmes. I saw Engelbert Humperdinck, the pop singer, for the first time. I could follow the films and plays when there was no dialogue without having to ask Ena what was happening.

In May, I returned to the Queen Victoria. Peter Rycroft examined me. He sounded happy but reserved. Then he examined the inner eye.

'I can see some fibrous tissue,' he said to his secretary.

He did not elaborate. He would write to me, he said, with the date of an appointment to visit an optician in London to obtain another pair of spectacles.

Chapter Thirty-Five

Ena's godmother had died and had left her a silver teapot. Later that month, we travelled to Oxford to collect it from one of the trustees of the will.

'This is from your godmother,' said the trustee reverently, as she handed the teapot to Ena. It was hanging in a green cloth bag, looking rather like the head of John the Baptist. 'Be very careful when you open it. It's a Queen Anne.'

Outside, Ena pulled the draw-string of the bag and gingerly extracted the teapot. She examined it carefully. It had been damaged but expertly mended and the damage was scarcely noticeable.

'A Queen Anne!' said Ena excitedly. 'Darling, we're in the money, even if it *is* damaged!'

A Queen Anne silver teapot would be decidedly out of place in our council house in Tongham and, as our finances were low once more because of my renewed quest for sight and consequent loss of wages, it seemed only sensible that we should sell it.

The same afternoon, Ena went into Aldershot and took it to a jewellery shop. She was offered eighty-five pounds for it. She declined.

'If it's worth eighty-five pounds to someone in Aldershot, think how much we could get from one of the big jewellers in London!' she said.

The following day, we went into Sotheby's, the world-famous auctioneers in New Bond Street, in the West End of London. They examined the teapot thoroughly.

'I'm sorry, madam, it isn't Queen Anne,' said one of their experts. 'It's George the Third. Unfortunately, it appears to have been dropped and damaged. In the circumstances, it would not be worth more than thirty pounds.'

Several jewellery shops to which we offered to sell Ena's teapot expressed no interest. Then, further along New Bond Street, we entered Asprey's, a famous, fashionable and expensive firm of goldsmiths, silversmiths and jewellers, which numbered the Queen among its customers. The teapot was in a brown-paper carrier-bag.

'Try and look dignified,' Ena whispered to me. 'As if we're going to buy something, not sell something.'

A haughty-looking assistant inspected us across the shop floor as we entered. Presumably deciding that appearances could be deceptive and that we were a pair of rich but eccentric buyers, he unrolled a length of green baize and laid it expectantly on a glass-topped showcase.

'Good morning, madam,' he said in a condescending voice. 'May I help you?'

Ena nonchalantly drew the green cloth bag from the crumpled carrier-bag, removed the teapot and placed it proudly on the green baize top.

'How much will you pay for this?' she asked innocently.

The assistant's face fell.

'I'm sorry, madam,' he said in a superior voice. 'We do not buy second-hand silver here.'

He picked up the teapot by the handle, holding it between finger and thumb as if not wishing to be contaminated by such an unsavoury object and handed it to Ena. He rolled up his green baize.

We turned to leave, crestfallen and shamefaced.

'Come on, darling,' Ena whispered. 'Let's walk out with dignity.'

We lifted up our heads and tried to move majestically to the door but I suspected that, in reality, we were creeping out.

The only money we had between us amounted to thirty shillings, which proved that appearances are deceptive only sometimes. We could not afford a proper lunch.

'Never mind,' said Ena. 'We can afford a cup of coffee and a bun, if nothing else.'

Although we had approached numerous establishments without success in an attempt to sell the teapot, Ena was determined not to give up.

'We'll try some more,' she said. 'There are plenty of jewellers in London.'

'I feel as if we've tried them all already,' I told her.

'Hancocks is near here,' she said. 'We'll go there next.'

On the way, I glanced towards the windows of the shops we were passing.

'I can see you, darling!' I told her, surprised. 'I can see your reflection in the windows!'

I stopped to look.

'Come on,' Ena said, trying to pull me away.

'No, darling, I want to see you in the window.'

Ena sounded slightly agitated.

'Heads are turning, Nino,' she whispered. 'People are looking round to see what you're doing.'

We walked along the road.

'I can see four stalks, darling!' I said excitedly, peering just in front of us.

'They're not stalks,' Ena said. 'They're girls' legs!'

'They're long legs, darling!'

'They're wearing mini-skirts. That's why their legs look long.'

I had never seen a mini-skirt, much less a young girl wearing one. The last time I had seen girls' legs, skirts had been down below the knee, not up round their bottoms. The legs seemed incredibly long and thin and, as the two girls disappeared from view, I was delighted to discover that there seemed to be no shortage of girls in mini-skirts.

'Nino!' said Ena, clearly embarrassed. 'You can't go around with your head down like that, staring at the girls' legs. People are looking. You'll get yourself arrested!'

I did not care. It was just like being a child all over again, seeing sights I had never seen before, not only the long, shapely legs of English girls but the bustle of London, the double-decker buses, the cars, the crowds hurrying along the pavements and in the West End stores.

At Hancocks, also jewellers to royalty, the rich and the famous, in Burlington Gardens, our reception was much more welcoming than the one we had received at Asprey's.

Ena plonked her battered carrier-bag on top of the show-case.

'I've been offered eighty-five pounds for this George the Third teapot and I think it's on the low side,' she told the assistant. 'How much will you offer me for it?'

'Let me take it to my directors, madam. They will be able to make you an offer.'

While we were waiting for the directors to examine the teapot and consider what offer to make, an American tourist walked in with a small girl, obviously his daughter. They looked around.

'What would you like, honey?' he asked eventually.

'That big silver gee-gee,' said the precocious child.

'How much?' her father asked, pointing to the beautiful, solid-silver horse.

'Six hundred pounds, sir,' said the assistant.

'Wrap it up!' ordered the indulgent father.

Ena and I looked at each other. After spending ten shillings on our lunch-time snack, we had only one pound left between us, scarcely enough for the fares home.

'How about a diamond bracelet, darling?' I joked.

After half-an-hour, the assistant returned with his directors' verdict.

'I'm afraid it's not George the Third, madam,' he said sadly. 'It's George the Fourth. In addition, it has been damaged and mended with lead on the inside, instead of with silver. But we can offer you fifty pounds for it.'

The trustee of the will had assured us that our teapot was Queen Anne. Sotheby's had decided that it was George III. Now Hancocks had decided that it was George IV.

'Yes, please!' said Ena, before he could change his mind. 'We'll take it.'

We walked from the shop calmly and sedately. Outside, we danced a jig on the pavement. Ena waved the cheque in the air.

'Fifty pounds!' I chortled. 'We're rich, darling!'

'Let's go and cash it quickly,' said Ena. 'Before they decide it's George the Fifth!'

The bank telephoned Hancocks to ensure that it was in order for them to pay cash before the cheque had passed through an account. It was. Ten crisp, five-pound notes were counted into Ena's hand. She put the notes into my own hand so that I could feel them and look at them. We had never held so much money in our hands.

'Let's go and have a good nosh!' I said.

Ena was hungry and readily agreed. We walked to a pleasant restaurant and blew three pounds on a mouth-watering meal. Then we went shopping and bought gifts for the children, a doll for Linda and football boots for the boys. They were the first presents we had ever bought for the children with cash. We had never had the money to do so. Always, previously, the children's toys had been bought through Christmas clubs, into which we had paid small amounts of money each week to spread the cost over the whole year.

It was one of the happiest days of our lives. I had seen, *really* seen, in a big city for the first time in twenty years. We had more money than we had ever had before. And we had gifts for the children.

Soon afterwards, Ena and I visited New Bond Street again, this time for a consultation with an optician to be tested for new glasses which, according to Peter Rycroft, would enable me to see even better.

I was taken to a darkened room. Ena sat on a chair beside me. Lens after lens was slipped into the special spectacle frame fitted over my eyes. I could not see properly with any of them. The numbers and letters, even the big ones, on the illuminated eye-test chart in front of me were decidedly unclear.

Why could I not see them? Had Ena not cleaned my lens properly that morning? My sight on some days, I knew, was better than on others. It was a fact that did not perturb me as, usually, when Ena gently polished my little window, my vision improved. On this day, though, when Ena polished the lens while the optician patiently waited, there was no improvement.

I tried desperately to read the letters and figures but, when the test was finished half-an-hour later, all that I had been able to read were a large letter A and a smaller letter O, both of them at the top of the chart.

'Maybe it's just one of your bad days, darling,' Ena said as we left the premises. I knew that she was trying to reassure me but I was not convinced.

I was even less convinced when, in July, Peter Rycroft informed me that a piece of skin was coming adrift from round the sight-giving unit. Ena was instructed to keep pushing it back with cotton wool on the end of an eye-stick until I could be admitted for a two-day stay while it was trimmed under anaesthetic. At the end of two days, I was discharged. The skin had not been removed. Nothing had been done.

With each day that passed, I was seeing less and less. My sight was beginning to dim. By August, everything I looked at had become distorted. I could still play football, although sometimes I missed the ball completely.

'Daddy!' said Paul to me one day when I swung my foot at the ball and failed to connect. 'You're not concentrating!'

The brown ball that we had always used was now scarcely visible to me. I sent Paul to buy a white one, which I could see much better.

A few days later, however, when the white ball was accidentally lost, the boys brought out the brown one again. I could not see it at all.

'Daddy!' they complained. 'You're missing the ball again!'

The boys became shadows moving on a green background.

I stumbled indoors and asked Ena to clean my lens again.

'Don't let the children know, darling,' she urged. 'It will only worry them.'

Even my new telescopic lens, like opera glasses with only one eye-piece, did not seem to help when I held it to my eye that evening. The Beverley Sisters were on television, in *Sunday Night at the London Palladium*. They appeared on the screen only as a blur.

'Perhaps it's just one of your bad periods,' Ena said. 'Perhaps tomorrow, darling, everything will be all right.'

I could tell that she was desperately worried.

That night, I woke up suddenly with a sharp pain in my left eye. On the following morning, everything was even more hazy. Ena cleaned and polished the tiny lens. There was no improvement. Soon I could see nothing.

After six months of sight, I was blind once more.

Peter Rycroft was no longer on the staff of the Queen Victoria Hospital. I was seen by Mr Werb and a new consultant. I was not to worry, they said. They would be able to clear up the problem.

Five weeks later, however, the sight-giving unit was ejected from my eye. It was left hanging on my cheek like a loose tooth, still attached to my eye as if on a thread. For weeks, the eye had been gradually rejecting the unit. New scar tissue had been forming. Finally, the scar tissue had pushed out the tooth root and the lens. In another operation at the Queen Victoria, scar tissue was removed. So was the vital unit that had given me my sight.

At the beginning of November 1967, I received a letter from Peter Rycroft inviting me to attend his new consulting rooms (which he had taken over from his father) in Harley Street, centre of London's medical world, where the country's leading – and most expensive – specialists held their consultations with rich, private patients.

His examination was thorough. He seemed hopeful.

'My advice, Mr Fettel, is that you should continue to try for your sight. I know what went wrong with the operation and I would like to perform it again. It is up to you whether you stay with me or go back to East Grinstead and ask them to try again. But I want you to know that I am prepared to do it again.'

'You gave me my sight,' I told him. 'I don't want to change surgeons.'

'Good! Come and see me again on December the twelfth.'

At our next meeting, Peter Rycroft explained that he no longer had a hospital where he could perform his operations but that he was opening a new eye clinic. He would operate on me there in less than two months' time, in the early part of February 1968.

'This time I hope we shall succeed,' he said.

He was talking excitedly. Afterwards, when I had recovered from the operation, he would fit a cosmetic contact lens which would look like an eye and would improve my appearance.

Christmas and New Year were happy, family occasions. February, and my sight-giving operation, was drawing closer. Next year, perhaps, I would *see* my children's faces as they opened their presents on Christmas morning, *see* the fairy lights winking on the green, tinsel-draped fir tree, *see* the mouth-watering, golden-brown turkey being lifted from the oven and placed, steaming, on the table.

One week into the New Year, I was busy operating my capstan at work when a workmate brought a copy of that day's London *Evening Standard* to me. It was a Monday. Another week was just beginning . . . another week nearer to the vital surgery that could make me see . . . surgery that was now less than a month away.

'Here, Kosta!' he said. 'Isn't this the bloke who did your eye?'

He read aloud a news item from the newspaper. The headline was, *Surgeon in mystery M4 death crash*.

'Mystery surrounds a fatal accident on the M4 motorway at Datchett on Saturday night,' he read on. 'The body of eye surgeon Mr Peter Vere Rycroft, 39, of The Mead, Dorney Reach, Taplow, was found in a bus stop lay-by half-a-mile from the scene of the accident.'

Peter Rycroft, the only man in Britain who, as far as I was aware, was performing the miracle operation that could give me my sight, was dead.

Chapter Thirty-Six

The accident had happened in a heavy snowstorm. Peter Rycroft had been killed instantly. One of his three young sons had been seriously injured.

I was totally demoralised. Not only had the medical world lost a brilliant young surgeon, I had lost a good friend . . . a friend who had shown more interest in, and enthusiasm for, my case than any other doctor before him. To him, I was not just a number . . . not just a patient even. I was a person. I had liked him long before I had been able to see him. The interest, the devotion, the enthusiasm, the humanity, the youthfulness, the *joie-de-vivre*, had all been there in his voice. His special qualities had helped not only me but countless others. With me, however, he had held a special place. He was the man who had given me my sight. His death, only four weeks before the planned repeat operation that could make me see again, was a shattering blow.

'It's the end,' I told Ena disconsolately. 'It's finished.'

Ena wrote to Peter Rycroft's widow expressing our sympathy, sorrow and gratitude for what he had done for me. Margaret Rycroft, in reply, wrote that she knew of my case. At Christmas, only two weeks before her husband's death, they had both visited Professor Strampelli in Rome. The two men had discussed my case and her husband had asked why the unit had been rejected by my eye. The professor had given an explanation and, armed with the new knowledge, her husband had been excitedly awaiting a second attempt to give me my sight.

'Go to see Strampelli,' she urged me.

It was a lovely dream. To travel to Rome, however, to have a consultation with the great professor, to undergo intricate surgical operations, cost money. I had none.

Spring arrived. The sun's rays grew warm. The daffodils in the garden opened up their tightly-closed buds. The sweet, fresh smell of the newly-mown grass filled the air. My depression lifted. My spirits revived.

Rome was out of the question. East Grinstead was possible. I decided to return to the Queen Victoria Hospital. The verdict, however, was not encouraging. Nothing could be done to my eye for the moment, they said. In the future, perhaps . . . in two or three years' time maybe . . . something might be done. In the meantime, they would continue to see me. Would I return for a further consultation in six months?

The faint hopes that were held out of improved techniques possibly increasing my chances of sight in the future were, I felt, intended simply to keep up my spirits. In reality, I was convinced, my chance of seeing again had gone with Peter Rycroft's death.

I was right, too. Although I was unaware of the fact at the time, on 10 July 1968, a letter was sent from the Queen Victoria's corneo-plastic unit to my general practitioner.

'I regret to report that we have had no success in dividing the skin-like membrane that covered this patient's left cornea,' it said. 'The condition does appear hopeless at the moment, but we will see him from time to time in case there are any new developments in this field.'

Six months later, on my return, the verdict was no more hopeful. If anything, it was even more pessimistic. Nothing could be done. My eye was hard, like cement, covered in scar tissue. They were unable to see the cornea at all. Would I come back in a year's time?

My heart sank. My hopes vanished completely. At first, I had been told to come back in six months. Now it was a year. In addition, nobody seemed to want to know me. Two years before, when I had been able to see, I had been shown off round the hospital like a prize exhibit. People had shaken me by the hand and clapped me on the back. Now, now that I could no longer see, I was almost ignored.

'Excuse me!' I said impulsively. 'Can I say something?'

'Certainly.'

'Before Mr Rycroft died, he told me he wanted to do the operation again.'

There was a sudden silence. The atmosphere became decidedly tense. Yes, yes, they knew all about that, they told me testily. I could rest assured, however, that nothing could be done for my eye. If I was not happy with that verdict, I was perfectly free to consult whoever I wanted.

It was clear that another operation would not be performed at the Queen Victoria. In addition, everything had changed. The entire atmosphere was different. Sir Archibald McIndoe . . . Sir Benjamin Rycroft . . . Peter Rycroft . . . they were all dead. The brilliant nursing sister who had been such an important member of the specialist eye team had resigned. The team of doctors and nurses in whom I had had so much confidence and trust were no more. Different eye specialists, different medical specialists of any kind, held different views, different opinions. That I knew. Peter Rycroft had wanted to operate. The present team did not. Undoubtedly, the new specialists were just as clever, just as brilliant, just as technically advanced, as the former ones had been. Undoubtedly, they were acting in what they were convinced were my best interests. Undoubtedly, their sincere and considered opinion was that the operation that Peter Rycroft had planned would not succeed, that it was still too much of an experimental operation, that its success-rate had still to be proved, that there were too many difficulties to be faced without the means of overcoming them and that, even though it had restored sight in some cases, in my own it was doomed to failure.

That, though, was no consolation to me. I was in the dark again . . . and I did not like it. Although I had accepted my blindness, I was unable to rest as long as the faint glimmer of hope that Peter Rycroft had given me was still there. Until that hope was finally extinguished, I was willing and anxious to take any chance that remained open to me.

In addition, I was stung by the refusal of the Queen Victoria's surgeons to operate . . . and by the blunt invitation to go elsewhere if I were not satisfied.

My pride was hurt. Margaret Rycroft's words sprang into my mind. I lost my temper.

'Right!' I declared heatedly. 'I will go to see Professor Strampelli!'

Chapter Thirty-Seven

It was an idle boast. I had no money to visit Professor Strampelli. In my moment of annoyance, though, determined to show them that I was not defeated by their refusal to operate, I had made my empty gesture of defiance.

The rest of 1969 passed. The following year came and went. I continued in my job as a capstan operator. Ena obtained a new post at her hospital, as sister in charge of the out-patients' department, which meant regular hours and no weekend working. The children were growing up. There was no longer the need for an *au pair* girl. It was a happy home. Only the death of Tina the dog, from natural causes at the age of fifteen, caused any sadness. We had a lot for which to thank God.

In the evenings and at weekends, I listened to the radio and television and read my braille books. I had accepted my blindness and had become an accomplished braille reader. Always at the back of my mind, however, was the name of the famous Italian eye surgeon, Professor Strampelli. Until I had consulted him, I could not be content. Until I knew his verdict, even though it might be unfavourable, I could not be satisfied. I needed to know if anything could be done to restore my sight. Only the knowledge that nothing could be done for me, that nobody in the world could help me, that no lingering hopes could be retained . . . only that knowledge could resign me to spending the rest of my life as a blind man. Only then could I be really happy at spending the rest of my life in the dark.

For more than two years after making my angry declaration that I would go to see Professor Strampelli, I received no treatment for my eyes. The letter addressed to the Italian surgeon that I had been given before leaving the Queen Victoria remained sealed in a drawer at home. I had had no money then for a trip to Rome. I had no money now. The dream remained as far away as ever.

Then, one day in April 1971, Ena returned home from work clutching a copy of a women's magazine. She was clearly excited. Inside was a special offer of cheap autumn and winter holidays for 'hard-working housewives' in Paris, Switzerland and Rome. Four days in Rome in October, including return air fares and hotel accommodation, cost thirty-three pounds.

'We're going!' she announced decisively.

'What are you talking about?' I said irritably. 'We haven't two beans to rub together.'

'We're going!' she repeated.

'We can't afford a holiday!'

'But don't you see, darling? It wouldn't just be a holiday. It's your big chance to see Strampelli while we're there!'

Strampelli! For the moment, I had forgotten about my blindness, about my hopes of obtaining a once-and-for-all verdict on the chance of regaining my sight.

'Ah!' I said, impressed. 'I see what you mean now!'

It was a good idea. The special four-day trip cost little more than a third of the normal scheduled return air fare between London and Rome – and there was hotel accommodation included in the bargain. It seemed too good an opportunity to miss but, although I was desperately keen to consult Strampelli, I was anxious about our lack of money.

'Let's go and see him just for fun!' Ena urged, sensing my doubts. 'He's a great surgeon. Let's go just to see if he can do anything for you.'

I quickly succumbed to her persuasions. As Linda was flying to Istanbul on a students' charter flight and Paul was spending part of the summer at a Boy Scouts' camp, Adrian was the only one without a holiday planned. We decided to take him with us. Ena booked the same day. The cost of ninety-nine pounds for three of us, including accommodation, was only seventeen pounds more than a day return trip for one person by scheduled airliner.

Ena wrote to Professor Strampelli, giving him details of my case history, telling him of Peter Rycroft's plans and asking him to see me during the four days in October that we would be in Rome.

Two months passed. There was no reply. Our hopes began to fade. Finally, our hopes had gone completely.

'Let's face it, darling,' I told Ena. 'He's not going to see us. But never mind. We'll have a nice holiday, anyway.'

A week later, a letter arrived from Rome. In Italian, it said: 'Please report to the Istituto di Cura "Villa Benedetta" on Wednesday, 27 October, 1971, at 1500 hours.'

It had worked! Ena's opportunism had paid off! I was going to see Strampelli!

At last, I had obtained the chance for which I had been waiting. Strampelli was a genius, a brilliant eye surgeon, the pioneer of the particular surgical technique that provided the only possible chance of my sight being restored. If the great Strampelli decided that nothing could be done for me, then I would be satisfied.

The weeks passed slowly. Linda went to stay with my relatives in Istanbul. Paul went camping. Ena and I worked feverishly, earning the money that was needed for the trip. Each day that passed was one day nearer to my appointment with Strampelli but, still, October seemed an age away.

Then, suddenly, the day of our departure arrived. It was Monday, 25 October 1971. I was out of bed by five o'clock. We kissed Linda and Paul goodbye. A friend from the village was moving into the house to look after them.

Because of my blindness, we were allowed to board the BAC 111 charter jet at Gatwick Airport ahead of the other passengers. Ena buried her head in my shoulder as the aircraft hurtled down the runway. Adrian, in the window seat, was thoroughly enjoying it. I had had three gin-and-tonics before boarding the plane and I was past caring.

The aircraft's nose lifted off the tarmac. It powered its way through the clouds and into the sky.

'Strampelli, here we come!' I shouted, my voice scarcely audible above the engine noise.

An Italian courier from the travel company was waiting to greet our party in the airport reception lounge. She introduced herself as Geanna. We answered our names to Geanna's roll-call. Our luggage was loaded on to a waiting coach. We drove for an hour through the warm Roman evening to the Hotel Villa Radieuse. On the way, Geanna, on the coach intercom, pointed out places of interest and provided details of hotel meal times and free coach tours that had been arranged.

The Hotel Villa Radieuse was beautiful, Ena said. Our bedroom was almost like a large apartment and it had a balcony, too.

On the following morning, we inquired where we would find the Villa Benedetta, and the *studio* of the famous Professor Strampelli. Rome, as we had seen already, was a big city. The clinic and the consulting rooms could have been miles away. They weren't. They were fifty yards down the road, opposite each other.

After breakfast, we went on one of the free sight-seeing tours, to the Vatican Museum and St Peter's. Ena described the beautiful sculptures and paintings. In St Peter's, we listened to the guide describing *Pieta,* Michelangelo's famous marble group of exquisite beauty. The beauty of St Peter's Basilica, however, defied description. Ena found it so breathtaking that it was literally indescribable. Fortunately, even though I was unable to see the beauty, I had no need of anyone to describe the peace and tranquillity of the place to me. I could *feel* it for myself. Ena led me to the memorial to Pope John, later to become Saint John, in whom I had a special interest. Years before, when I was a boy in Istanbul and he was a cardinal and Apostolic Delegate from Rome to all the Middle East, he had blessed me during my confirmation. It was an event that had stayed in my mind as I had grown into manhood and I had been delighted when my favourite cardinal had become the Holy Father. At the Sistine Chapel, Ena described Michelangelo's famous murals. They sounded fantastic. By the time we returned to the hotel, we were all exhausted.

Wednesday dawned. It was the day of decision, the day when I would receive the verdict on my eyes from probably the one man in the world with any hope of giving me my sight, the genius who had pioneered the miraculous surgery known as osteoodonto-kératoprosthesis. Yes, it was possible that I could see again. No, it was impossible.

We breakfasted on coffee and rolls, looked in the shops and then took a taxi to the Villa Benedetta. We wanted to inquire what fee the professor charged for an initial consultation.

'Oh, darling, the clinic grounds are beautiful!' Ena exclaimed. 'There are palm trees and lots of lovely shrubs.'

The clinic was run by the Order of the Sisters of St John the Baptist. We walked up steps of white marble. We reached the foyer. Nuns in black habits greeted us. Nurses in smart white-and-blue uniforms went about their business. We were directed to a reception desk manned by one of the nuns. In Italian, I told her my name and my business.

'*Ah, Signor Fettel! Si, si!*'

I asked for details of Professor Strampelli's fee.

'*Trenta cinque mila lire.*'

Ena squeezed my arm.

'How much? How much?'

'Thirty-five thousand liras,' I told her. 'That's about twenty-three pounds.'

It was a shock. We had expected the consultation fee to be about five pounds . . . ten pounds at the most.

'What shall we do?' Ena wailed as we wandered out into the street. 'We only have ten pounds to spare.'

'By the time we've paid the fee, we'll only have twenty pounds left for all our other expenses,' I calculated. 'And we still have two days to go.'

Ena was not beaten.

'We'll go to the British consulate,' she said. 'They'll help out if it's very urgent!'

Ena telephoned from the hotel. She spoke to the consul.

'Come and see me,' he said.

We told him the full story. Ena asked him if he would cash a cheque for fifteen pounds. He seemed reluctant. Finally, he agreed.

'We don't do this for everyone, Mr Fettel,' he said. 'But it seems a rather unusual story so I will cash your wife's cheque.'

An official went away with Ena's hurriedly-scribbled cheque and returned with fifteen pounds' worth of liras.

'You've saved us from a difficult situation,' I told him. 'Thank you.'

'Don't tell anyone about this . . . please,' he said. 'Otherwise we shall be flooded out with poverty-stricken tourists.'

After lunch at the hotel, I strolled with Ena and Adrian along the Via Aurelia and turned left into the Circonvallazione Cornelia. The nun at the clinic reception desk directed us to the waiting-room. I sank into a soft, plush seat. I was nervous.

'Can I have a cigarette, darling?'

'No,' said Ena. 'Sorry. There's a notice that says *Vietato fumare*.'

I longed for a cigarette even more. Ena described to me the other people in the waiting-room. From their conversation, I could tell that they were of many different nationalities.

'There are crucifixes and religious pictures all over the clinic, darling,' Ena said. 'We're sitting right underneath a beautiful wooden crucifix. I wonder if it's a good omen?'

'Do me a favour, darling,' I said. 'When we first go into the consulting room, tell me how many of them there are.'

I had always found it a help to know how many people were present in a room. Knowing the numbers seemed to put me more at ease. It assisted me to visualise the scene, to know where various people were sitting or standing, to differentiate between the voices.

Half-an-hour passed. I tapped my foot impatiently. An hour went by. Every so often a name was called. One of the patients

in the waiting-room shuffled out. Nuns bustled busily into and
out of the room. The packet of cigarettes was burning a hole in
my pocket.

'Signor Fettel!'

I jumped to my feet as though I had been given an electric
shock. I straightened my jacket and tie. I cleared my throat and
asked if Adrian could come into the consultation with Ena and
me.

'*Si, si, signor!*'

We were led into the consulting room.

'Four people!' Ena whispered quickly.

A firm hand gripped mine in a friendly handshake. My hand
was taken into both of his.

'Please come in,' Professor Strampelli said in English. 'I have
heard a lot about you. *S'accomodi.*'

He guided me to the examination chair. I sat down as requested. His greeting was warm. His voice was deep. It sounded
kind but tired. I could tell from the fact that it came from high
up that he was tall, certainly taller than I. He shook hands with
Ena and Adrian and then sat opposite me. I handed him the
letter that I had been given for him on my last visit to the Queen
Victoria Hospital almost three years before. He read it.

'They do not think anything can be done for you,' he said.

He began to examine my eyes. I was shaking with nerves. I
was approaching one of the most important moments of my
life. Would he, too, like the eye specialists in England, conclude
that I was a hopeless case? Or would he be able to help me?

He asked a number of questions about my case. His English
was by no means perfect, particularly when he was trying to
question me about medical symptoms. He was searching for
technical words that he was not used to expressing in English
and I had difficulty in understanding him.

'*Io parlo Italiano,*' I told him.

'*Oh, bene, bene!*' he exclaimed.

The conversation continued in a mixture of Italian and
English.

'Take off your dark glasses,' he said finally. I felt a hand on
my shoulder. I thought it was Ena. I handed her my glasses.

'*Grazie!*' said the voice of one of the nuns.

Professor Strampelli began to press my left eye. Then he
explained that he would shine three coloured lights into my eye.
He wanted me to see if I could identify the colours.

'Do you see the colour of that light?' he asked.

'Yes. White.'

'And that?'

'Green.'

'Bene! And what is that?'

'Red.'

'Bene, bene! Are you able to see this shape?'

He shone a special light into my eye, Ena told me later.

'It looks like a tree.'

'Bene. I'm going to press your eye. Tell me if you see a green sparkle near your nose. Do you see it?'

'No. Nothing.'

He sounded disappointed. He pressed harder.

'Do you see anything now?'

'No. Nothing.'

He was silent for a moment.

'I will ask your wife to explain to you exactly what I want you to do,' he said.

He demonstrated on Ena, pressing her eyeball until she saw the sparkle near her nose.

'Nino,' she said. 'He wants to know if you can see anything near your nose. Come on! I'm willing you to give the right answers!'

'I understand that,' I told her. 'But I don't see anything.'

Professor Strampelli pressed again. Suddenly, I saw little blue-green discs flashing by my nose. They lasted for less than a second. Then they were gone.

'Lo vedo! Lo vedo!' I shouted. 'I see it! I see it!'

He sat back in his chair. He smacked his hands on his thighs.

'Bene, bene, bene!' he cried.

He asked me to identify the colours and the shape again. He pressed my eye once more.

'When did you last see?' he asked.

'Four years ago.'

'How long did your sight last?'

'Five months. Nearly six.'

'Peter Rycroft was my great friend. He came to spend Christmas with us in Italy.'

'I know,' I said.

His examination was thorough. He seemed pleased with some tests, disappointed with others. The longer his examination continued, however, the happier he sounded. His voice was smiling.

Finally he leaned back in his chair.

'I can make you see,' he said.

It was not the answer that I had expected. My hopes had not been high. His words came as a considerable shock. My initial delight at his verdict was quickly subdued, however, when he added a cautious proviso.

'But no tooth, no operation,' he said. 'Do you have your own teeth in your mouth? Without teeth I can do nothing.'

'I have my bottom ones,' I told him.

I removed my top dentures. He examined my teeth. He asked the sister to call another professor.

'He is the dental surgeon who takes the X-rays,' he explained.

Professor Strampelli did not seem impressed by my available teeth. At East Grinstead, all my top teeth had been removed with the exception of my two eye teeth. One of those had been used in the operation that had restored partial sight. All that was now left at the top was the solitary eye tooth. Although I had all my bottom teeth, they were not in first-class condition.

My one remaining eye tooth had been filled and was not ideal, Professor Strampelli explained. Nor were my bottom ones. He sounded disappointed. His voice took on a lower tone. It seemed that there was no suitable tooth.

'No tooth, no operation,' he repeated.

He looked into my mouth again. Suddenly, his voice seemed brighter. There was one tooth at the bottom that interested him, he said. Yes, that one was a distinct possibility.

At the Queen Victoria, when they had extracted my top teeth, they had wanted to remove all my bottom ones, too. I had declined. I had told them that I would keep my bottom teeth and the last remaining eye tooth at the top . . . just in case they might come in useful some time. It had proved an extraordinarily fortunate decision.

If none of the roots were suitable he would not be prepared to attempt the operation, he said, but he would send me to have X-rays taken of my jaw so that he could see the roots for himself.

My face fell. I said nothing. It was already costing twenty-three pounds just for a consultation with the professor. To have X-rays taken meant that we would have to pay more money. I shuddered to think how much they would cost.

Strampelli seemed to read my thoughts.

'Ah, wait!' he said. 'Perhaps you had better have them taken in England as they do them free there. You can send the X-rays to me here.'

In French, he explained to me the mechanics of the operation he intended to carry out provided that there was a suitable tooth root he could use. It would take place in three stages, he said. First of all, I would have to attend the clinic for one month, during which time he would take mucous from my lips and place it over my left eyeball.

'Like this,' he said, touching my eye.

Then in another operation, he would remove the tooth, cement the sight-giving lens into a section of the root and bury the unit in my cheek just below the eye.

'Here,' he said, touching my cheekbone.

The sight-giving unit would remain in my cheek for three months, during which time I could return home. The object of implanting it into my face was to enable the surrounding tissue to adjust to the foreign body so that, when it was eventually implanted into my eyeball, the problems of rejection would be reduced.

After three months at home, I would have to return to the clinic. If all was well and the tooth root had not become infected, the final sight-giving operation would take place. The unit would be implanted into my eyeball, carefully aligned with the retina at the back of my eye.

The professor also explained that, in the early operations, he had cut the tooth root so that it looked like a little disc with a hole in the middle and had grafted the whole disc, with the lens cemented over the hole, into the eye. Now, however, he used only half of a disc, so that what went into the eye looked like a half-moon shaped root with the lens attached.

'That never comes out,' he said. 'It stays for ever.'

'I understand.'

'Go to England now, have your X-rays and send them to me. If the roots are good, we will send you a letter calling you to the clinic.'

'I put myself entirely in your hands, *professore*,' I told him. 'I am prepared to take the chance. If we don't succeed, don't worry. It will not be the end of the world.'

'*Bene!*' he smiled.

There was one matter that was worrying me . . . and worrying me considerably.

'Now, Professor Strampelli, there is something I must speak to you about,' I said hesitatingly. I was clearly embarrassed.

'The question of payment. I haven't much money. Can you tell me how much it will cost?'

'*Per me io non volio niente,*' he said. 'For me I want nothing.'

I smiled broadly.

'That's very generous of you, *professore.*'

'There is only one thing,' he added. 'The clinic will cost one million liras.'

I calculated quickly. It was about six hundred and seventy pounds.

'But, professor,' a nurse interrupted. 'There's the anaesthetist's fee as well.'

'That will be nothing,' he told her, presumably deciding that if he himself could give his services free then so could the anaesthetist.

He shook my hand warmly. Then he took Ena's hand and my hand together and clasped them in both of his.

'If your teeth are good, we will operate,' he said.

Outside, Ena paid the equivalent of twenty-three pounds to the nun at the reception desk. At last, I lit a cigarette.

Numbed by Professor Strampelli's provisional agreement to operate, we strolled back to the hotel in silence. Soon the numbness wore off. We were brimful of joy. We told Geanna, the travel courier, our news.

That evening, as we were touring the sights of Rome by coach, Geanna suddenly made an announcement over the coach intercom.

'Ladies and gentlemen,' she said. 'I have a wonderful announcement to make. In this coach there is a blind gentlemen from England who has come with his wife on this tour especially to consult a famous eye surgeon in Rome to see if he can bring back his sight. I have much pleasure in telling you that the surgeon has given new hope for sight and agrees to operate!'

The entire coach buzzed with excitement. Passengers stood up, clapping and cheering. I felt hands patting me on the back and on the shoulder. I was self-conscious at the reaction and, at the same time, near to tears at their obvious happiness for me. When Ena spoke, I could tell that she had a lump in her throat.

At the Trevi Fountain, known to tourists from all over the world and immortalised in the Hollywood film *Three Coins in a Fountain,* in which the title song was sung by Frank Sinatra, Ena squeezed my hand.

'You're supposed to throw a coin in the fountain and make a wish, darling,' she said.

We were short of money but I sorted out a coin from my loose change. I threw it into the fountain. I wished that the next time I came to Rome, I would be able to see.

Ena threw a coin into the water and made her own wish.

'Did you wish, darling?' she asked.

'Yes.'

'Tell me what you wished.'

'No, you're not supposed to tell.'

'You've got a funny smile on your face,' she laughed. 'I think I can guess, anyway.'

'I'm sure you can.'

She read my thoughts and squeezed my hand again.

'The next time we come here, darling, you will see Rome,' she said.

Suddenly, I felt very tired. I was still tired on the following day. Ena and Adrian went on a coach trip without me. I stayed at the hotel and slept. On their return, they described to me the summer palace of the Emperor Augustus at Tivoli, built high up among the olive groves of the hills, its magnificent fountains formed by the power of waterfalls.

Later in the day, we returned to St Peter's. Following the consultation with Professor Strampelli, I felt that I wanted to pray at the memorial to Pope John, to which Ena had led me on our visit to St Peter's two days before. I asked Ena to leave me alone. I needed to be on my own. I knelt before the memorial depicting Pope John blessing the prisoners.

'Pope John, hear my prayer,' I said. 'Give me strength. When I come to Rome next time, let the operation be successful. Let me succeed in seeing this time. You put your hands on my head and blessed me when I was a boy at my confirmation in Istanbul and you were a cardinal. Now that I am blind and in need of your help, bless Professor Strampelli, guide his hands well, bless my eyes and make them see . . . '

My prayer ended. It was silent and peaceful in St Peter's. I knelt before the memorial for a long time, wondering whether my prayer would be answered, whether next time I would see St Peter's.

There was nothing more to be done in Rome. I longed for Friday to arrive so that we could return home, so that I could have the X-rays taken of my jaw. Finally, it did. At the airport departure gate, Geanna, our courier, suddenly kissed me on the cheek. Unknown to me, her kiss left a huge lipstick mark. It was not until the aircraft had taken off and we were on our way to England that Ena removed it with her handkerchief.

'I didn't want to wipe it off straight away,' she laughed. 'I was quite proud of it. It looked as if all the girls in Rome had kissed you goodbye!'

Immediately after breakfast on the following morning, I rang my dentist to tell him of the urgent need for the X-rays. Even though it was Saturday morning, he told me to visit his surgery straight away. I was apprehensive about the result.

'Are there any good roots?' I asked anxiously as he surveyed the X-ray plates.

'I can tell you now that you have six jolly good roots that he could use,' he said.

It was wonderful news. No matter how many roots might be suitable, however, there was still the agonising problem of how we could possibly pay the clinic's fees of six hundred and seventy pounds, plus the cost of air fares and a hotel room for Ena. It was impossible for us to find such a large amount ourselves. We had virtually nothing. There was only one way we might get it. We would have to beg for it.

Straight away, Ena began to write dozens of letters explaining the reason that we needed money and asking for help. She wrote to several organisations dealing with the blind, to Catholic charities, to army charities and to Surrey County Council. Their replies were all the same. It was not possible for them to make a grant. It was too much money to spend on one blind person. In desperation, she wrote to the Queen. The reply, from Buckingham Palace, was sympathetic but regretted that the Queen had no funds available for assisting such cases as mine. There seemed to be nothing more we could do.

Ena, however, would not give up. At three o'clock one morning, towards the end of November, she suddenly sat up in bed and awoke me from a deep sleep.

'Darling!'

'What is it now?'

'We will get the money – we *will*!'

'You've written to everyone already and got nowhere.'

'But, Nino, I've got it! I've had an idea!'

'Oh, Ena!' I groaned. 'Not another of your ideas!'

'I'm going to do a walk!'

'Go back to sleep!'

'I'm going to walk the length of the Hog's Back,' she announced. 'In the middle of winter. In bare feet.'

Chapter Thirty-Eight

Ena's idea was that she should perform a sponsored walk along the Hog's Back, a famous Surrey beauty spot and centuries-old road running between Guildford and Farnham that was once part of the old Pilgrim's Way of Chaucer's *Canterbury Tales*. She would persuade well-wishers to sponsor her and pay however much they could afford for each mile she completed.

Painful though it was for me to think of Ena tramping such a long way, her feet blue with cold in the chill December weather, I had to admit that it was the sort of hare-brained idea that might provide the answer to our problems. Reluctant though I was to agree to such a physically-demanding act, I knew that nothing I said or did would prevent her carrying out her plan.

Local and national newspapers soon heard of Ena's heroic stunt. News stories were published telling of her plan to raise money for my operation. The public were not slow to respond. Some agreed to sponsor Ena on her walk. Others simply sent donations of money.

On the Saturday morning after the newspaper stories appeared, there was a knock at the door. I opened it.

'Are you the chap who wants to see?' asked a man's voice.

'Yes.'

'Well, here is a tenner towards it. God bless you. I admire your guts.'

The man walked away. Ena joined me at the door. She looked at the ten pound note clutched in my hand.

'Darling, he's in a big chauffeur-driven car!' she said.

Each time the postman called there were letters containing one pound notes and ten shilling notes. One old lady sent a book of postage stamps worth five shillings. Post Office workers in Aldershot started their own collection.

The unexpected response from so many different quarters quickly made it obvious that the entire appeal for money needed to be put on to some sort of official basis. As a result, a trust fund was formed with Pearl Bannister, the Post Office employee who had started the collection among her colleagues, and two priests from Tongham churches – one Church of England and one Roman Catholic – as trustees.

Ena sought sponsorship from three well-known national

manufacturing companies, offering to perform her mid-winter walk wearing Dunlop plimsolls instead of in bare feet and keeping up her energy by eating Mars bars and drinking Ovaltine. In return for the publicity that would ensue to the firms, she asked for a donation. Unfortunately, all three declined.

She wrote to *Nationwide,* a popular BBC television current affairs programme, and to *Today,* its equivalent on Independent Television, asking them to sponsor her on her walk. Although her offer failed to produce any response from the *Nationwide* producers and although *Today* declined to sponsor her, it did arouse the interest of the latter programme. Sandra Harris, an interviewer with the Thames Television programme's team, visited us and took copious notes in preparation for a filmed item dealing with the planned walk.

Three days later, the television crew arrived. We had expected about three men. There were twelve. The house was quickly turned into a television studio. Floodlights were set up. Microphones were put into position. Cables snaked across the floor. Sandra Harris sat with us, talking about Istanbul, about anything, to relax us and take our minds off the activity around us.

Suddenly, they were ready. Lights were switched on. A voice started counting.

'Five, four, three, two, one. Okay, start rolling!'

The interview began. Sandra Harris had an easy-going, relaxed interviewing technique and both Ena and I quickly forgot that we were being filmed for a programme that would be seen by millions of television viewers. We answered her questions confidently and naturally.

After a while, the producer stopped the cameras. The interview ended temporarily and continued out in the garden, where the two boys were filmed playing football. Then Linda was filmed singing excerpts from well-known operas, accompanied by Ena on the second-hand piano that her parents had given us, just like the two of them did almost every day.

Ena and I and the three children were invited to lunch with the television crew at the nearby Hog's Back Hotel.

'Daddy,' said Linda in a horrified voice as we drank our coffee. 'Paul is smoking!'

One of the young technicians had jokingly offered him a cigarette and, being Paul, he had taken it, lit it and was smoking it quite happily.

After lunch, there was more filming. Finally, everything was in the can. The crew left at about five o'clock.

The programme was shown on Tuesday, 7 December, 1971, four days before Ena was due to walk the Hog's Back. We gathered excitedly round our television set. It was introduced by Eamonn Andrews. Ena's voice was clear yet soft. Linda's singing was beautiful. The item lasted for fifteen minutes.

Immediately the programme had ended, the telephone rang. It scarcely stopped ringing all that evening. We were inundated with calls from friends and well-wishers, some of them complete strangers.

The following day, the telephone rang again. Ena took the call. I heard her weeping quietly as she spoke to the person at the other end. She put down the receiver.

'What is it, darling?' I asked anxiously, trying to comfort her, fearing bad news.

'Darling,' she said. 'That was Sandra Harris. An anonymous viewer has donated one thousand pounds so that you can have your operation!'

They were tears of joy. Ena flung herself into my arms. That evening, on the *Today* programme, Eamonn Andrews gave viewers the news of the generous donation. The donor's letter was read out.

Sandra Harris had tried to persuade Ena to drop her plan for the walk now that the one thousand pounds had been donated. She felt that the physical exertion would be too much. Ena, however, had been in training for some time, walking barefoot in Tongham and the surrounding area, trying to harden the soles of her feet, and felt physically equipped to tackle it. In addition, she feared that, if she abandoned the walk, the many generous people who had already contributed to the fund might think that she had obtained money by false pretences, that she had never had any intention of carrying out the walk.

'I'll do it,' she said. 'I'll do it as an act of thanksgiving to the wonderful man who has provided the money.'

Saturday arrived. I awoke Ena at dawn. I kissed her.

'Darling, I wish you wouldn't do this for me,' I told her. 'My poor wife has to run barefoot through the streets now!'

The weather had been cold and wet but the morning was dry, the wind less cold and the sun began to shine. Well before eight o'clock, the road was swarming with newspaper reporters and photographers. The police were there in force.

Ena kissed me lightly on the lips. She was dressed in shrunken jeans, thick socks, a duffel coat and, on top, a striped fluorescent jacket provided by the police so that she would be readily seen on the road by drivers and, thus, avoid a possible accident.

'I feel like a pregnant wasp in this!' she joked.

She set off, accompanied by Adrian, who was determined to walk with his mother for the whole of the twelve-mile route.

Ever since news of Ena's planned walk had first broken, ever since she had started training for it, she had had to contend with many cruel jibes from unthinking people. She was nothing but a publicity-seeker, some of them said. Others complained that she was making a complete fool of herself, as if in some way her foolishness reflected on them. Her answer to the hurtful remarks was always the same. If her critics had a blind husband and raising sufficient money was essential to give him a chance of sight, what would they do?

Now she was to carry out her promise, her barefoot walk, and they could all think what they liked. How brave she was!

At ten o'clock, Sandra Harris arrived at the house with a TV cameraman. Linda made coffee. As we drank it, and as I talked with Sandra, my thoughts were with Ena. She should have been almost half-way by then. At eleven o'clock, Sandra could stand the tension no longer.

'Come on, Nino!' she said. 'Let's go in the car to see how she's doing. You, too, Linda. Maybe we can persuade her to stop walking.'

We drove the one mile from the house to the Hog's Back and then along the road to Guildford.

'There she is, Daddy!' Linda's voice was a mixture of pride and excitement. 'Daddy! Mummy's still walking quite fast!'

Sandra stopped the car and wound down the window. Ena sounded breathless and tired but she declined Sandra's suggestion that she should give up the walk, climb in the car and be driven home.

'I'm all right, really,' she insisted. 'I'll meet you all back at the Hog's Back Hotel.'

She walked on. Sandra sighed. We drove on to the Guildford end of the Hog's Back, where a crowd of photographers was waiting to picture Ena arriving, flanked by two police cars, at the six-mile half-way stage.

Ena's pace on the return leg of the walk was considerably reduced but, by a quarter to one, she had almost completed the twelve miles. When she was still fifty yards away, Sandra clapped me on the back.

'Nino,' she said. 'You have a wife in a million!'

Ena stumbled into the hotel car-park and into my arms. She

was completely exhausted but happy. She put her arms round my neck.

'I've done it, darling!' she cried. 'I've done it! I've done it!'

The photographers clustered round as Sandra presented Ena with the cheque for one thousand pounds. In addition, the walk had earned twenty-six pounds from sponsors.

Ena had been encouraged on the walk not only by Adrian but also by her sister, Dorothy, and her husband, Colin Malcolm. All three had completed the whole twelve miles with her. Young Adrian was more exhausted than any of them and had suffered blistered heels. Ena's feet, without shoes for the entire walk, were in surprisingly good condition.

We retired with Sandra to the hotel for a drink. The lounge bar was crowded with the county set, sipping their Saturday lunch-time gins-and-tonic and pints of draught bitter. Beautiful young dolly birds with cigarettes in holders were draped nonchalantly over the bar. They gazed in astonishment at Ena in her shrunken jeans, woolly socks, duffel coat and fluorescent jacket.

'Dah-ling!' drawled one of them, who (according to Ena) looked as though she had never walked further than from her luxury country residence to the E-type Jaguar in the drive. 'Who on earth is that queer woman over there?'

I did not care. Ena's bright idea, and her courage, had earned the money needed for my operation – and I knew that I had the most wonderful woman in the world for my wife.

Chapter Thirty-Nine

Christmas came and went. Ena and I returned to work. The children were still on holiday from school. On 30 December, I made my usual lunch-time telephone call home to ensure that the children were all right.

'There's a letter from Italy, Daddy,' said Linda.

I could not contain my curiosity until I went home from work that evening. I could not wait. I had to know what the letter said. An Italian workmate jumped into his car and collected the letter from the house. We read it together. I was to report to Strampelli on 10 January 1972, for the first of my three operations.

It was four o'clock in the afternoon by the time we arrived at the Villa Benedetta. We sat in the waiting-room for three hours before Professor Strampelli was able to see us. He examined my eye.

'Right,' he said. 'We will operate next Saturday.'

It was Monday. Ena had only two weeks' holiday from work. I would scarcely have recovered from the operation by the time she had to leave. I knew that she would be loath to leave me until I was well again.

'Please could you operate tomorrow, Professor?' I asked. 'My wife has to be back home next week.'

He thought for a moment.

'We shall see, we shall see. Now will you go to administration?'

At the administrative office, a civilian clerk noted my details.

'Deposit, please,' she said.

'Pardon?'

'Have you brought a deposit?'

'What deposit?'

'You must pay a deposit of five hundred thousand liras.'

It was half of the clinic's total fee, about three hundred and thirty pounds. The question of a deposit had not been mentioned before. We had expected to pay the bill at the end of my treatment. We had brought with us only about fifty pounds.

'We have the money in England,' I told her. 'You could ring the bank to check.'

'We must have a deposit,' she insisted. 'How much can you put down now?'

'Thirty-five thousand liras.'

It was about twenty-one pounds. She laughed sarcastically.

'You had better go back and see Professor Strampelli,' she said sourly.

We walked away. Everyone sounded so unfriendly. We had been travelling since seven o'clock that morning. It was now eight o'clock in the evening. We were exhausted and hungry after such a long journey without food and by the three-hour wait to see the professor. Disappointed by the cool reception, Ena began to cry.

'Let's go back home,' she sobbed.

'No,' I told her. 'I've started this – and I'm going to finish it. We're staying here.'

Strampelli's assistants tried to reassure Ena. Everything would be all right, even though we did not have the deposit, they said. We were sent back to the office.

Ena was still sniffling when we left the administrative clerk.

'*Perchè piange?*' one of the nuns asked me. 'Why is she crying?'

'We have not brought enough money for the administration,' I told her. 'She is tired and she has to get back to her hotel before it gets any darker. She is upset because she has to leave me.'

'*Vostra moglie puo dormire qui,*' she said. 'Your wife can sleep here.'

'Don't worry,' I said to Ena. 'She says you can stay here.'

Ena started to cry again. She put her head on my shoulder and wept. She had taken enough. The worry of how we could afford the clinic's fees had been mainly hers. The task of organising the fund-raising and her sponsored walk had been hers. The walk itself had been exhausting. She was mentally and physically wearied. Now that the time had come for my operation, she was fearful of what lay ahead for me. Suddenly, she could take no more.

'Thank you, thank you very much,' she said to the nun when she had recovered her composure.

The nun led the way to my room on the second floor. It was ten o'clock. The corridors were quiet. She took my hand and guided me round so that I would know its layout. On the left, as we entered the door, was an armchair. The bed was in the middle of the room, its head against the wall. To the left of the bed was a locker with a telephone on it and, to the right, a chest of drawers with a compartment that pulled out to turn into a camp bed. Against the opposite wall was a table and chair. Facing the foot of the bed was a door leading to the bathroom, which contained a lavatory, washbasin, bidet and shower.

We had not known that each room had a camp bed on which the patient's spouse could sleep. Nor had we known that husbands or wives of patients were welcome to stay at the clinic. A room had already been booked for Ena at the Hotel Villa Radieuse, where we had stayed on our first visit to Rome to consult Strampelli. It was already paid for and, in addition, the hotel reception desk would be expecting her. Despite the nun's kind offer to let her stay with me, Ena decided to go to her room at the hotel.

I settled in. I was given a bowl of soup. As I undressed for bed, a nun entered to give me an enema.

'You are having the operation tomorrow,' she explained.

'Tomorrow! But I thought it was on Saturday!'

'No, tomorrow.'

On the following morning, Ena rang from the hotel. She was as surprised as I was that Strampelli had apparently acceded to my request and had decided to operate that day.

'No smoke, no eat,' said one of the nuns in broken English.

Blood samples were taken from my ear and finger. An electrocardiograph monitored the performance of my heartbeat. My jaw was X-rayed. Ena arrived. She kept me company until three o'clock in the afternoon. Then the nuns arrived to prepare me for the operation.

One of the nuns told me to take off my pyjamas. I was given a short gown to wear. I climbed back into bed. The nuns started to push the bed out of the room. It was my first operation in a foreign country and I was apprehensive. I could not see where I was going. What were they going to do to me? Unlike in England, there were no men around, only nuns. The nuns even appeared to act as porters.

Ena accompanied me as far as the lift. She kissed me on the lips. The gates clanged shut. The lift ascended two floors. In England, I had always been given the anaesthetic and rendered unconscious before being taken into the operating theatre, but here I was wheeled straight in. The bed stopped alongside the operating table.

'Jump up here,' said one of the nuns.

I eased my body on to the narrow table. I lay flat on my back.

There were no pillows. My stomach was empty of food. A wave of nausea swept over me.

For the first time, I heard male voices. One man took hold of my right arm, pulled it away from the table and placed it into a hanging loop. Another man did the same with my left arm. Someone lifted my legs and placed an ice-cold, steel cylindrical object underneath my thighs. I felt as if I was strapped down in the electric chair.

A needle sank into my arm and, after ten seconds, I knew no more.

'Keep still, darling.'

I regained consciousness to the sound of Ena's voice. Knowing that she was near me was the best aid to recovery that I could have had.

'It's all over, darling. Don't worry. Everything is all right.'

I could tell that there were bandages across my eyes and more bandages across my mouth. The inside of my mouth was packed with gauze. My mouth was extremely painful. As my mind cleared, I remembered the reason. Strampelli had been planning to take mucous from my mouth to graft on to my eyeball.

I took Ena's hand and brought it to my lips but I was unable to kiss it. All that it touched were the bandages, not my lips. I wanted to greet her, to tell her I was all right, to say 'Hello, darling,' but no words came out, only groans.

The groans turned into choking sounds and I was vaguely aware that I was vomiting and that the vomit was spewing out from the hole that had been left in the bandages. Nuns were packing towels round me to soak it up. Most of it seemed to be going down my throat and I choked again.

'Keep still,' said the voice of one of the nuns. 'Turn your head to the right.'

Ena was holding my hand. I squeezed her hand to try to reassure her. I was aware that she was speaking to me.

'Please keep still, darling. Don't move. Just vomit. It's all right.'

I was worried about the vomiting. I could tell that it was going over Ena, soiling her clothes. She sensed my concern.

'It's all right,' she said. 'Do it in the bed. It doesn't matter. Don't worry.'

I realised why it was that Ena was repeatedly urging me not to move. If I moved my head too much, the operation could be ruined. The delicate graft might not take.

Someone was at my bedside. A needle went into my arm. I slipped into unconsciousness.

When I awoke on the following morning, a nun brought me a cup of lemon tea. Ena fed it to me through a tube. It was my first drink for twenty-four hours. It tasted beautiful, soothing.

'It's like nectar,' I told her.

My bottom lip was extremely painful and gripping the tube between my lips was agony. It was difficult for me to suck the lemon tea through the tube and I managed to drink only a few sips. Ena washed me. I began to feel better.

'Give me a cigarette, darling,' I mumbled through my sore and swollen lips and mouth.

'No,' she said. 'You're not allowed to smoke.'

Nuns came in to clean the room. Ena left the hospital to buy fruit and newspapers. The morning passed in a haze. Ena sat at my bedside, talking to me and reading from the newspapers.

In the afternoon, Professor Strampelli visited me. He took off the bandages and put some drops in my eye. He seemed pleased with what he saw.

'*Bene, bene*,' he said. '*Molto bene!*'

The operation was satisfactory, he said, although the eye was much more badly damaged than he had previously thought.

I was confined to bed for three days. By that time, my mouth was less uncomfortable. I was feeling better. I was allowed out of bed.

Ten days after the operation, Professor Strampelli came to my room. The following day, he said, I would be going to the operating theatre. The tooth that was needed to make the sight-giving unit would be removed from my jaw and implanted into my cheek. Unfortunately, it was not possible to remove the tooth as in an ordinary extraction. That way, the root and the nerves would be damaged. To avoid the possibility of harming the precious root, my tooth would have to be cut out, dug out.

On the following morning, I was wheeled to the operating theatre and, like the first time, spread-eagled on the table with my arms in loops. It was a Saturday, almost two weeks since we had flown out from England. This time, before I was given the anaesthetic, Strampelli came into the theatre. He examined my eye and started to probe it. I felt sick. For some reason, I was almost on the point of vomiting. I started to take deep breaths in a bid to keep the nausea at bay. I wished that they would hurry and give me an injection so that I would go to sleep and know nothing more about it. Finally they did.

When my brain cleared and I became more aware of my surroundings, I felt round my mouth with my tongue to find where the agonising pain was coming from. One of my bottom teeth was missing. So was the gum that had surrounded it. There was a huge gap, a hole, where the gum had been cut away both at the front and at the back, right down to the jawbone, right down to the root of the tooth. The gum had been cut away also on either side of the tooth that had been removed (dug out rather than pulled out) and the roots of those teeth were exposed, too. The enormous cavity that had been left was packed with gauze. I could feel stitches in my mouth. Bandages covered my left eye and cheek, into which the tooth root and lens had been buried in a bid to overcome rejection problems. Two saline drips were attached to my feet.

Although the pain in my mouth was worse than any I had experienced for some time, I was happy. I was happy because I knew that this was the last operation before the final one, the one that could give me my sight.

One evening soon afterwards, when I had almost recovered, the nuns were fussing round me, plumping up my pillows, straightening the bedclothes, tidying the room and arranging the fruit in the bowl. Their attentions were rather more meticulous than usual. There was a simple explanation.

'Signor Fettel,' said one. 'You have a very important visitor this evening. The Mother Superior is coming to see you.'

They departed. Another nun opened the door. Someone walked in.

'I am the Mother Superior of the clinic,' said a voice. 'It is a great honour to meet you all the way from England.'

'It is a great honour for me to meet you, Mother Superior,' I said in Italian.

She sat by my bedside.

'I shall have to come to you to improve my English,' she said.

We talked for a few minutes. The conversation led to a discussion about the Pope. She could arrange for two cards for the audience hall at the Vatican, she said, but it would be for Professor Strampelli to decide whether I could be allowed to attend.

The following day, I asked him.

'I don't see why not,' he said. 'But the next time you come to Rome you will be able to *see* the Pope.'

The Mother Superior arranged for two seats in the audience hall for the following Wednesday. Thanks to the efforts of Ena's mother back home in England, money from the trust fund had been transferred to us in Rome. Our financial situation had improved. We took a taxi.

The audience hall was crowded. As we sat there among the throng, Ena described the scene to me – the colours, the Swiss Guard, the people of different nationalities, the layout of the hall. We waited for half-an-hour. Suddenly, there was a lot of clapping.

'His Holiness is coming along on a chair carried by the priests,' announced Ena excitedly.

Pope Paul spoke to his audience in seven languages. Then a cardinal announced that His Holiness would bless us all and that the blessing would be carried to our families at home and abroad. Any religious possessions such as rosaries or crucifixes would also be blessed by His Holiness.

'Oh, darling!' said Ena, disappointed. 'We haven't anything with us that he can bless!'

The entire audience was going wild. Hands clutching rosaries and crucifixes were stretched out towards His Holiness. Those at the back held them up in the air. Our seats were good ones. We were only two aisles away from the one down which the Pope was being carried.

'What a shame, darling!' I said. 'We should have thought to bring something.'

'Never mind!' said Ena. 'Stand on your chair instead so that His Holiness can see you better!'

She helped me on to the chair and stood beside me on her own chair.

'Is he nearly here, darling?'

'Yes, darling. He's right in front of you now! Oh, Nino! He's looking straight at you!'

It was a moving and thrilling moment for me and, as Pope Paul passed by, I thought of Professor Strampelli's words.

'The next time you come to Rome you will be able to *see* the Pope.'

Chapter Forty

Ena and I returned home with an appointment to visit Strampelli again in six weeks' time for a check-up. If all was well, I would need only a brief examination in the out-patients' department. Consequently, we booked a day return flight between London and Rome, generously paid for by Ena's brother, Nigel.

Other patients were waiting when we arrived at the clinic but we were ushered straight into the consulting room.

'How are you?' Professor Strampelli asked.

'There seems to be a piece of fibrous tissue sticking to my eyeball, *Professore*,' I told him. 'Will you have a look?'

We had been extremely worried but I tried not to let the concern show in my voice. He examined my eye and touched the mucous membrane with an instrument.

'Don't worry,' he said. 'When you come again in May we will separate it.'

He began to write on a notepad.

'Do you have to be admitted?' Ena whispered anxiously. I shook my head.

Professor Strampelli carried out the same tests as previously, shining red, green and white lights into my eye and the special one that gave me the impression of a tree. Then he pressed my eyeball with his finger.

'Can you see the sparkle?'

'Yes, I can.'

'*Bene, bene!*'

He asked Ena what she had been using to clean my eye and instructed her to ensure that it was kept meticulously clean. Then he showed her some photographs of my eye that had been taken during my previous stay.

The condition of my eye was very satisfactory, he told me. The mucous membrane over the eyeball was perfect and there were no signs of rejection of the unit from my cheek. He would see me again in May for the final operation. He turned to his assistant and asked him to book a date. The entire consultation was over in fifteen minutes.

Outside, I lit a cigarette. Both Ena and I were happy. We had been dreading that I would have to be admitted. Nevertheless, it seemed a long way to have had to come for a fifteen minute consultation.

'What a waste!' I said. 'We needn't have bothered coming.'

'Never mind,' said Ena happily. 'It's been a nice day out. And at least we now know that everything is all right.'

'It's an expensive day out, darling,' I said. 'It's cost Nigel two hundred pounds!'

At the airport, we celebrated in the restaurant with spaghetti bolognese and a bottle of red wine. Our return flight left at ten-past-five. Dorothy and Colin, Ena's sister and brother-in-law, were waiting to collect us at Heathrow Airport. It seemed incredible that we had been to Rome and back in one day.

My next admission day, 24 May 1972, arrived. I was excited. I thought back to when Peter Rycroft had given me partial sight. I had been fascinated then by the sight of something that Ena and the children had probably never even noticed – the sight of the centre-piece of the kitchen window-frame, shaped like the letter H. Sometimes, I had sat at the kitchen table, smoking a cigarette and just looking . . . staring at that unremarkable shape that, for some odd reason, I found so fascinating. Now, when I came back from Rome, would I be able to see not only the window-frame but also the kitchen taps? Would the miracle happen? Perhaps not. At least, if the operation were not successful, I would have lost nothing. At least, in my old age, I would not regret having had the opportunity to see and not having taken it.

We drove straight to the clinic. After three hours in the waiting-room we became convinced that we had been forgotten. Ena spoke to a nun.

'*Un momento!*' she said. '*Un momento!*'

It was seven o'clock before Professor Strampelli was able to see me. We had been waiting for four-and-a-half hours.

He examined my eye and then sent me to another room for ultra-sound X-rays to be taken. I lay on a couch. A doctor placed an electrode over my eyeball. The results were taken to Strampelli.

'Everything is all right,' he said to Ena. 'Your 'usband will see.'

Outside, we met a Dutchman who was at the clinic for a check-up after having had the same operation that I was about to have. Unlike me, he had had sight-giving units implanted into both eyes and, happily, was able to see. It was a great encouragement. He was full of praise for Strampelli.

'Professor Strampelli is a good man,' he said. 'Look – I can see!'

'How long were you in?' Ena asked.

'Six weeks,' he said.

'How long will I be here, Giovanni?' I asked.

'The same,' he answered. 'Six weeks.'

Six weeks! It was a shock. We had understood that my stay would be for only three weeks. That was the period for which we had paid in advance. If I had to stay for an extra three weeks, we would be in financial difficulties again. In addition, Ena had only four weeks' leave from work. We started to worry again.

'But Giovanni has had the operation on both his eyes – not just one like you're going to have,' Ena said, trying to cheer me up. 'Maybe it's only half the time for one eye.'

A young nun picked up our suitcase and took it to our room. This time, knowing that Ena was welcome to stay at the clinic, we had not booked an hotel room for her. She was to sleep on the camp bed in my room.

I slept fitfully. Breakfast was brought to me on a tray. Ena ate in the clinic restaurant.

During the following two days, I underwent various medical tests. Blood samples were taken. Chest X-rays were examined to ensure that my lungs were in condition to withstand the anaesthetic. Ena described the view to me from our room, the buildings outside, the people in the street. I heard the sound of a petrol engine starting up.

'It's one of the doctors going off on a little moped,' Ena laughed.

I awoke early on the Saturday, the third full day after our arrival. It was the day of my operation. The fateful moment had arrived. There was no turning back.

Ena and I had each other. We had our children and our families. We had a home and we had jobs. We had a lot to be thankful for. Were I to regain my sight, it would be an extra blessing, an added bonus to our happiness. We had nothing to lose. We could only gain. The operation was worth the risk.

I was longing for success . . . praying for success. It had to be successful. If it were not, it was the end of my hopes. Even if success were to elude me, however, at least I would not reproach myself for not having taken the chance. At least, I could then resign myself to a lifetime of blindness.

Our room was only about fifteen yards from the clinic chapel and, since our arrival three days before, we had delighted in listening to the nuns each evening singing vesper hymns and, each morning, singing the prayers at mass. One of the nuns, an important member of Strampelli's team, was a particularly accomplished soprano. Her voice stood out from the rest. She was always the one to start to sing. The others followed.

'You have a very nice voice, Sister,' I said to her on my second day in the clinic.

'I was trained to sing,' she said happily, pleased that I had noticed.

That morning, Saturday, the day of my operation, I had a sudden desire to join the nuns at the seven o'clock mass. Ena guided me into a pew. The theatre sister who would be in charge at my operation that afternoon was sitting in the pew immediately in front of us. The entire congregation, apart from ourselves, consisted of the clinic nursing staff, all nuns of the Order of the Sisters of St John the Baptist.

It was a simple mass in Italian. A priest gave an address. His words were directed at the nursing nuns. They should always remember, he said, that the work they were doing was God's work and that they had been especially chosen by God to do it, to care for the sick, to relieve suffering. The sick needed them, he said, needed them as they themselves needed God.

To me, the nuns were saintly creatures who dedicated their lives to helping others, working seven days a week from half-past-seven each morning until eight o'clock or even nine o'clock in the evening.

There was an electric atmosphere in the chapel and yet, at the same time, it was peaceful. I was uplifted. The hymns and psalms and responses filled me with a feeling of well-being and of calm. I did not fear the operation.

'O Lord, give me strength,' I prayed. 'I have had many trials and tribulations. Let everything turn out right in the end. And let this be the end.'

My big day had arrived. I thought of Strampelli and his promise that I would see the Pope. Ena had described His Holiness to me but it was not the same as actually seeing him. Would I see him in two weeks? In two months? Or never?

Back in my room, while Ena had breakfast in the restaurant, I sat in the armchair and prayed again. I prayed that God would give strength and courage to both Ena and me, that He would bless my wife and children, my mother and sisters, Strampelli and the nuns, and all the people who had made my operation possible, especially the unknown man who had donated the one thousand pounds. I prayed that God would guide Strampelli's hand on my eye, that He would make me see, and that He would spare the great surgeon for many more years to carry out his wonderful work.

Ena returned from breakfast. She obtained permission to take me for a walk. We bought the *Daily American*. She read the news to me.

Soon, the time came for me to undress and get into bed. I was given an enema, followed by an injection. At four o'clock, two nuns arrived to wheel me away. Ena kissed me goodbye. The lift gates closed.

In the operating theatre, a woman doctor attended to me.

'I am going to give you an injection to make you pass water,' she said. 'Don't worry if you get a pain in your tummy.'

The needle went into my left arm. I felt a bottle put into my hand.

'Keep that bottle beside you because you will pass lots of water,' said the woman doctor.

She was right. After ten minutes, I started to make water and, once started, I feared that I would not stop. By the time the doctor was ready to give me the anaesthetic, the bottle was so full that some of the urine spilled out on to the sheets.

'Scusate sorella,' I said to one of the nuns. 'I spilled the bottle.'

'Non faniente,' she replied. 'It's nothing.'

I climbed on to the operating table. The anaesthetist tapped the back of my hand. He gave me an injection. I could hear voices and the clatter of surgical instruments but none of the voices was that of Strampelli. I went to sleep.

I was barely conscious but I could sense that I was in my own room. There was no pain. Someone was kissing me.

'Don't move, darling. Don't worry. I'm here. You've had your operation. Everything is all right.'

For a moment, I did not recognise Ena's voice. When I did, I tried to give her a smile but I suspected that the way it turned out was not what I had intended.

'You have a catheter – a tube that's passed into the bladder,' she said. 'It's there so you won't have to mess about with bottles.'

My head began to clear. I became aware that my eyes were bandaged.

'What time is it?' I asked.

'One o'clock in the morning. You were in the operating theatre for four hours.'

I could feel something heavy on the top of my head. My hand reached up to it. Ena gently drew my hand away and kissed it.

'Nino, darling, it's an ice bag,' she explained. 'A two pound bag of ice cubes to keep your head cool.'

There was something hard on each side of my head, pressing against my face.

'There are two hard cushions on either side, darling,' Ena said, reading my thoughts. 'They're to stop you moving your head. It's important that you keep still. You look like a mummy – and you must lie like one!'

'There's something in my foot.'

'A glucose drip. There are two – one in each foot.'

I lapsed into silence. Ena was unsure whether I was still awake.

'Darling, can you hear me?' I nodded. 'Professor Strampelli came into the room especially to see me. Do you know what he said? He said "Your 'usband will see in . . . " – and he held up five fingers – " . . . five days." What do you think of that, darling?'

In five days' time! Could it be true? Exhaustion suddenly overtook me. Before I could answer Ena's question, I drifted off into a deep sleep. I had time only to smile . . .

The cold of the ice bag woke me up. I remembered what Ena had told me just before I had fallen asleep.

'Did Professor Strampelli really say that, darling?' I asked. 'That I would see in five days? Or was I dreaming?'

'Yes, darling, he did.'

The night passed slowly. I slept fitfully. Each time I awoke, I reached out with both hands, trying to take Ena's face between them, trying to kiss her. Gently, she placed my hands back on to the bedclothes. I repeatedly asked her what time it was. It seemed that I was wakening about once every hour.

At various times during the night, I became aware of Ena's fingers on my wrist taking my pulse and of her hands massaging the calves of my legs. On several occasions when I woke, I felt her hands round my diaphragm, pressing, massaging.

'I'm giving you some physiotherapy, darling,' she explained. 'Will you breathe in? Take a deep breath.' I breathed in. 'I'm going to press on your rib-cage as you breathe out.' All the air in my lungs seemed to be expelled as I breathed out. She pressed my chest three times, squeezing out the air.

'Darling, are you undressed?' I asked.

'Not yet.'

'When are you going to lie down? When are you going to get some rest?'

'Soon now.'

'You must have some sleep.'

I tried to raise my head.

'Please don't move, darling. Please keep still.'

'I feel sick.'

'Please don't be sick!'

Even though I was only half-conscious, I realised the reason for Ena's obvious concern. If I were sick and moved my head, the newly-implanted unit, the unit that could give me my sight, could become dislodged. Professor Strampelli's vital work could all be ruined.

The nausea passed. I thought again of Strampelli's words.

'Five days' time, darling? Did he really say that?'

I smiled and fell asleep.

I knew no more until soon after dawn. I was awakened by the sound of the nuns singing at the Sunday morning mass. It sounded beautiful.

'Open the door, darling, so that I can hear them better,' I asked. The clarity of the angelic choir increased.

Ena washed me. I drank a glass of lemon tea through a tube. A nun entered and removed the ice bag. It was a relief to have the heavy weight taken off my head. A few minutes later, however, I heard the ominous rattling of ice-cubes. Another bag was put in place.

'Not another one!' I said.

'*Si, Signor Constantino!* For a fortnight!'

At half-past ten, I heard a trolley outside my room. There was the rattle of instruments as it was wheeled in. Strampelli entered with an entourage of doctors and nuns. My right hand was lying across my chest on the outside of the bedclothes, palm down on the white sheets. He patted the back of my hand, twice.

'*Bene, bene!*'

The day passed in a doze. Each time I wakened, I sought confirmation from Ena about what Strampelli had said. Was she certain that he had said five days? Yes, she was positive. I could not wait for the five days to pass.

At lunch-time, I was wakened to drink a bowl of soup. My appetite had not yet returned, however. By the time I had taken seven spoonfulls, I had had enough.

At intervals throughout the day, I was given injections. Ena held my head so that I would not move it as I swivelled my hips to expose my rump for the nun's needle. After each injection, I thanked the nun who had administered it. After the fifth, she could contain her curiosity no longer.

'Why do you thank me, *Signor Constantino?*' she asked.

'Because you are helping me to get better.'

'But I hurt you with my needle – and then you thank me!' she said, puzzled.

'You have to do your duty,' I told her, smiling.

The reason for her bewilderment was that Italian patients would never have considered expressing gratitude for an injection. They had a pathological dread of hypodermic needles, were notoriously bad patients when receiving injections and, invariably, maintained a continuous barrage of shouts and screams until it was all over.

On the Tuesday, three days after my operation, Strampelli and his retinue arrived late. The sister looked at Ena and waved her hand towards the door.

'*Signora . . .*'

'I've got to go, darling,' Ena said, kissing me. 'I'll see you later.'

I could hear people gathering round my bed.

'*Buona sera!*' said Strampelli.

'*Buona sera, Professore!*'

'How are you feeling?'

'*Molto bene, grazie!*'

'I am opening it and dressing it,' he announced.

What? After only three days? I felt myself going cold. One of the other doctors echoed my thoughts.

'Shouldn't it be left for another day or two?' he asked.

'No,' said Strampelli. 'I'm going to do it now.'

I heard the snipping of scissors as my bandages were cut away.

'Bring that light nearer, sister,' Strampelli ordered.

Somebody pushed the trolley and the instruments on it clattered.

'Keep that nurse quiet!' he barked.

My eyelids had been stitched together. I felt an instrument snipping at the stitches. There was a sudden feeling of release and the lids came apart. I could see light coming into my eye. It was from the hand-light that sister was holding.

'*Aqua physiologica*,' said Strampelli. I felt water splashing on my eye and trickling down my face. I felt him polishing the little window through which he was hoping I would be able to see. It was like someone polishing my eye with a circular movement.

'Put the light behind his head,' Strampelli ordered. The sister moved behind me with the light. Immediately she did so, I could see something. I could see two fingers facing me, immediately in front of my eye . . .

'*Vede?*' Strampelli asked. 'Can you see?'

'*Si, professore!*' I cried. '*Due dita!*'

'*Bene, bene!*'

From the moment that Strampelli had started to take off my bandages, an electrifying silence had hung over the room. Suddenly, it buzzed with suppressed excitement. The sister squeezed my shoulder. Strampelli put down one of the two fingers and tucked it into his palm.

'How many?' he asked.

'*Uno.*'

He put up two more.

'How many now?'

'*Tre.*'

'And now?'

'*Cinque.*'

'Now we will give it a rest,' he said.

Cream was squeezed into my eye and my eye and head were bandaged.

'Have patience,' said Strampelli. 'I will see you tomorrow.'

Ena was waiting outside the door.

'Your 'usband can see,' he told her quietly.

She rushed into the room.

'Ena!' I shouted. 'I can see!'

'Professor Strampelli's just told me, darling,' she said breathlessly. 'What could you see?'

'Two fingers! Three fingers! Five fingers! I got it right every time! Darling, it was terrific!'

'How well could you see them? Were they clear?'

'A little foggy – but fairly clear.'

'Oh, Nino! I'm so excited! So are you – you're trembling, darling!'

'I can't help it! It was so wonderful! I've made it, darling! I can see!'

Suddenly, I realised that I was holding my arms straight down at my sides, rigidly, under the sheets, almost as if I were lying at attention. The previous few minutes had been so tense that my fists were tightly clenched.

During the rest of the evening, Ena and I could talk of nothing else but what I had been able to see. A nun came in and replaced the ice bag with a fresh one but I did not mind. Not even the ice bags bothered me now.

On the following afternoon, Strampelli – or The Lion as Ena and I had nicknamed him – called again to see me. Ever since our arrival, we had been amused to hear the sound of his voice when he was angry. Even when he was right up on the top floor, we could hear him bellowing at his trembling assistants and, because his roars of rage resembled those of the king of the jungle, we had decided to call him The Lion.

He washed my eye, polished the lens and held up his fingers. I was correct each time.

'Can you see them clearly?' he asked.

'Not clearly,' I told him. 'It's like a little fog.'

The next day was the first day of June. It was my birthday. I was forty-eight. It was also the Feast of Corpus Christi, a feast day that (like most feast days in Italy) was marked by a public holiday. Rome was taking its ease. One of the nuns entered.

'Here is a birthday present for you, *Signor Constantino*,' she said.

I was surprised and pleased.

'What is it?'

Something was held in front of me. She took my hand and placed it over a flower in full bloom. I could smell the scent of roses.

'They are beautiful roses from the clinic gardens,' she told me. 'Red and yellow but mostly beautiful pinks.'

She put them in a vase. All the nuns were wearing their best white habits for the important religious festival. The Mother Superior came in, obviously excited.

'*Signor Constantino*,' she said. 'The archbishop will be coming past your window today. There is to be a big procession to the quadrangle outside, where the archbishop is to administer Holy Sacrament. They are building the altar now. Can you hear them? Anyway, will you tell your wife that she is to throw rose petals out of the window before the archbishop?'

'The archbishop's coming,' I told Ena. 'She says you are to strew his path with rose petals.'

Two nuns came in bearing huge pot plants which they heaved up on to the window-sill, where they balanced precariously. The bustle of activity continued well into the morning. Ena reported that men were putting out hundreds of chairs in the quadrangle and that the huge altar was almost completed.

Professor Strampelli arrived at ten o'clock. His wife was with him. Ena stayed in the room as he washed my eye. He held up two fingers.

'How many?'

'Two.'

'How many now?'

'Three.'

'Bene, bene!'

As he finished the test he turned his hand before moving it out of the line of my 'tunnel vision'. For a moment, the back of his hand was in front of my eye and, in that fraction of a second, I saw something that caused me to gasp in astonishment and wonderment. I saw the tiny, black hairs standing up on the back of his hand . . .

The room was silent. I sensed that signals were passing between Strampelli and his assistants and that they did not want me to know what they were doing.

Strampelli held something in front of my eye and moved the light behind my head.

'Cosa è questa?' he asked. 'What is this?'

Five seconds passed . . . seven . . . ten . . . before my brain began to interpret the message that my eye was signalling to it. Gradually, I began to recognise the object in front of my face. There was a definite colour to it . . . yes, it was red . . . and there were leaf-like shapes that seemed to be wrapped around each other. Yes, they were petals! It was a rose! A red rose!

'Una rosa!' I shouted, unable to control my glee.

The room boiled with the babble of excited voices. The doctors and nurses all began speaking at once. Sentences in Italian rippled round my ears. Strampelli himself was thrilled. He clapped his hands and turned to Ena.

'There you are!' he said. 'He sees for you!'

He held up a chart about three feet away.

'Vede?' he asked. 'Can you see?'

'Numero uno.'

The large figure one, black on a white background, was the only number on the chart. The chart moved. A new number appeared.

'*Sette – nero,*' I said. 'Seven – black.'

The professor was satisfied.

'*Basta!*' he said. 'Enough!' He turned to Ena. 'Come and meet my wife.'

My eye was dressed. They departed. Ena went to the door with Signora Strampelli and stood talking outside. When she returned she was overjoyed.

'Darling, wasn't that marvellous? It was so thrilling for everyone when you were able to see that rose!'

She confirmed what I had suspected from the silence that had preceded the appearance of the rose in front of me – that they had been signalling to each other. Using sign-language, Strampelli had indicated to one of the nuns to pass him a rose from the vase containing my birthday present.

'There were tears in sister's eyes,' Ena said. 'They've all been praying for you to see – and it was like a miracle to them for you to see that rose on the Feast of Corpus Christi. Their happiness was unbelievable!'

Ena was silent for a moment.

'What is it, darling?'

'It was just something that Signora Strampelli told me outside. I was saying how wonderful it was to think that you had had your last operation and she said maybe it was your last, maybe it wasn't. She thought her husband wanted to do a bit more. Something to do with your lids.'

It was rather a blow. I had thought that I was finished with operations. I was not prepared for another.

In the afternoon, the Mother Superior brought me a big box of sweets for my birthday. She was looking forward to the festival, she said. Ena was rather nervous about what was expected of her when the procession came along and asked me to find out exactly what she had to do.

'Tell her that in England it's not the custom to throw rose petals at archbishops,' she said. 'Supposing I throw them and they hit him in the face?'

The Mother Superior chuckled when I translated.

'Just throw the petals as he comes into view,' she explained to Ena.

The sounds of chanting drifted into the room from the main church in the courtyard. Nuns raised the half-drawn blinds. Ena stood by the open window. I was lying flat on my back in bed.

'The archbishop is coming down the steps with all the other priests,' Ena reported. 'They're all coming this way, walking in procession . . . the archbishop, the priests . . . and mothers and fathers with little children all holding candles in front of them! Nino, I'll never be able to throw these petals! I'm frightened of hitting the archbishop!'

One of the maids came into the room. Ena siezed her chance. 'Ask her to show me what I'm supposed to do,' she urged. I did. The maid obliged. She waited at the window with Ena until the archbishop approached. Then she scattered the petals into his path. Ena took her courage – and the petals – into both hands and followed the maid's example. A vigorous round of applause broke out from the crowd below. Ena stopped in surprise. For a moment, she imagined that what they were clapping was her own praiseworthy petal-strewing performance.

The service began . . . the Benediction of the Blessed Sacrament. A smell of incense drifted in through the window. The choir and the congregation in the quadrangle sang the *Tantum Ergo* and the *Sacramentum*, the benediction hymn.

'Oh, darling, this reminds me of my childhood!' I told Ena excitedly. 'I used to be an altar boy in Istanbul and, every Corpus Christi, we used to walk in procession through the churchyard scattering rose petals from a big basket looped over my arm -- just like you're doing now. And that benediction hymn – I remember my mother used to go to benediction every day!'

It was a moving experience for me. I had not heard anything like it for thirty-one years. Not since leaving home to join the army in 1941 had I been present at a religious procession or at the scattering of rose petals.

That night, I went to sleep a happy man. It was my birthday. The benediction service and the quaint custom of the rose petals had revived many happy childhood memories for me.

And, on the same day, I had seen my first rose for twenty-six years.

Chapter Forty-One

As Professor Strampelli was dressing my eye on the Sunday, eight days after my operation, I turned my head to the left and, immediately, saw someone standing there. I could not detect a face but I could tell that the figure was dressed in white.

'I can see the sister,' I told him.

'Patience. You will see much better!' he replied. 'You wait!'

On the following day, however, the sensitive hearing that I had developed since losing my sight allowed me to overhear an aside he made to his chief assistant. It filled me with foreboding.

'I am anxious about this eye,' he muttered.

Instead of re-bandaging my eye, he placed a round piece of perforated metal over it, almost like a saucer with holes in it and covered with gauze.

He departed without another word. Ena was waiting outside the room. He swept past her without speaking. He did not even smile. The anxiety he had expressed was the first suggestion there had been that there was any cause for concern.

'Don't worry!' Ena urged. 'Every surgeon worries about something.'

That same evening, a huge omelette was brought in for my dinner. At least four eggs must have gone into it. I was surprised. It was not the usual sort of evening meal served at the clinic. Ena was suspicious.

On the following morning, her suspicions increased. Breakfast consisted of two eggs, extremely lightly boiled. I swallowed them like medicine.

Lunch was a normal one of pasta and fruit but, no sooner had I finished it, than a boiled egg appeared.

The soup at supper was followed by another enormous omelette. The sweet was an egg pudding.

Ena's suspicions were confirmed. Her own nursing knowledge told her that eggs were prescribed for protein deficiency.

Strampelli swept in with his retinue. It was the tenth day after my operation – the day on which I was expecting to see Ena. According to what I had been told, patients were not permitted to see their spouses until the tenth day because of the emotion that was always aroused. When delicate eye surgery was involved, tears could ruin everything.

It was clear from Strampelli's voice that he was not happy. Ena left the room. His assistants seemed nervous. He was shouting at the nurses.

He examined my eye, pulling my face roughly in doing so. It was in complete contrast to his normal gentle manner. He put his knee on the bed to hold my face more firmly.

'A piece of tooth is showing,' he announced sombrely to his assistant. 'I will have to take him to the theatre. Straight away. Tonight.'

'But, Professor, the anaesthetist has gone!' said the sister.

Strampelli's voice rose into a roar.

'Then go and get him!' he shouted at her.

The sister rushed out. A few minutes later she returned, crestfallen. She could not find the anaesthetist.

'He has gone, Professor! Everyone has gone!'

'Either find him or ring up someone else to do the anaesthetic!' he shouted. 'If we have to wait up until midnight, the operation has to be done tonight or this man will lose his eye!'

'Yes, Professor!'

He turned to me.

'You are going for an operation,' he said.

I said nothing. I realised that, if a piece of tooth were showing, it meant that the mucous membrane had not healed properly over the tooth root. The professor was obviously extremely upset and I decided that it would be better not to ask any questions.

Ena came into the room.

'Darling, I have some bad news,' I told her.

'What is it, darling?'

'I have to go to the theatre.'

'But you've only just had your dinner!'

'It can't be helped.'

'Why can't they do it with a local anaesthetic?' Ena asked, clearly agitated. 'You're very good with a local. You keep extremely still. You don't move your head.'

'They say it must be a general anaesthetic.'

'Nino, you're very precious to me,' she said. 'You can't have a full anaesthetic when you've just had your food.'

Strampelli had left the room for a few minutes and, when he re-entered, Ena asked him if the operation could be done with a local anaesthetic. It could not. Two anaesthetists came into the room.

'But he's just had a meal!' Ena protested. There was a slight note of hysteria in her voice. 'It will be too dangerous!'

Strampelli was unmoved.

'Madam!' he said grimly and deliberately. 'All emergency operations are dangerous!'

His words did nothing to allay Ena's fears. She clasped my hand in both of hers.

'Oh, Nino!' she cried. 'I want you alive – not dead! Let's pack up and go home now!'

She was on the verge of tears but I knew that there was no turning back. I squeezed her hand.

'No, darling!' I told her. 'We must go on. Please help me to be strong!'

In twenty-six years – in Egypt, England and Italy – I had had seventy-four operations but never before in the whole of that time had I heard anyone suggest that what I was about to undergo was dangerous. For the first time in seventy-four operations, I prepared myself for the theatre with thoughts of death in my mind. I feared that, this time, I would never see my wife and children again.

Despite my fears, the risk was one that I had to take. I prepared myself through prayer. I gained strength from it. Inside fifteen minutes, I was in the theatre and under the anaesthetist's spell.

Downstairs, the nuns tried to comfort Ena. They could see her anguished expression and tried to make light of the emergency.

'Una piccola interventione,' they said. 'A little operation.'

Ena was not convinced. They tried to reassure her even further.

'Uno punto!' they said. 'One stitch!'

An hour passed. Two hours. Three. The nuns' piccola interventione was turning into a marathon. By the time that I had been in the theatre for four hours, Ena was thankful that I was having no more than uno punto.

Suddenly, she saw a priest coming down the stairs from the operating theatre. A nun was with him. For one awful moment, she was convinced that the priest had just come from the theatre after giving me the last rites and that he and the nun were now on their way to break the dreaded news to her. Ena's stomach turned over. Her heart stopped. Her hands trembled. The priest and the nun walked past without a word.

No sooner had they gone than a nurse, seeing Ena's miserable face, tried to cheer her up.

'Be 'appy!' she said.

Ena was in no mood to be cheered up, however.

'How can I be happy when my husband is up there fighting for his life?' she snapped. 'You're not married! You don't know what it's like!'

It was a somewhat unkind remark, certainly not one that Ena would have made in normal circumstances. In her emotional, over-wrought condition, however, it was, perhaps, both under-standable and forgivable.

It was seven o'clock in the evening when I was taken to the theatre and midnight when I was returned to the ward. As I revived, I became aware that Ena was showering my face with kisses. The ice bag was back on my head but there were no drips attached to my feet.

'Darling, you're back safely,' Ena said.

I stretched out my hands to her face.

'How long have I been away?'

'Five hours. It's now midnight.'

Strampelli came to see me on the following afternoon. He explained the reason for the emergency operation. A stitch had come loose, which had to be repaired. He had also stitched up the lids to protect the tooth root. At the same time, he had carried out an operation that he had been planning to do later. He had taken a piece of skin from my temple and had grafted it on to my eyelids.

'It was a good opportunity to do it when I had you up there in the theatre,' he said.

'When can I get up, *professore?*'

'But for the operation, you could have got up today,' he said. 'But now . . . three days.'

'And in three days . . . will I see?'

'When I open your lids,' he said, 'you will see.'

According to the nurses, my eye had required not one stitch, as they had told Ena, but three.

'Tre punti,' they told me.

Three days passed. I was still kept in bed. Three more days were required before I could get up, they said. On the sixth day, however, my confinement to bed was extended yet again. I was having five injections every day. I had already been immobile for sixteen days.

Seven days after my emergency operation, Strampelli ex-amined my eye. He asked for cotton-wool. He cleaned it. He asked for scissors. He began cutting. Dead flesh, rotten and smelling, began to fall on to my nose and face. It was a smell and a feeling that I had experienced many times before. I knew that the skin-graft on my eyelids had died.

'Necrosis,' Strampelli confirmed.

'Can I get up now?' I asked morosely.

'No,' he replied. 'Another three days in bed. Have patience!'

'When is he going to open my lids?' I asked Ena when he had gone.

'Maybe tomorrow,' she said.

'When am I going to see that rose again?'

'Maybe tomorrow.'

Tomorrow was a long time coming. For four weeks, I was obliged to lie flat on my back, not moving my head. Finally, I was allowed to get up.

I persuaded Ena to look underneath the metal saucer that still covered my face to see what condition my eye was in following the emergency operation. She was reluctant but, eventually, lifted it up and peeped underneath. She was not overjoyed by what she saw. The lids that Strampelli had stitched up had actually begun to grow together, just as an operation incision knits together after stitching.

'I don't know how he's going to open them, darling,' she said. 'I'm afraid it's going to mean another little operation.'

'It doesn't matter,' I told her. 'Just as long as he opens them.'

When it had become obvious that I was not going to be discharged from hospital in time to return to England with Ena at the end of her four weeks' leave, she had telephoned her mother and asked her to speak to the matron of the Cambridge Military Hospital, explain the circumstances and seek an extension of her leave. Mrs Argyle had done so and the matron had readily agreed to extend Ena's absence on compassionate grounds. By now, however, the extension granted by the matron had almost expired. Ena was worried. It was nearly time for her to return but, if I were to have another operation, she was loath to leave me.

We decided to put our problem to one of the sisters, an American nun who was secretary to the Mother Superior.

'It's like this, sister,' I told her. 'My wife has to go back to England in a couple of days and we don't know what is going on. Professor Strampelli hasn't opened my lids. My wife doesn't want to leave me if I have to have another operation. She'll cancel her flight and stay here.'

'I'll try to find out what's happening,' she assured us. 'The only way to do it is to pin Professor Strampelli down when he's in your room tomorrow. Give me a list of what you want to know.'

On the following day, as Strampelli was examining me, she seized her chance.

'May I please speak to you, Professor Strampelli?' she asked in Italian.

'Later! Later! In the examination room.'

She ignored his instruction and produced a piece of paper on which she had noted the questions we wanted answering.

'How long will Mr Fettel be staying here?'

The professor glared at her and then at the list in her hand.

'I don't know,' he snapped. 'I can't tell.'

She decided to abandon her prepared questions. She put the list away.

'His wife is worried. She has to go home. She wants to know whether he has to have another operation.'

'No more operations,' Strampelli told her. 'He will stay another week or two. Then he will go home. Tell the *signora* to go home without worry. In September, he will come back here and I will open his lids. Then I hope he will see like he did before.'

'The *signora* wants to thank you for all you have done for her husband.'

He waved his hands expressively as if to say that he did not require any praise. It was nothing.

All the while he and the sister had been speaking, Strampelli had been sitting on my bed holding my hand. By now, there was a smile in his voice.

He left. Ena followed him and, outside the room, took his hand in a gesture of thanks. He led her back by the hand. He removed the metal saucer from my face and showed her my eye.

'I have stitched the lids and joined them – thus,' he said. 'When he comes back in September, I hope he will see again.'

Giovanni, the Dutch patient, had been right when he had forecast that I would be at the clinic for six weeks. Even so, even though I was disappointed that I would not be returning home with Ena as planned, I was relieved now that I knew what was happening. Strampelli had decided to play safe. Instead of opening my lids now and discovering, too late, that the action had been premature, he had decided to wait for three months to allow the eye more time to accept the unit. In the meantime, as a protection for the tooth root, my lids would remain closed.

Happy though I was that the uncertainty was at an end, I could not subdue a slight feeling of regret that my blindness was to continue for at least another three months. I had been able to see for ten days – ten days in which I had seen Strampelli's fingers, the white uniform of the sister and a red rose – and it had been wonderful. To send me home now for three months with my lids closed was rather like dangling a carrot before a donkey and then taking it away, like tossing a bone to a dog and then snatching it back.

Ena was leaving for home on the following day. It was Saturday, 24 June 1972, exactly four weeks since the day of the operation in which the sight-giving unit had been implanted into my eye. She was taking most of my belongings with her so that I would not have a heavy suitcase to carry when I returned home alone.

After lunch, Strampelli came to say goodbye to her. He took the metal saucer from my face, showed her my eye again and told her not to worry.

Ena lay down on the bed. She needed to rest before the flight. A taxi had been ordered.

'I shall say goodbye quickly, darling,' she told me. 'I shall kiss you once and then I'll go. I don't want you to see me in tears.'

The room telephone rang. It was the taxi. She kissed me. She was gone. I was alone and blind in a strange country.

From the courtyard, Ena's voice floated up through the open window.

'Goodbye, darling Nino! Take care!'

The taxi pulled away.

Forty minutes later, the telephone rang. It was Ena. She was at the airport.

'Nino, it was hell leaving you,' she said. 'I did not dare look back. If I had looked back out of that taxi window I would never have gone.'

There was a knock at the door. The Mother Superior's secretary, the American nun who had tackled Professor Strampelli about our worries, came in.

'Mr Fettel,' she said. 'I have something for you. Before your wife left, she gave me a letter for you. Come outside into the sitting-room and I'll read it to you.'

She began to read.

'My precious, darling Nino,' the letter began. 'I have asked the sister to read you this letter after I leave today because I want you to know how much I love and need you. It isn't just a part of me but *all* of me that I am leaving behind in your little room at the clinic. I have promised you that I will not worry, but I go as a walking robot back to our precious children and back to duty and work. Not until we are together again, my darling Nino, will I become *me* again. For these few weeks I have spent with you have taught me many things. They have made me realise that I am married to the most unselfish, courageous and good man. They have made me realise that we are as one person in our love.'

The sister's voice broke. She stopped reading. Tears were pouring down my face.

'My darling, darling Nino,' the letter continued. 'That is why it is so very hard for me to go today. But, as you have the courage to remain behind, then I will borrow some of your courage and go back to our precious children. I will live for those brief, wonderful moments when I shall hear your voice, your darling voice, on the telephone, and I shall live for that moment when you tell me that you are coming home. You are my world.'

The nun's voice broke completely. It was several seconds before she could continue.

'I promise I will take care how I cross the roads,' the letter ended. 'I love you, darling, always. Ena.'

The sister stopped reading. The tears were running down my cheeks and dripping off the end of my nose and off my chin on to the backs of my hands. It was the most moving letter I had ever heard. Nothing before in my life had touched me so much. In that moment, when I was all alone and blind in a foreign land, my wife was telling me that I was important to her ... that we belonged to each other ... that I was wanted ... that I was needed ... that I was loved ...

'I'll get you a towel to wipe your eyes,' said the sister. She brought one from my room.

'Thank you, Sister,' I said.

They were the first words I had spoken from the moment that she had started to read. I dried my eyes. We sat in silence again.

'She's a wonderful girl,' she said at last.

'Yes, Sister,' I said. 'She is.'

Chapter Forty-Two

After nearly three months at home in Tongham, Ena and I returned to the Rome clinic for my final operation . . . the operation to open my lids.

It was Thursday, 14 September, 1972. We were shown to a double room on the ground floor. Unlike the previous rooms I had occupied, each of which had a camp bed for the patient's spouse, this one had two single beds. Ena's additional comfort was assured.

My hopes were high. I was optimistic about the outcome. During my time at home, even though my eyelids were closed, I had fancied that I could see reflections. While out walking with Ena both in Tongham and in nearby Aldershot, I had thought that I could see the movements and colours of passing cars . . . reds, greens and blues. Once, in Aldershot, I had asked Ena if a woman walking in front of us was wearing a patterned dress of black and white dots. She was.

I could not understand it. Was I really seeing them? Or was I imagining it? Back at the Rome clinic, I asked one of the sisters. Yes, it was possible, she said. It could happen. I could be seeing the light reflected through the crack between my lids. I was thrilled . . . excited. I knew that the retina and the unit were functioning as they should.

On the following day, Strampelli examined me and pressed the eyeball.

'Have you any pain?'

'No.'

'I will open your lids tomorrow,' he announced. 'If everything is as it was on your last visit, I hope you will be able to see.'

'*Grazie! Grazie tanto!*' I said. 'Thank you! Thank you very much!'

He was silent for a moment as he washed his hands in the basin.

'Could you repeat what you just said?' he asked.

'*Grazie! Grazie tanto!*'

He left without another word.

'What was that all about?' I asked one of the nuns. 'Why did he ask me to repeat it?'

'He just wanted to hear you thanking him again,' she said. 'None of the rich patients who come here ever think of saying thank you. They think their money buys the clinic, Professor Strampelli and everything. He just thought it was very refreshing to hear a patient say thank you.'

At three o'clock on the Saturday afternoon, I donned my gown and climbed back into bed, ready to be wheeled to the operating theatre. Ena left. We were both prepared for a long job. I expected another operation of four or five hours. In fact, it was over within an hour.

When I awoke, I did not know where I was. I could tell that I was not in my own room. It was a strange one. My eyes were bandaged. There were voices round me. People were walking past. There were the sounds of footsteps and of the clashing of metal bowls.

'*Signor Fettel!* The Professor will see you in ten minutes.'

The voice in my ear was not Ena's but that of one of the nurses. Ena was not there.

My mind cleared. I was in the recovery room next to the operating theatre.

'Let us have the bandages off.' It was Strampelli's voice. '*Aqua physiologica.*'

He washed my eye and polished the lens. My lids had not been parted. Instead, a hole had been punctured in my top lid so that the lens became exposed. He asked the sister to put a light behind my head. I saw two fingers held up in a V-sign.

'Churchill!' I cried.

'*Vede?*'

'*Si, Professore!* Churchill! Victory!'

I could see the two fingers clearly, much more clearly than during my ten days of sight in May and June. As Strampelli held them aloft in the British prime minister's famous wartime victory sign, I realised that they represented more than simply a device for testing my sight. They symbolised my own incredible victory . . . a victory achieved by Strampelli and me together.

I could see again! The past year, since I had first come to Rome to visit the great professor, had not been wasted. The five operations I had undergone at his skilled hands had not been in vain.

The prayer that I had prayed in an Egyptian hospital twenty-six years before – 'Lord, let the miracle happen so that I will see again one day' – had been answered.

After twenty-six years and seventy-six operations, the miracle *had* happened.

This time, I knew, nothing would go wrong. The mucous membrane had healed over the tooth root. The sight-giving unit had been in my eye for nearly three months, time enough for it to be accepted.

The room buzzed with excitement. There were murmurs of wonderment. Everyone started talking at once.

'Go and tell his wife!' one of the nuns urged.

'That will do for the moment,' Strampelli said, patting me on the head.

'You will see even better when you get some glasses,' said one of the nurses as she placed a pad over my eye.

I was wheeled in my bed to the lift and along the ground-floor corridor towards my room. One of the doctors ran on ahead.

'He can see!' he shouted to Ena. 'He can see!'

Ena was in the room.

'I can see, darling!' I told her excitedly.

They left us alone.

'Tell me! Tell me!'

'I saw Strampelli's fingers . . . much more clearly than before!'

'No, it can't be true!'

'Yes, it *is* true!'

Ena took my hand and kissed it.

'I'm so relieved! I thought you'd come back covered in drips! I can't believe it!'

'How long have I been away?'

'About two hours.'

'I've been waiting in the recovery room for a good hour.'

'Darling, if only I'd known! I've been sitting here wondering what was happening to you . . . imagining you still in the operating theatre.'

'You've been in here the whole time?'

'No, I couldn't stand it. I was so sad that I had to go out to church. I don't like seeing the room with your bed not there . . . with you not there. Darling, are you sure you saw those two fingers?'

'Yes, I'm sure.'

'So it's all been worth it after all . . . '

I took her hand.

'I want to thank you, my darling, for all your patience . . . over so many years . . . '

'Not my patience! Yours!'

'Without you, this would not have been possible.'

'Don't be silly! You're the one who has had all the suffering!'

'But I know you have, too . . . '

She cuddled me to her. I was still trembling with excitement.

'Have a sleep now, darling,' she said. 'You must be tired.'

I was too excited to sleep. I had seen two fingers and it had whetted my appetite. I was longing for Sunday to come so that I could see more . . . so that I could see my Inneta.

'*Buona sera, Signor Constantino!*'

It was the maid. She had come to lay the supper. Even she seemed happy for me. Her voice was brighter than usual. Her greeting came wrapped in a warm smile.

We ate supper. Although I had to stay in bed, I was able to sit up.

'We must let the family know now,' Ena said.

'No,' I told her. 'Let's try to keep very calm until tomorrow.'

'Please let us ring our *bambinos*!' she pleaded.

I relented. I put a call through. Linda answered.

'Hello, Daddy!'

'I can see, Linda!'

'Are you sure, Daddy? Are you sure?'

'I can see Professor Strampelli's two fingers!'

'Will you be able to see me when you get back?'

'Of course I will! But don't tell anyone until we get home.'

I spoke to Paul and Adrian.

'When are you coming home, Daddy?' Adrian asked.

'I don't know. But Mummy is coming home next Friday.'

I spent a restless night, waking every two or three hours. Each time I woke, I switched on the light to make sure that I could still see it creeping in through the holes in the metal saucer that was still protecting my eye. I could.

'I still can't believe it!' I told Ena happily.

On the Sunday morning, Strampelli arrived with one of the nuns. As soon as the metal saucer was removed, I could see light through the gauze pad over my eye. When the pad was removed, I could see Strampelli's two fingers. He polished the lens, put a light behind me and examined my eye.

'Let's see if you can see colours,' he said.

He was very calm. He held up a little bottle of eye drops. I could tell that it was a bottle and that, round it, was a label in three colours. The colours were in bands running round the bottle's circumference. I read from the top colour down.

'*Verde. Bianco. Rosso.*'

'Bene! Bene!'

He held up a small eye-chart.

'Vede?'

'Uno. Sette.'

'We will try you with letters.'

The silence in the room was electric.

'Ay. Dee.'

'Bene! Madam – come here! Sit down on the bed.'

Ena sat at my shoulder.

'Do you see her?' Strampelli asked.

I could see a face but the light from the window was shining into my eye.

'I see a little. But not clearly.'

'When we give you glasses you will see better.'

'He doesn't want to see my ugly mug,' Ena said.

On the contrary, I did. Very much. I knew it *wasn't* an ugly mug. Her face was close to mine. I could see two eyes, a nose and a mouth but I could not recognise it as Ena. It was like looking at a negative photograph. Nevertheless, it was thrilling to see Ena's face. I was longing for us to be left alone so that I could see it at my leisure.

I turned momentarily. My hand pointed at Strampelli.

'Oh, Professor!' I cried. 'You are wearing glasses!'

'Si!' he said, obviously pleased. *'Bene!* Now I want you to tell me one more thing. What is this?'

The object that Strampelli held up looked like two steel knives, pointed and crossed. I could not identify what it was. I was puzzled. Why were they crossed like that, at an angle of ninety degrees?

Suddenly, the memory cells in my brain leapt into action. There was a flurry of feverish activity in my personal computer. Memory flooded back . . . memory of something I had last seen twenty-six years before and the appearance of which I had almost totally forgotten.

'Scissors!' I shouted.

'Bene!' beamed the professor.

Immediately after breakfast, we sat by the open window, staring out. I was longing to discover just how much I could see. Ena was spurring me on. She kept turning my head in the direction of different objects but my eye had not yet learned to focus into the distance and I could see only with difficulty. Gradually, my vision improved. The more I tried to see, the more I saw.

'I can see something over there,' I told Ena. 'What is it? It's like a pole on the roof!'

'Yes,' said Ena. 'It's a television aerial.'

'There are three of them. One small, one medium and one large.'

'That's right, darling! The big one is nearest to you. The others look smaller because they're further away.'

They were the first television aerials I had ever seen.

'They look like spiders, darling! Like daddy-long-legs!'

Ena laughed.

'Look left,' she said. 'About six feet from the big television aerial.'

I did.

'Now look down,' Ena continued. 'What do you see?'

'There's a window! It's green!'

'Yes, it has green shutters! The shutters are closed. Now look at the next window.'

'The shutters are closed there, too!'

'Now go down about two feet.'

'Another window! The shutters are open! The windows are open!'

'Can you see who is there?'

'A woman! Wonderful!'

After a while, as the sun grew brighter, the clinic garden and perimeter wall came into view. The back of the apartment block beyond, the one with the green shutters and television aerials, became much clearer. I could see trees in the strip of green and more apartment windows.

'Have another look at the roof,' Ena urged. 'Can you see anything else apart from the television aerials?'

'Chimney stacks!'

'And can you see the chimney pots on the chimney stacks?'

'I can, darling!'

'How many can you see?'

'Seven . . . eight! No . . . nine!'

'Can you see anything on those chimneys over there? The three close together?'

'They look like little chamber-pots, darling!'

'They're not, I assure you!' she laughed. 'They're hoods – to stop the smoke going into the rooms when it's windy.'

'Something's happening over there,' I told her. 'The window is opening.'

'Can you see what it is?'

'A woman standing there.'

'Can you see what she's doing?'

'She's shaking something . . . she's shaking the bed-sheets, darling!'

'Darling, how marvellous!'

'Oh, what a shame! She's going in . . . the window is closing . . . '

All day, from straight after breakfast until late at night, I sat staring out of the window, watching the shutters opening and closing, fascinated by the everyday activities of the occupants. My elbows were on the window-sill. My chin was cupped in my hands. I was totally absorbed by the sights I was seeing even though, to anyone else, they would undoubtedly have appeared boringly mundane.

Towards late afternoon, a man appeared at one of the green-shuttered windows. He glared in my direction.

'Darling,' Ena said nervously. 'That looks like one of the husbands . . . '

The man shouted down to another man at the window beneath. They both stared hard in my direction.

'Darling,' said Ena. 'They must think you're a peeping Tom!'

The two windows slammed shut simultaneously. The shutters were closed. They stayed closed.

I laughed.

'Not a peeping Tom, darling!' I chuckled. 'More likely they're a couple of jealous husbands who think I fancy their wives!'

Ena smiled thinly.

'Don't stare too much at the houses, though,' she urged. 'Or they'll come and arrest you! Anyway, come on, darling! It's time you were coming in. Have some sleep.'

'No, darling. I must look!'

'You'll strain your eye!'

'Just another five minutes, darling!'

I craned my neck out of the window to catch the last rays of sunshine. I stayed there, fascinated, watching the shadows moving slowly across the houses and I did not leave until the dusk brought down a curtain in front of my eye. Reluctantly, I allowed Ena to close the window.

Even then, I could not bear to stop using the sight that had been given to me. I picked up a British European Airways' magazine that we had been given on the aircraft. Although I could not distinguish between the different advertisements for cigarettes, perfumes and watches, it was still a delight simply to sit looking at the brilliant colours.

Later that evening, Ena was lying on my bed reading a book to me. I was sitting in the chair listening to her. There was a knock on the door. Two of the nuns had arrived to rub me with spirit to prevent bed sores. They were in a jovial and playful mood because I had regained my sight and, surprised at finding Ena on my bed instead of me, they took hold of her arms, unfastened her summer dress down the back and rubbed her with the spirit. Ena squealed.

'The *signora* is the patient now!' they chortled.

At bedtime, as usual, they came to inquire whether there was anything else we wanted and, as usual, kissed Ena goodnight.

'What!' I protested. 'No kiss for me?'

They laughed. They could not let me go to sleep disappointed, they said, kissing me on both cheeks.

During the night, I woke up and lit a cigarette. I could see not only the match flaring up but also the red end of the cigarette glowing in the dark. Each time I drew on it, pulling more oxygen through the tobacco, the lighted end glowed more brightly and I could see that it illuminated the room.

'Be careful, darling!' Ena cautioned. 'Don't burn yourself!'

On the Monday morning, in the bathroom, I held out my left hand to discover if I could see it. I could. I picked up the razor that my father had given me when I had left for the army as a boy of seventeen nearly thirty-one years before. I could see that, too.

Breakfast was served in the room. I could see the cup and the coffee pot and the bread.

I sat in an upright chair at the right-hand side of the window, staring out at those fascinating green shutters. Ena sat opposite me in an armchair, at the left-hand side of the window. The shutters were still closed over the windows of the two apartments from which the two men had glowered at me on the previous evening.

'Maybe they're not going to let me take a look at their wives today, darling!' I joked.

'I don't blame them a bit,' said Ena. 'But I think it's more likely to be just because it's so early. They're probably still in bed.'

I turned to look at her. The bright, morning sunlight was flooding in through the open window. It was falling directly on to Ena, bathing her in a warm glow, lighting up her features, glinting on her fair hair. My heart leapt as, for the first time, I saw her face completely clearly. I could see her eyes, her nose, her mouth, her hair. She was smiling at me. It was thrilling.

'What is it, darling?' she asked, seeing the expression of wonderment on my face.

'I can see you, darling!'

'Can you?'

'Keep still, darling!'

'I'll try!'

'I've lost you!'

'Can you see me now?'

'No!'

'I'll move my head . . . '

'That's it! Hold it! Don't move!'

I gazed and gazed. It was a lovely, small face. I was fascinated by her eyes blinking.

'My neck's getting stiff!'

'Sit still, please!'

I gazed again. I looked and looked.

'Please can I move my head now? My neck's aching!'

'No, no! Keep still! I must keep on looking at you!'

'What am I like?'

'You're lovely!'

'What do you like about me?'

'Your eyes.'

'Stop looking at my horrible old nose! You know I don't like it!'

'Don't be silly! I've known your nose with my finger for the last twenty years. It's beautiful . . . '

'You're just saying that.'

I leaned forward and kissed her right on the tip of her nose.

'It's a lovely nose,' I told her.

'You've got a good aim!' she giggled.

Ena bought the *Daily American*. I was able to read the main headlines. She obtained permission to take me for a walk. The clinic corridors were dark. She had to lead me.

We stepped out of the half-light of the main entrance into the clinic courtyard. I felt the hot sun glaring down at me. The whole scene was bathed in sunshine, almost as if it were lit up by powerful floodlights. I could see a large building of sand-coloured stone and realised that it must be the main church in the courtyard, the Church of St John the Baptist. Hanging over the entire scene was a cloudless Roman sky of brilliant azure blue. I stood in the entrance for several minutes, taking in the breath-taking view. It was a revelation.

We walked through the gardens. I could see flower beds and pathways and palm trees.

'Darling!' I said, running my hands over the palm trees. 'This reminds me of Egypt all those years ago!'

We passed through the outer gates set in the perimeter wall of the clinic grounds. The road outside was busy.

'Just look at the traffic!' Ena exclaimed. 'It's going so fast. We're never going to get across this road!'

'I don't care if we have to wait all day to cross it,' I told her determinedly. 'We're going to cross it!'

We walked further up the road to the traffic lights and waited on the pavement for them to change in our favour. I was fascinated by the speed of the passing traffic, by the colours and shapes of the different vehicles.

'That one was a car,' I said. 'Now a lorry . . . '

'You're right, darling!'

'There are lots of little red cars,' I said, intrigued. 'They are like little ladybirds!'

'They are little red Fiats,' Ena explained.

My head was moving excitedly and repeatedly from left to right and back again like a spectator at a tennis tournament.

We crossed the Circonvallazione Cornelia and walked to a little café which we had patronised together occasionally in the past and which Ena had frequented on her own at times when I was confined to bed or to my room.

Sitting at the cash-desk was the same plump, middle-aged woman we had talked to previously and with whom Ena had conversed in broken Italian on the occasions when I had not been there. We had come to know many of the regular customers and some of them were inside drinking coffee.

Previously, whenever they had seen me, I had been wearing the dark glasses of a blind man. Today, I was wearing spectacles with clear lenses. They stared open-mouthed when we walked in.

'*Mio marito vede!*' Ena announced happily, putting an end to their obvious uncertainty. 'My husband can see!'

The café owner continued to stare at me for several seconds. Then she gave a little cry of delight and rushed from behind her cash-register. Tears were streaming down her face. She kissed Ena on both cheeks.

'Miracle!' she cried. 'Miracle!'

The regular customers who knew me crowded round, clapping

me on the back. Many of them, including grown men, were weeping.

'*Magnifico!*' they shouted. '*Magnifico!*'

'*Signora! Signora!*' The café owner tugged at Ena's sleeve. How many years was it, she wanted to know, that I had been blind?

'Twenty-six,' Ena told her.

'*Giorgio! Mario! Questo uomo è venuto dal Inghilterra! Dopo ventisei anni vede di nuovo!*' she announced for the benefit of those customers who did not know. 'Giorgio! Mario! This man has come from England! After twenty-six years he can see again!'

'*Magnifico!*'

'*Il Professore Strampelli l'ha operato!*' she continued. 'Professor Strampelli has operated on him!'

'*Uno uomo magnifico!*' they shouted. 'A magnificent man!'

The woman flung her arms wide in an expressive gesture of joy.

'*Il capucino a la casa!*' she cried. 'Coffee on the house!'

They waved us off. We continued our walk.

'What's that?' Ena asked.

'A car.'

I was fascinated by the houses, the chimneys, the lamp standards, the people passing by. In particular, the colours held my attention.

'She's wearing green . . . that car is red . . . '

I noticed that the petrol-pump attendants all wore different-coloured overalls. I could see the blue sky. I could see the advertisement hoardings . . . the names over the shops . . . chocolates on display . . .

At one shop, I could even read a notice in the window. '*Saldo*', it said. 'Sale'.

It was a sale of shoes.

On our way to lunch, we went into the Church of St John the Baptist inside the clinic grounds. We wanted to pray. After being outside for so long in the bright sunlight, I found it difficult to adjust to the half-light of the church. It seemed dark inside. Ena had to lead me by the arm. She took me to the left-hand side of the church and stopped just before the sanctuary.

'Can you see what it is?' she asked.

'Not clearly.'

'It's a statue of Our Lady. The Madonna and Child.'

As my eye became accustomed to the darkness, more details

of the statue gradually came into view. I could not see it perfectly but I could tell that it was on a pedestal, that it was about five feet eight inches high and that the Madonna's face was almost life-size. Round her head was a lighted halo, a glittering crown of tiny, star-shaped electric light bulbs glowing in the gloom. One arm was holding the Child. Hanging from her free arm was a beautiful crystal rosary that shimmered in the flickering light from the many candles that stood round her feet in coloured glass pots, casting a kaleidoscope of reds, yellows, blues and greens. As the wicks burned low, the light from the candles seemed to glow more brightly. The colours of the glass pots shone more vividly. The rosary took on the appearance of a glinting diamond necklace.

'Darling,' said Ena. 'I'm going to light a candle. Which colour would you like?'

'Blue, please. Light me a blue one.'

I knelt before the Madonna and Child and gazed up at the lighted halo.

'Thank You, Lord,' I prayed. 'For the miracle . . . for letting me see my wife . . . for Professor Strampelli . . . for everything . . . '

We left the church. Outside I could see a flight of white marble steps leading down from the church doorway. I could see a row of black tiles along the front edge of each step.

Ena was clutching my arm, as she had done for the past twenty years. Hesitantly, I prepared to take my first faltering step, as I had done for the past twenty-six years.

At that moment, in the bright morning sunshine, the white marble seemed to become incredibly clear. The contrasting black edging stood out starkly . . . vividly . . . almost as if it were in relief.

Suddenly, as I was about to begin my uncertain descent, peering down nervously to see where I was putting my feet, I stopped.

Slowly, I disengaged Ena's arm from mine and, alone and unaided, strode confidently down the white marble steps.

Epilogue

It was wonderful to see my daughter and two sons again for the first time in six years. How different they looked! They were no longer children but teenagers . . . young adults. Even Adrian, the youngest, was fifteen.

Friends whom I had known by their voices for years appeared as complete strangers to me. They delighted in playing games with me by keeping silent, making me try to guess from their faces who they were, laughing uproariously when I bestowed on them the most unlikely identities. I was distinctly unsuccessful in matching the faces with the voices that I had known for so many years. In only one instance was I correct.

Six years before, when Peter Rycroft had given me my sight, I had found television almost unbelievable. Then, I had seen only black-and-white pictures. Colour television was a revelation.

Outside the home, I was fascinated by mini-skirts, the revolutionary designs of new cars and aeroplanes (I had never seen jet aircraft before), modern hairstyles and with-it fashions. Only my boss at work seemed to have the sort of hair-cut I remembered, with a central parting. Kipper ties were out of this world. Men's shirts, which I had known only to be either blue or white, seemed to be in all the colours of the rainbow and many more besides. Even more incredible, some of them even had floral designs!

Most awesome of all, however, was the wonder of Nature. For hours on end, I sat totally absorbed, staring at the sights that other people seemed to take for granted, the sights at which even Ena and the children scarcely seemed to give a second glance – the sweet-smelling golden daffodils in the garden with the furry honey-bees busily collecting their pollen . . . the sturdy oak tree, heavy with ripe acorns, about to shed its fruit in the same wondrous way it had done for centuries . . . a field full of cows, their gently-coloured brown-and-white hides blending perfectly with the green of the lush meadow beyond . . . the endless cobalt blue of a cloudless summer sky . . . the fluffy, snow-white cotton-wool clouds hanging in the heavens as if suspended from some invisible thread . . . the full moon, mysterious and unfathomable on a crisp-frost winter's night . . .

Difficult though it was for me to adjust to sight after so many years of blindness, it was almost equally difficult for Ena. At first, she kept forgetting that I could see. For many years, as she took her morning bath, it had been my practice to sit perched on the end of the bath chatting to her . . . talking over our plans for the day . . . discussing what we would do on our return from work that evening. On one morning soon after my return from Rome, as Ena took her bath, she had an uneasy feeling that she was being watched. She glanced up, suddenly remembering that I could see, and was embarrassed to find my good eye following her every movement.

'Nino!' she said shyly, covering her confusion with her flannel. 'You've got a naughty smile on your face . . . '

Two months after the visit to Rome that had restored my sight, I returned to the Villa Benedetta for a check-up. My eye was satisfactory.

I saw the Pope.

In March 1973, at a further check-up in Rome, Professor Strampelli declared himself pleased with my progress. One day, he said, he would graft on new eyelids and make me look beautiful for Ena by inserting a contact lens that looked like an eye. A hole would be drilled through the pupil of the contact lens to enable the lens of the sight-giving unit in my eye to look out on to the world.

Unhappily, on 24 November 1974, unexpected complications arose. After two years of sight, I was in the dark once more.

Ena wrote to Professor Strampelli and, in January 1975, we flew to Rome to consult him. At the initial examination, the professor's opinion was that there was still some slight hope. The diagnosis was inter-ocular haemorrhage and infection. He placed me on a series of steroid injections. After one week of treatment, I returned to England. There was no improvement in my vision. Ena was instructed to continue the treatment by giving me the injections at home.

When the course of treatment had ended, we returned to Rome. I was a patient for four days. There was no change in my condition. Still, Professor Strampelli was hoping that my sight might return.

It was not to be. In May 1975, severe pains developed in my eye. Soon afterwards, English eye specialists decided that the surgical removal of the whole sight-giving unit was necessary. The operation was carried out in the Cambridge Military Hospital, Aldershot, in August.

320 The Night Before Me

I accepted my blindness. I readjusted to a life of darkness. I had had the wonderful gift of sight for two incredible years. I had seen my wife and three grown-up children. I had seen my mother and two sisters. I had seen the Pope.

There were no regrets.

I am deeply and eternally grateful to all the dedicated doctors and nursing staff – in Egypt, Britain and Italy – who, over a period of more than a quarter of a century, worked so hard to help me.

It is my hope that my story may provide some inspiration for those who read it, that those who are faced with adversity and despair may derive strength and courage from it. Were it to prove of help to the blind, who might read it in braille or hear it as a 'talking book', I should feel particularly pleased.

Perhaps, having read my book, others will feel encouraged to follow the philosophy I have pursued throughout my life, no matter how difficult the periods through which I was passing: Keep on fighting. Never give in. In life, there is always hope.

What of the future? Who knows?

For the moment, I have accepted my life as it is.

I am content.

Constantine Fettel
Tongham, England
June 1977